DETAINED

DETAINED

D. ESPERANZA
GERARDO IVÁN MORALES

PRIMERO
SUEÑO PRESS

ATRIA

NEW YORK AMSTERDAM/ANTWERP LONDON
TORONTO SYDNEY/MELBOURNE NEW DELHI

ATRIA
An Imprint of Simon & Schuster, LLC
1230 Avenue of the Americas
New York, NY 10020

First Primero Sueño Press/Atria Books hardcover edition October 2025

PRIMERO SUEÑO PRESS / ATRIA BOOKS and colophon are trademarks of Simon & Schuster, LLC

Manufactured in the United States of America

1 3 5 7 9 10 8 6 4 2

Library of Congress Cataloging-in-Publication Data is available.

ISBN 978-1-6680-3377-7
ISBN 978-1-6680-3379-1 (ebook)

To all immigrants and anyone facing adversity: may your courage, resilience, and dreams light the path to a brighter future. This book is for you.

To our parents, our family, Gerry, Malena, and my sister Paulina: thank you for your unwavering support, love, and belief in us. Your sacrifices and strength inspire everything we do. This journey would not have been possible without you.

—D. ESPERANZA & GERARDO IVÁN MORALES

Llevaron unos niños a Jesús para que les impusiera las manos y orara por ellos, pero los discípulos regañaban a quienes los llevaban. Jesús dijo: «Dejen que los niños vengan a mí y no se lo impidan. Pues el reino de los cielos es de quienes son como ellos». Después de poner las manos sobre ellos, se fue de allí.

Then little children were being brought to him in order that he might lay his hands on them and pray. The disciples spoke sternly to those who brought them; but Jesus said, "Let the little children come to me, and do not stop them; for it is to such as these that the kingdom of heaven belongs." And he laid his hands on them and went on his way."

MATTHEW 19:13-15

Yo digo al Señor: «Tú eres mi refugio,
mi fortaleza, el Dios en quien confío».

You [. . .] will say to the Lord, "My refuge and my fortress, my God, in whom I trust."

PSALMS 91:2
Reina Valera and English Standard Versions

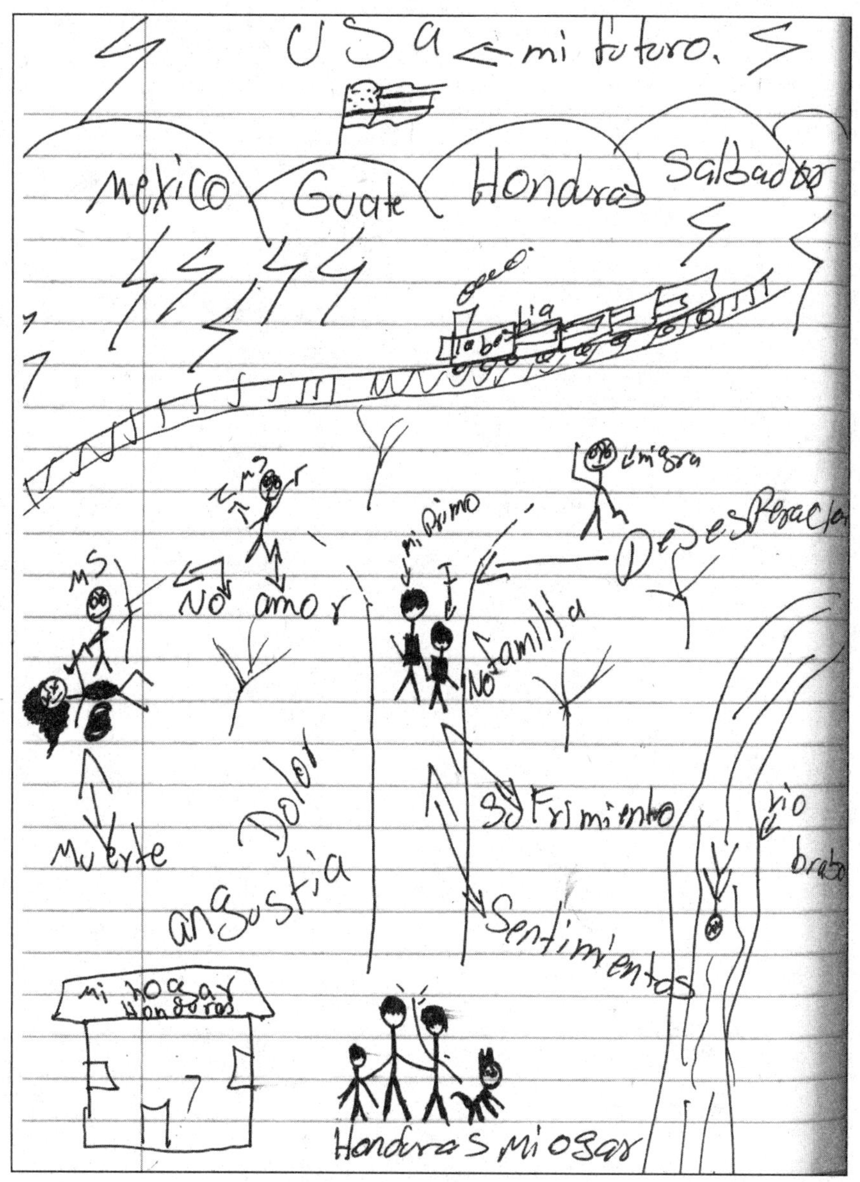

In detention, I made this drawing of my entire voyage to the United States to seek asylum with my cousins. "Suffering, despair, anguish, pain, death, no love, USA, my future?"
Photo taken by Iván Morales.

AUTHOR'S NOTE

When I was fourteen years old, I spent five months in captivity in Texas, at centers run by the U.S. government and its contractors. In the Tornillo Influx Facility, the provisional tent city where the Trump administration relocated underaged migrants in 2018, I met Gerardo Iván Morales (I always called him Iván), an immigrant from Mexico who had come to Tornillo to support and protect detained minors like me. Iván was like the big brother I never had. He was the first person to see my poetry and he encouraged me to write about my journey from Naranjito, Honduras, to the U.S. border, and through the migrant detention system.

When I was transferred out of Tornillo, I left those pages, along with a goodbye letter, as a gift for the Alpha 13 family that helped me survive in that place. Years later, Iván and I reconnected, and he suggested we try to share my story with the world. This book is based on a translation of those entries and my memories, reconstructed and stylized here as a journal. Some names and details have been altered for privacy and clarity. But at its core, this is my life story as I wrote it at age fourteen, lying in my bunk and scribbling in a black-and-white, wide-ruled composition book.

PART I

THE JOURNEY

Naranjito

Dear . . .

Hmm . . . Um . . . It still feels like I should be addressing this to someone, but I don't know who, since I don't expect anyone to ever read this. I'm not even sure I'll ever reread it. But whatever, I'll just start writing. I'll introduce myself to whatever imaginary reader is out there and see what happens.

Here goes.

My name is D. Esperanza. I just turned thirteen yesterday. My whole life, I have lived in a small pueblo in Honduras called Naranjito. It's a tiny town with a big church, and mountains on all sides. There are trees and plants and stray dogs all around, and if you go just a little bit outside of town, there's lots and lots of haciendas.

My parents left for el Norte when I was six months old. I always thought of them as leaving when they were old, but Tía was just saying yesterday, because it was my birthday, that they were only a few years older than me when they left. When I was little, I didn't get why they couldn't come back to be with me, or why I couldn't go to be with them. I thought they just got in a car or something and drove there. Now I know that it's a long trip to el Norte, and it's dangerous, so they don't want to put me in danger by asking me to come. And they can't come back to visit, because they might not let them go back to el Norte if they ever leave it.

After they got to el Norte, my parents had another baby, my little sister, who I've never met. When Mamá told me over the phone, it was kind of exciting and sad at the same time, because she's my sister, but she's in a whole different country, you know? She's old enough to talk a little bit now, and my parents try to get her to talk to me, but she's still so small that she doesn't say much. But I'm excited to meet her one day.

I live with Tía (Tía is really my abuela, but me and Miguelito call her Tía because she always says she's too young for us to call her Abuela). I also live with my cousin Miguelito, and we used to live with my uncle Felipe, too. Tía has been taking care of me and Miguelito since we were little. She does most of the cooking and cleaning, and she's always active, always moving around the kitchen and stuff. She tries to never make the same meal twice in the same week. On Sundays, she takes us to church, and almost every night she makes us say the Rosary, even though it's really boring.

Felipe was Mamá's brother and Tía's son. He spent almost every day driving microbuses, because even though my parents send back as much money as they can, it wasn't and still isn't enough to pay for food and medicine for Tía's cough.

Miguelito is eleven, two years younger than me. Felipe was his papá. We're cousins, but we might as well be brothers, since we've lived together our whole lives.

There's also our dog, Caramelo. He's scrappy, with pointy ears and two dark rings on his face, like he has two black eyes. You can't exactly say he's a member of the family, because he's a dog and not a person, but I love him just as much. I got to name him because I was the one who found him. Or, really, he found me. He was sitting outside the house one morning when I walked out the front door. I stopped to pet him and then kept walking, but he followed me all the way to school. Obviously, they wouldn't let him into the building, and I forgot about him during the day. But when I left for work after school, he was there waiting for me. And again the day after that. And the day after that.

Everybody in Naranjito knows Caramelo is my puppy because we're together all the time. They all laugh that I named him Caramelo even though his fur is black, not caramel-colored. Everyone calls street dogs like him "perros aguacateros" because they're always eating avocados that fall off trees, and that's definitely true of Caramelo. He's obsessed with avocados. He eats everything except the seed, which he brings to us like a trophy. Some days, he'll bring us seven or eight avocado seeds.

Sometimes I wish I could sleep with him, especially when I miss my parents, but Tía won't let him inside the house. She pretends she doesn't like him, because he's dirty and leaves green avocado poop outside our house all the time, but occasionally, when she thinks me and Miguelito aren't looking, she'll leave scraps or leftover bones outside the door for him.

Anyway, I don't write very often, and holding the pen for this long is making my hand cramp. Writing about how Felipe used to live with us is also making me feel kind of weird, so I'm going to think about what I'll say, and write more tomorrow. I think I actually really like writing like this. It feels good.

FIVE MONTHS LATER

I haven't forgotten about you, it's just . . . a lot has happened. I was going to write more yesterday or the day before, but I was too tired after getting back from the hacienda. Anyway, it gave me time to think of some other stuff I want to say about the past few years.

Now that I'm working so much, I understand money a lot better. I've always known we're poor, at least in theory, because that's why Mamá and Papá left in the first place. Sometimes Felipe used to talk about how we were poor, too. He'd complain about work and how much stuff cost. He'd say that before I was born, the plantaciones bananeras ruined the economía. I didn't know what that meant when he said it, and I still don't. Before everything got bad, I didn't understand money stuff at all. I assumed everything was fine because on Sundays at church, when Padre Juan passed a basket around, Tía would always put money in. And when I left for school, if she had been up all night coughing and she was too tired to make me lunch, she would draw a cross on my forehead and press a coin into my hand so I could buy a baleada for lunch.

Honestly, until I was twelve, I don't think I had any problems. I know I'm supposed to say it was hard growing up without my parents, and obviously I miss them, but I've never felt like an orphan or anything. It's like, I know there's this gap in my life, but the gap isn't empty. Does that make sense? I have my family. I have one photo of my parents from before they left, where they're holding me as a baby in their arms. They're posing for the photo and smiling. The photo is old and falling apart, but it's in a glass frame, and when I talk to my parents on the phone, I imagine I'm talking to the people in that photo. I know they're older now, but that's still who they are to me. They're not here physically, but they're in my life. They always call me on my birthday, Christmas, Semana Santa . . . they never miss those. Mamá always says she misses me, always reminds me that she's there for me: it's a relationship that we keep up through promises, phone calls, letters . . . I know that my parents aren't here because they're busy providing for me and Miguelito. And I know that one day, once my parents have saved enough money, I'll either go join them or they'll come back here.

Sometimes I get impatient for that to happen and I ask Mamá when I'll be able to join them in Nashville. When I was little, I didn't think about them being gone very much, but when I got older, I started to see my friends' parents pick them up from school and it would give me this weird feeling in the bottom part of my chest. I love Tía and Felipe—they've been like parents to me. But I look at that photo of Mamá and Papá from when I was little, and I get a little jealous of the baby they're holding in the picture, even though I know it's me.

Talking about this with Tía helps. She says I should count my blessings and "agradecer lo que ya tengo," because when I was still going to school, there were lots of other kids whose parents weren't around, and a lot of them had it way worse. She reminds me that there are other kids in Naranjito who never got to go to school at all, or who dropped out after first or second grade because they had to work.

Then I realize me and Miguelito have been lucky: my parents send back money, we didn't have to work when we were little, except sometimes when Felipe would give us money to ride with him in the micro. We'd help older passengers get inside, clean any trash people left and stuff like that. Felipe always made us sit in the back, where it was safer, but he'd talk to us the whole time and glance at us in the rearview mirror. It wasn't very hard, since it was just a microbus that couldn't fit more than fifteen people. It's not like it was a full-size bus. I didn't have to start working for real, en el campo, until after fourth grade. And even then, I didn't have to quit school, I just had to spend a few hours in the afternoon or on Saturdays stirring soil, or washing and feeding livestock. Then I'd ride my bike home and do my homework.

Mamá always says on the phone that she feels bad that I've had to work at all. But at least half the kids in my class did something similar, and, like I said, me and Miguelito were the lucky ones. I was happy to help bring in money, and I didn't mind being busy. Felipe always called me "hiperactivo." Even if I didn't have to go anywhere, I'd still ride my bike all around Naranjito and to other nearby pueblos. Or I'd go play fútbol with the boys in my class and come back with my clothes so dirty that Tía would get annoyed. She's always trying to explain consequences by telling me and Miguelito about "causa y efecto." I didn't take care of my clothes (causa), so she had to wash them (efecto). She was annoyed at me for getting my clothes dirty (causa), and next time she might not let me play fútbol (efecto).

I also always felt lucky because I had my best friend, Cami. We met at school in third grade when Cami saw me writing a rap during recess. I was embarrassed to show her at first, but she told me she liked singing and making music too, and she was impressed with my rhymes (they probably weren't very good, but I was little back then, and I've gotten better). Later, we became close with another girl named Daniela, who had a computer in her house, and if I didn't have to work after school, we'd spend the afternoon looking up karaoke versions of songs on YouTube. We'd spend hours singing.

I love music. I like rock most of all, but I love rap and reggaetón too. Actually, there isn't any kind of music I don't like. I even like songs in other languages like Portuguese or English. Even though I can't sing along and I don't understand what the words mean, the songs still make me feel things.

That's why I was writing a rap during recess—I knew I was just a kid, but I wanted to write music good enough that I could perform it someday. Once I was friends with Cami and Daniela, we'd write and record songs together, even though we didn't have any instruments. Then, when we got tired of singing, we'd play Need for Speed or Call of Duty on Daniela's PS3. Or we'd watch *Dragon Ball Z* or *Naruto* or some other animes together.

I used to always ask Tía if we could invite Cami and Daniela over to our house, too, but she said no girls allowed. Sometimes on the street, she would point at other boys who were a few years older than me. She'd say their parents had let them invite girls over (causa). Then she'd point at the babies in their arms (efecto).

I used to have friends who were boys, from my class, and we'd go play fútbol or go fishing together. Occasionally, I'd come back with a fish and Tía would cook it for a dinner. But I've never had a ton of male friends. Most boys in my class always wanted to go looking for snakes, and snakes creep me out. I got along fine with them, but I didn't really like them enough to want them to come over. Cami and Daniela were the only close friends I needed.

So that was how things were until everything started to go wrong. But

I've written a lot tonight, and I don't want to go into the bad stuff yet, so I'll write again soon.

A MONTH LATER

Naranjito

I know it's been a while since I've written in here. I've been really busy working, but today is Sunday, so I have a little bit more time to write. To be honest, I think part of the reason I haven't been writing is because I don't want to talk about all the bad stuff. But I do think it'll be good to write it down. Writing makes me feel a little better, for whatever reason.

First, there was the microbus. That was on a Sunday, too. I'd just talked to my parents on the phone for the first time in a few weeks. After I hung up, Felipe asked me and Miguelito to come with him to work. He always used to try to get us to help him when he was driving the microbus because he worked a lot, and we wouldn't get to spend much time together otherwise. Or maybe he wanted us to learn to be microbus drivers. It's a more stable job than working on a hacienda, and it's safer, too. It's supposed to be, anyway.

Miguelito said he didn't want to go, because it was the birthday of a friend in his class. Miguelito is obsessed with birthdays, he always remembers everyone's, it's his favorite thing. But a week before anyone's birthday, Miguelito is already planning.

So it was just Tío Felipe and me. It was dark by the time we'd dropped off all our passengers, and he was driving back to the station where he parked the micro overnight. I felt impatient, because I'd just started sixth grade and I had a lot of homework. But I'd had to work the day before, and then on that Sunday I'd had to go to church, and then I was helping Felipe, so I hadn't finished my assignments yet. We were doing word problems in math. ("Adriana sembró 10 hileras de maíz con 8 plantas cada una. El 20% murieron. ¿Cuántas plantas quedan?") Figuring out how many of Adriana's corn plants survived was fun but hard. Word problems took me a long time.

Tío Felipe could tell I was worried about finishing my homework, but he said the most important thing was to focus on the present. Deal with the future in the future. He gave us speeches like that all the time, full of life lessons, and he'd always conclude them with some kind of proverb like *No hay mal que por bien no venga* (Every cloud has a silver lining). Maybe he hoped that if he said them enough times, we'd never forget them. If that was the plan, it worked, because he said them so often that I could already predict what proverb he was about to say just then: *Paso a paso se va lejos.* One step at a time, you can travel far.

"You can worry about your homework when we get home," he said. "Paso a paso, se va—"

Felipe never got to the end of the proverb.

It happened fast. He was looking at me in the rearview mirror when I heard screeching wheels outside. I looked out the window and saw a bus—a real bus, a yellow-school-bus-size bus—slam into the driver's side of our microbus at full speed. There was a crash, and the sound of metal bending and glass shattering. I flew out of my seat. Then there was another crash, and then another, and then the smell of something burning.

I don't know how I got out of the microbus. I don't remember. There were people all around. They must have been trying to talk to me, but I couldn't hear. I was sitting on grass. The bus was upside down on the grass with me. The wheels were still spinning slowly in the air.

There was blood all over my leg, but I didn't feel any pain at all. I wondered for a second if it was somebody else's leg. After a few minutes, I realized I had just been in a car accident. I still couldn't make sense of the sounds I was hearing, but I started looking at the adults all around me to see if any of them were Tío Felipe. For the first time, I wondered why microbuses don't have seat belts.

I don't think I ever passed out, but I don't remember going to the hospital. Somehow, I got there. A doctor checked all my injuries and said that miraculously, I wasn't hurt too bad. I just broke my right ankle and got a lot of scrapes and bruises. So that was the good news.

Tía had tears in her eyes when she gave me the bad news: the bigger bus had slammed right into the driver's side of the micro, and Felipe didn't survive. She said he probably died instantly.

This was a few months ago, but it's still kind of hard to think about and write about. Sometimes when I wake up, I forget for a minute that Felipe isn't here anymore. I know Tía cries a lot about it. I wished Mamá and Papá could've come back for the funeral. At least then I'd get to meet my baby sister. But I know coming back is complicated.

1

Cuando I nasi no tube la oportunidad
de conoser a mi mamá ni mi Papá
Solamente conosi a mi abuela mi Primos
y mi tio cuando yo tengo memoria
recuerdo cuando yo iba al quinder
de ai llo fui ala Primaria de ai
llege ala secundaria bueno todo era
feliz Happy Pero cuando ocurrio
una tragedia con mi tio

nosotros ibamos en un autobus
y derepenten Pum un choque feo yo
y mi Primo sobrebibimos mi tio murio
las ultimas Palabras fueron (Los amo
mucho mis hisos) y fallesio Pasaron los
años termine la Primaria y entre
ala secundaria siempre estube nose
solo tres años solo no tenia muchos
amigos amigos no conosido
compañeros en ton ses conosi a
una Persona qe se llama
fue una
amiga qe era como yo comensamos
adescubrir lo qe nos gustaba

Written by me, this is my very first entry inside my actual black-and-white notebook detailing the story of my life from the very beginning when I did not have the opportunity to know my mom and dad growing up.
Photo taken by Iván Morales.

THE NEXT DAY

Naranjito

Finally I've managed to write for two days in a row. Success! I think I can wrap up all the bad stuff that happened with one more entry. Then what'll I write about? I could talk about the things that happen day-to-day, but compared to the past few months, that'll be pretty boring. Anyway . . .

After the micro accident, things started going wrong so fast that they all blurred together. It has almost felt like horrible things are bound to happen over and over, like some kind of punishment. Afterward, I had to stay in bed because of my broken ankle. But if I could have walked, I still would've stayed in bed. Miguelito is the same way. For two weeks after the accident, he didn't go to school. He has barely left the house since then. He's gotten really close to Caramelo, so Tía made an exception to her rule, washed him, and she has been letting him come inside. Miguelito falls asleep with him almost every night.

As soon as my foot was healed enough for me to walk, I had to quit school and start working full-time because, otherwise, without the money Felipe had made, we wouldn't be able to afford the house and food and Tía's medicamentos. Tía asked my parents to start sending a little more money every week, but they have to pay for things en el Norte too, especially to care for my baby sister. Miguelito still isn't working. Tía thinks it's important for him to stay in school because he's still so young.

Tía also made an exception to her no-girls rule and let Cami come over sometimes too, during the daytime, since I couldn't see her at school anymore. But it didn't last long, because Cami had even more bad news. She was dropping out of sixth grade, too. Her parents were worried about how gangs were starting to do bad stuff in other pueblos near Naranjito, and they were taking her to los Estados Unidos where she'd be safer.

The same day Cami told me that, I called my parents and asked if I could come join them in Nashville. I said we could all go, me and Miguelito and Tía. They said no. When I asked why not, they just said it was complicated and we'd be together one day, but not now. Then they changed the subject.

I didn't say anything at the time, because I've never had a fight with my parents, but I guess what's a notebook for if it isn't to say the things you can't say in real life?

Between you and me, it's not fair that I can't be with Mamá and Papá. I was really mad when I hung up the phone. Nobody stopped them from going to el Norte, and they were barely older than me when they went. If I'm not in school and Cami is gone and Felipe isn't alive anymore, why should I have to stay here?

Now you know pretty much all the bad stuff that has happened in the last year. I feel a little better now that I've actually "talked" about it.

I'm kind of liking this writing thing. I'll write more tomorrow.

THE NEXT DAY

Naranjito

Three days writing in here in a row. But today I'm writing because it turns out the bad stuff isn't over yet. Today, Tía brought me and Miguelito to church. That should've been my first clue. She always brings us to church on Sundays, but today is Tuesday. Afterward, she bought us rosquillas to eat and said we had to talk about something serious. She told us that her sickness was getting worse and that we were going to have to put our faith in Cristo and be strong because she wasn't going to be around for very much longer.

We'd known she was a little sick . . . she'd been coughing for years. It was actually pretty annoying because me and Miguelito sleep in her bedroom, and she coughs so loud that it wakes me up, and then I can't fall back sleep. But we never thought about it very much. We never thought it meant that she was going to die.

She told me I'd have to look after Miguelito the same way she and Felipe had looked after us. She said she would love and protect us desde el cielo, and one day we would all be together again.

I cried and hugged her and told her it wasn't true, that she just needed to get a better doctor. I said I'd work even harder to make more money so she could go to San Pedro Sula and maybe there they could give her medicamentos that would make her better.

But she just shook her head and talked to me in a way she never had before, the same way she always talked to Felipe. She said I'm big now, and I have to understand. She doesn't want to get my hopes up, and she's not going to waste the little money we have just to make things a little slower. She said "Dios tenía un plan para todos" and he would always be with us. He had protected me in the microbus accident, and he would protect me even after she was gone.

Miguelito didn't say anything, but when Tía hugged both of us at the same time, he started to cry with long, heavy sobs that shook his whole body.

I haven't cried like that yet. It doesn't feel real.

THREE WEEKS LATER

Naranjito

I know I haven't written in, like, three weeks . . . I've just been working and trying to help Tía, and when I'm not helping her, I'm talking to Miguelito about stuff when he gets sad.

I guess things are getting worse. For the past few weeks, Tía seemed to be getting a little weaker, but she still went to church almost every day. Then, one morning, after she'd been coughing all night, she told us to come with her to the hospital. We've been here for four days. The nurses are nice to me and Miguelito, and they're always explaining what's going on. They say we're good nietos. Yesterday, they showed me radiografías of Tía's lungs: there was a shadow where there wasn't supposed to be one, and they said that meant she wouldn't be alive for much longer.

Causa y efecto.

TWO DAYS LATER

Naranjito

Six days at the hospital. Tía keeps getting quieter, her breathing is getting shallower, and her face is starting to change color and even change shape, it's like the skin is sitting on her face in a different way than it ever has before. I've been trying to avoid looking at her because it makes me feel weird and sad and guilty, like I'm seeing something I'm not supposed to, like I'm watching her get dressed or something. It feels like dying is turning her into a different person.

But actually, if I think about it, it's me and Miguelito who are turning into different people. We have always been like siblings, but I think it's during these past few days that we've become brothers for real. It's hard to explain, but for as long as I can remember, our family was Tía, Felipe, Miguelito, and me (and also Caramelo, but I think dogs go in a different category). Four people in a family of four. After Felipe was gone, it was like the meaning of "our family" shifted, so four people's worth of family had to exist in just three of us. And now, in the hospital, while Tía is dying, it's like her share of the weight is slipping onto us too, and between the two of us, me and Miguelito have to become a family of four. I feel this love and worry for Miguelito that's different from anything I've ever experienced before. I know it's weird, but yesterday, I just turned to him and said, "Miguelito, when we get back, you have to do really good at school, okay?" He looked kind of confused, but he nodded.

I have a feeling we'll be going back soon, but I'm not sure I want to. I'm not ready to say goodbye. I'm not ready to become a family of two.

THE NEXT DAY

Naranjito

Day seven. Padre Juan came today to say some prayers over Tía. He said some prayers with me and Miguelito, too. He told us he would do her funeral, and that he was sure she would go "directamente al cielo." He said it was important for us to keep going to church even though Tía wouldn't be there to force us to anymore.

So, I guess that means it's almost over, even if I don't want it to be. Does that make me selfish?

HOURS LATER

Naranjito

I know it's only been a few hours since the last time I wrote, but I wanted to let you know. Tía is gone. The last thing she said to me and Miguelito was "Dios los guarde y los proteja." God keep and protect us.

I guess I don't know what happens now. I don't know what to write, even. I'm not sure I'll know tomorrow either.

TWO DAYS LATER
Naranjito

Querida Tía:

Padre Juan says that because you're not here anymore, you're in Heaven, that I can talk to you and you'll hear me. Since you were the one who gave me this notebook, I figure that if I write to you in it, you can read it, too. I was thinking before you went to Heaven that I might show you my notebook after I'd filled up all the pages, and that maybe you'd be proud that I wrote so much. I hope you can be proud of me from up there too.

Love,
D.

THE NEXT DAY
Naranjito

Querida Tía:

It's weird being in the house without you. We're still letting Caramelo sleep inside. I hope you don't mind. I try to keep him as clean as possible, I promise.

We miss you. I've talked to Mamá every day on the phone since you died, and I told her that I'm writing to you in my notebook. She says to tell you that she misses you, too, and she's sorry she wasn't with you in the hospital. And she also asks for you to please watch over me and Miguelito extra carefully.

Love,
D.

TWO DAYS LATER

Naranjito

Querida Tía:

When Miguelito is crying all night, I don't know what to do except for hug him and offer to make him some rice or bring him some water. If there's anything you can do to help him be okay, please do it. I might start suggesting we say the Rosary at night, like you used to make us do, just so we have something to give the day some kind of, like, conclusion. And maybe it'll help him feel like you're still here.

I'm going to tell Miguelito that I think he should try to go back to school tomorrow. I need to start working again or else we're going to run out of money, and I think he'd be even sadder if he wasn't home alone all day.

Love,
D.

A MONTH LATER

Naranjito

Querida Tía:

Sorry it's been a few weeks. I've been working as much as I can, plus I've been learning how to do stuff I've never done before, like how to pay the dueño of our house for rent and electricity and water, how to cook, how to go to the tienda to collect the money Mamá and Papá send. So it has been hard to find time to write. A few times I've sat down to start writing, but it feels like if I sit still for too long, I'll start crying. But I'm not going to stop writing, ever, because I don't want you to think I've forgotten about you.

Now that you're not here to keep track of money, I understand that wc are poor for real. I look at how much we have (almost nothing), and I get this antsy feeling in my chest when I think about how much I'll make working (almost nothing), and how much we have to pay to stay in the house (so much). It felt less real when you were taking care of money stuff. Did you have any tricks? How did you keep from freaking out every week, worrying you wouldn't be able to pay for food or something? We must have always been this poor, I guess, but you and Felipe just didn't want me and Miguelito to worry about it. I don't know how you had any money to put in the basket at church or for me to buy a baleada at lunch. There was a reason Felipe was working all the time. Now I'm the one who has to work like crazy just so we can afford food and the house and electricity. And so Miguelito can stay in school. That's the most important thing.

I wake up at 4:40 every morning except Sundays, so that I can be outside by the time the señor comes around in his truck to pick up workers. The señor is . . . well, he's exactly that, a man who drives through Naranjito in the mornings to bring us to the haciendas for work. I have to be outside by five o'clock, or else he'll drive past. There are lots of people looking for work, so he doesn't need to wait for me.

Most days, the señor brings us to one of the haciendas outside the pueblo. We stay there all day, working in the heat. The sun almost makes you more exhausted than the work because there's no shade anywhere. My skin is starting to peel off like it never did before. Felipe's old hat doesn't fit me, and I can't decide if I should buy a new one at the tiendita. For now, at least, I figure that I don't need to spend the money, I can just put up with the sun.

When we show up at the haciendas, the señores in charge give us instructions. Every day, no matter what, we have to lead the cows to the river to drink. Some haciendas have more than five hundred of them, so it takes forever. I'm still not very good at it, because until I started working on the haciendas, I'd only been on a horse a few times. I'm trying to get better as fast as I can, but I keep falling off and hurting myself. The older workers tell me to be really careful because if you fall and don't get up fast enough, the cows might trample you. It sounds scary, but I'm not super worried about it, because every time I fall, these amazing dogs that help us herd the cattle show up out of nowhere to make sure I don't get stepped on. Once I'm on my feet, I always want to pet the dogs to thank them for saving me, but they disappear just as quickly as they showed up. So, after the señor drives me home at seven or eight at night, I make sure to give Caramelo extra snuggles, and I put some extra scraps outside the front door for him, if we have any. For the past month, snuggling with Caramelo has been the best part of the day.

Love,
D.

TWO WEEKS LATER
Naranjito

Tía, just a quick update: I gave in and bought a hat. The skin on my head was peeling, and it hurt so bad that I couldn't focus on the work. Plus, I couldn't see as well with the sun in my eyes all day. I bought the cheapest hat they had. It's the best 110 lempira I've ever spent.

—D.

A FEW WEEKS LATER
Naranjito

Querida Tía:

Today at the hacienda, they made us put hay into this hay-cutting machine that scares me a lot. It's big and louder than a motorcycle or any machine I've ever seen. I've only had to work with it one time before, and it gave me nightmares about accidentally getting my hand cut off. Since then, if there's any other work to do, I always ask the other men if they can operate the machine while I do one of the other tasks. They've usually agreed, maybe because some of them have kids my age and they feel a little sorry for me. But today there were no other tasks to do, so it was either work with the scary machine or don't go to the hacienda.

So, anyway, I guess I just wanted to pray that you would help me not have nightmares tonight about getting my hand chopped off. Please, thank you. Love you. Miss you.

—D.

THE NEXT DAY

Naranjito

Querida Tía:

There was no work on the haciendas today. I stood outside at five in the morning, but the señor never came. So I went to the tiendita to ask them if they needed any help doing odd jobs. Sometimes they do, and it's easier than working on the haciendas, but they pay way less. They didn't need help either, though, so I waited for a delivery truck to come through and asked the driver if I could ride along and help unload stuff. He said yes. Drivers almost always say yes when I ask for work. They're on tight schedules, so they'll take all the help they can get. Also, since I'm just a kid, they don't have to pay me as much as they'd pay an adult. It's a little fun, because I get to drive around the whole region unloading flour and sugar and stuff. The drivers are usually nice. I feel good helping them. But now my arms are like rubber, and I know that tomorrow my whole body will be so sore that it'll be hard to get out of bed.

I do all this work so Miguelito can stay in school. He has been depressed, obviously, since you and his papá died. I'm sad all the time, too, but I'm also tired, so I don't have energy to act sad, if that makes sense. I'm worried that if Miguelito had to quit school, too, he'd be way worse. And him and Caramelo are all I have left. Other than that, I'm alone all the time. He can see how hard I've been working, and he has been trying to stay positive for me. He's doing good in school, just like I told him he had to. And he's working, too, but just a little bit in the afternoons. I wish he didn't have to work at all, but if he didn't, we wouldn't be able to survive. I make less money than Felipe did because most of the señores give me less than they pay the grown-ups. They say that since I'm a kid, I'm not as helpful, so they can't pay as much. That really annoys me—they still expect me to work for as long and as hard as the adults.

Love,
D.

P.S.—no nightmares about the hay-cutting machine last night. Thank you ❤!

A WEEK AND A HALF LATER

Naranjito

Querida Tía:

I talked to Cami today. She's in los Estados Unidos now, and a few nights of the week I go to the tienda so we can talk on the phone, I feel guilty spending money to use the telephone. It's the only thing I spend money on that isn't technically necessary, and we don't even have enough to pay the dueño everything we owe him. But some days, it's the only time all day that I smile.

I talk to Cami more than I talk to Mamá and Papá. I love my parents, and I know they care about me, but we've never really known each other, so we don't have a lot to talk about. But Cami and me can talk about music, and her parents, and Miguelito, and the fun stuff we used to do. I tell her about work and money, and she tells me about all the new things she's doing, like eating at McDonald's. She's working, too—she has been painting houses. I can't believe how much she gets paid. She makes more money in two hours than I do in a whole day on a hacienda. She even has a cell phone now, she says everyone in los Estados Unidos has them. One time, she said if she worked for three hours a day for just four days, she would earn enough to buy a PS4. I changed the subject when she said that because it reminded me of the word problems I was supposed to do on the day Felipe died.

Either way, I didn't even know there was a PS4. I thought the PS3 was the newest one. Maybe the PS4 is only in los Estados Unidos.

She never bought a PS4, though. Most weeks, when she can, she sends me some of the money she earns. It was hard for me to take it at first. I felt bad, and I still feel bad. I don't want her to have to work so hard just to give me her money. But she has a really big heart, and she feels sorry for me and Miguelito. I used to thank her a lot every time we talked on the phone, but she asked me to stop.

There's another reason I take her money: Naranjito has been getting more dangerous. I know it was getting worse when you were around, but I didn't really pay attention to it, because you were here to look out for us. Sometimes, Tío Felipe would say stuff about the gangs and violence in San

Pedro Sula or Tegucigalpa, but it was just news. Like, it was a sad thing that was happening in the world, but it was far away, like the guerra civil en Siria or the victoria de Donel Tromp en los Estados Unidos. But since you've been gone, a lot of adults who know me and Miguelito live alone—like Padre Juan and some of the men I work with on the haciendas—have started to warn us that the gangs are becoming more present in other pueblos near here. The gangs are famous for kidnapping kids and forcing them to join. I'm worried that they might come for Miguelito. But I know that sometimes, if you give them money, they'll leave you alone. So we want to save up a little bit of emergency money, for when they finally reach us here. I haven't been able to save any yet, but I hope I can start soon.

So, please keep protecting us, Tía, especially Miguelito.

Love,
D.

TWO WEEKS LATER

Naranjito

Querida Tía:

Today, Miguelito asked about going to el Norte. He was nervous, but I know he's been thinking about it a lot. I think he's really set on it. I want to go to el Norte, too, obviously, but I know you and Tío Felipe didn't want us to, and Mamá and Papá wouldn't let us.

"¿Y si fuéramos al Norte?" he asked.

He said it when he was sitting under a mango tree, eating a mango, with yellow mango mush on his lips and cheeks. Which is especially confusing because Miguelito hates mangos.

I didn't really want to have that conversation, so to dodge the question I asked him why he was eating a mango when he hates them.

"I used to, but I changed my mind—it's tasty!" he said. Then he pointed up at the tree branches above him. "And it's free! But I think we should leave Naranjito because you'd get to go back to school and we could live with your parents and you wouldn't have to work all the time and we'd get to just be normal kids and—"

I love Miguelito. He's such a funny kid. Ever since he was little, whenever he's nervous, he talks in these really long sentences with a million *ands*. The longer the sentence gets, the faster he talks, and the harder it is to keep track of what he's saying. You have to interrupt him mid-sentence or he'll keep going until he runs out of breath.

"Okay, hang on, let me think about it for a few days, okay?" I said. Even though I've been thinking about all these things almost nonstop for months, ever since we came back from the hospital without you.

I think Miguelito had wanted me to decide right then and there, but I need time to think it through. And write to you about it. And sleep on it. Now I sound like Miguelito with the million *ands*.

I'm gonna go to bed now, but I'll write more tomorrow.

Love,
D.

THE NEXT DAY

Naranjito

Querida Tía,

I've been thinking about what Miguelito said: "You'd get to go back to school and we could live with your parents and you wouldn't have to work all the time and we'd get to just be normal kids." All of this made me really want to leave.

You'd get to go back to school. I wasn't the smartest kid in my class, but I was good at school. At the end of fifth grade, the profe told me I'm a good writer and gave me a bunch of books. I was going to read them, but then the microbus accident happened, and I never had time. They've been on the floor of your room for two years. Maybe if I went to school, I could read again and start learning how to write for real, instead of just scribbling rap lyrics in notebooks and writing letters to you.

We could live with your parents. When you and Felipe were here, you always made me feel totally loved and taken care of. But ever since you died, I haven't even hugged anyone except Miguelito and Caramelo. I don't like to think sad thoughts for too long, but whenever I talk to my parents, I feel this kind of . . . not *anger*, that's not the right word, but I feel this kind of unhappy, lonely feeling, and I don't know how to make it go away. Maybe going to Nashville will help.

You wouldn't have to work all the time. I've been thinking a lot about this today . . . and every day, if I'm being honest. I don't just feel lonely and exhausted. I feel trapped. Like, I'm not even making enough money to support Miguelito, and I'm never going to make very much more, because I'm not in school, so I'm never going to learn how to become like, an electrician or a musician or a video game designer or anything. I'm going to be stuck waking up at 4:40 in the morning and working all day and peeling dead skin off my forehead forever,. Other than leaving, I don't see any way to change that. I can't just keep doing this for another sixty years.

We'd get to just be normal kids. At the end of fifth grade, a few months before the microbus accident, we had a talent show, and Cami and Daniela convinced me to sing a song with them. I was super nervous, but once we started performing and I saw the other kids get into it, I felt really good about myself. After that, the three of us got really popular, and I was really, really happy. Going back to that part of life feels impossible . . . but maybe it isn't? I'm thirteen now. I know work and stress and pain are part of life, but can't there be time for friends and fútbol and music too?

It's really tempting, but I know going to el Norte is hard. We don't know exactly how to go, and it would take money (we don't really have a lot of that). And time. I think it takes like a week to get there, but I could be wrong . . . it might take longer. Everyone also says getting through México is really hard, that you have to be sneaky. People have told me that the police in México are really tough—they'll try to stop you from getting into México, and then they'll also try to keep you from crossing out of México into los Estados Unidos. The good news is that once you're across the Río Bravo—I don't know exactly where that is, but people say it's what you have to cross to get to the country—all you have to do is find la Migra on los Estados Unidos side, and as long as you're not a criminal or anything, they'll help you get to your family. Obviously we can't be criminals, because we're just kids.

But Miguelito is still pretty young. He's really sensitive, too, so I don't know if he could handle it.

Plus, we couldn't tell Mamá and Papá, because they would say not to go. And going without telling them feels weird. We also couldn't take

Caramelo with us. So for now, I'm going to tell Miguelito we should stay here and see if things get worse with the gangs. If they do, we can talk about going again.

Love,
D.

A WEEK LATER

Naranjito

Querida Tía:

Writing to you at 4:30 in the morning while I wait for the señor with the truck to take me to work on the hacienda. I haven't slept really. I don't know if I'd be able to. But I wanted to update you on what happened.

Last night, when I got back from the hacienda, Miguelito was crying like I haven't seen since you told us your sickness was worse. The kind of crying where snot was dripping into his mouth and his chest kept moving up and down and he couldn't even get words out. For a second, I thought he was hurt or sick. I ran over and asked him what was wrong. I said a prayer in my head: *Por favor, que no se muera Miguelito también.* He couldn't answer, so I looked all over his body to see if he was bleeding or something. He wasn't. He didn't seem hurt. I hugged him, and I started crying too, even though I didn't know what was wrong. I held him really tight and told him everything was going to be all right. I don't know if that was the right thing to say, it's just what people say in movies when someone is crying.

When his breath started getting a little more normal, he tried to explain what happened. A neighbor had come over with something wrapped in a blanket. She saw a dog get hit by a delivery truck before the truck drove away. She had recognized Caramelo.

We cried all night. Before sunrise, we dug a hole behind the house and buried him with two ripe avocados, one from each of us.

I think this is it. I think we have no reason to stay in Naranjito anymore.

We're going to Nashville.

We're going to have a family again.

We're going to go to school and learn English and make friends and be kids again.

And as soon as we get to our new home, we're going to adopt a perro aguacatero and name him Caramelo Segundo.

Love,
D.

THE NEXT DAY
Naranjito

Querida Tía:

I think getting ready to leave is going to be easy. Here's my plan:

Step one: Make as much money as we can for a few weeks, leave sometime in January.
Step two: Hitchhike, walk, or take buses to Guatemala.
Step three: Figure out a plan to get across Guatemala to the border with México.
Step four: Figure out a plan to get across México to los Estados Unidos.
Step five: Call Mamá and Papá and have them pick us up.

I'm the most worried about step five, because I decided I'm not going to tell my parents we're leaving. If I did, they'd definitely say we're not allowed to go.

Papá will be all encachimbado that we left Naranjito without telling him. It won't be the best way to start our real-life relationship. Not to mention, I don't know how far Nashville is from the border, but he'll be annoyed if he has to go on a long drive to get us, especially if he has to take the day off work.

And Mamá might be worried, because they've started calling every Sunday since you left, and I'll miss their call if it takes us more than seven days to get to los Estados Unidos. She'll think something bad has happened to me. Ever since you died, she has been more paranoid about us being safe. If we're not there to pick up the phone, she'll probably call other people in Naranjito to go check on us. When we get to the border, she'll be relieved at first that we're safe, but then she'll be encachimbada, too, just like Papá, because we made her worry for no reason.

I think you'd also probably tell us not to go . . . if you were here. Maybe not. I don't know what you'd think about the gangs getting closer. Maybe you'd want us to go.

Anyway, besides being worried about how my parents will react, we think it'll be fun. Miguelito is excited, partly because he's been wanting to go to el Norte for a long time, but also because neither of us has ever left Honduras. We're not sure how different it will be. It's like a little adventure. Plus, Tía Gloria and our cousins live in Guatemala, and we've talked to her on the phone before, so once we're on step three of our plan, maybe we can find a phone and call them.

Wish us luck.

TEN DAYS LATER
Naranjito

Querida Tía:

It's Sunday, which means I talked to Mamá and Papá on the phone. The conversation went something like this:

PAPÁ: Have they been making you do anything dangerous on the haciendas? (*I know he's been feeling guilty since Felipe died. He doesn't want me to have to work. But he can't send enough money for us to survive, so there isn't any choice.*)

ME: No. (*He doesn't believe me, though. I'm not a very good liar, as you know, Tía.*)

PAPÁ: Because if they are, you don't have to work there. We can find a way to send you more money. (*He isn't a very good liar either. I change the subject.*)

ME: I wish I was there. Can me and Miguelito come to Nashville?

PAPÁ: One day. Soon.

ME: Okay. Te quiero, Papá.

I almost told him about our plan. But I know he'd be against it. That was another one of Felipe's proverbs: *Es más fácil pedir perdón que pedir permiso.* Still, I feel bad for not telling him. He'll forgive me, though, right, Tía?

Love,
D.

THE NEXT DAY
Naranjito

Querida Tía:

Happy New Year, I guess. This is the first full year of my life I'm gonna spend without you, and with me and Miguelito going north, I think it'll be a year with lots of other firsts, too. I hope some of those will be good ones, to make up for not having you here anymore. More soon.

Love,
D.

TWO WEEKS LATER
Naranjito

Querida Tía:

I worked like usual the past few weeks, but I didn't pay for the electricity or anything else, and Miguelito skipped school so he could work too—not on the haciendas, but odd jobs wherever he could get them. We thought about selling some of our stuff so we'd have a little extra money, but it's a small town, and we don't want anyone getting suspicious and calling our parents. We don't have anything that'd be worth much anyway.

Today we went to the tienda to pick up the money my parents sent this week, and between that and what we've made in the past few days, we have 1,856 lempira. We know we can't use lempira outside of Honduras. In Guatemala, they use quetzales, in México, they use pesos, and in los Estados Unidos, they use dólares. We asked the man at the tienda how much our lempira will be worth in those countries. He typed on his computer for a minute, then told us that 1,856 lempira was equal to 587 quetzales guatemaltecos, 1,493 pesos mexicanos, and 76 dólares estadounidenses. It seemed unfair that our money was worth so much less in other money, but maybe stuff will be cheaper outside Honduras.

We went home and shoved some food, clothes, and water bottles into bags. As soon as I finish writing, I'm putting this notebook you gave me into my bag. First thing tomorrow, we're heading for the bus stop.

Bye-bye, house. Hasta nunca.

Love,
D.

THE NEXT DAY

Trinidad

Querida Tía:

All right, so we already made it to our first stop, Trinidad, another pueblo to the west of Naranjito. When I used to help delivery drivers unload their trucks in the area, we almost always stopped at the tienda here. It looks . . . pretty much exactly like Naranjito: green, peaceful, with a big white church in the middle of town.

Getting here in a truck is fast—the drive only takes like twenty minutes. But the walk felt like it took two hours. We tried to flag down a few cars that were driving by to see if they'd take us, but none of them stopped. It's hot, and we drank most of the water we packed, but it was okay because we knew we'd be able to refill our bottles as soon as we got here.

The bigger problem that I hadn't expected is that my right foot hurts. It healed pretty well after the microbus accident, but it still hurts sometimes when I'm doing something that involves a lot of standing and lifting on the haciendas. I've never had a problem just walking before, though. I guess I don't usually walk for more than two hours straight. Hopefully we'll be able to hitch rides most of the way to Guatemala.

We walked to a park in town, refilled our water, and rested under a bench. There's a bus stop here, and Miguelito suggested we try to get a bus to Guatemala. He doesn't want to keep walking.

At the bus stop, we asked some adults which bus to take to Guatemala. They all looked a little confused. Eventually, a woman told us there aren't any buses that go straight there, but there's a bus that goes north, and north is the right direction.

When the bus got here, we asked the driver if he'd let us ride for free. (It was worth a shot!) He just shook his head like we were crazy. So we gave him eighty lempira each and got on. We're just starting to drive now. I recognize some of the places we're passing—the señor has driven past them on the way to the haciendas. Miguelito is starting to fall asleep, so at least he'll get some rest. I'm gonna look out the window now, but I'll try to write to you again tonight.

Love,
D.

A FEW HOURS LATER
La Entrada

Querida Tía:

It's nighttime now. We're in La Entrada. By the time we got here, there was almost no one left on the bus, and the driver said we had to get off because this was the last stop. We found some benches here at the bus station to try to sleep on. A few other people are sleeping on them, too. Some of them look like they're just waiting for their buses, and other ones look like they don't have anywhere else to go.

The bench is really hard, and I think it's going to be hard to fall asleep. What if someone steals my bag while I'm sleeping? I guess there isn't anything valuable in it anyway. I'll close my eyes and see what happens.

I just wanted to let you know we're getting closer and we're safe. Though I guess you already knew that if you're watching over us. At least I hope you are.

Anyway, more tomorrow.

Love,
D.

THE NEXT DAY

Under a bridge somewhere

Querida Tía:

Today has been weird, this trip isn't going exactly the way we'd expected. I didn't sleep very well—besides the hard bench, the sounds of buses and people and announcements over the speakers kept me up.

This morning, we ate a few cookies and decided we'd try to get on another bus. But the tickets were way too expensive. So we just followed the road in the same direction as the bus. This whole time, Miguelito has been pretending that he's still as excited as he was when we left Naranjito, but after we woke up, I could tell he wasn't happy to be walking again. We're the only people we've seen walking. Besides us, it's just cars that rush past really fast. We get a little bit worried that they won't see us when they're going around curves.

We're not dumb. We knew it'd take a long time to walk all the way to Guatemala. We kept trying to flag down cars when they went by. Eventually, one of them started to pull over, and Miguelito and me looked at each other and smiled. We took off our backpacks—which had gotten really heavy—and tried to figure out what we were going to say to the driver. We didn't know if we should've told him we were going to los Estados Unidos or to México or what.

Miguelito's attitude suddenly changed.

"Is it safe?" he asked. He has always been like this: whenever he gets excited about something, out of nowhere he'll find a reason not to do it. It drives me crazy sometimes.

I know you always told us not to go anywhere with strangers, but a lot has changed since then. We're older, and we've learned how to fend for ourselves better ever since you've been gone.

"I think so," I said to Miguelito. "There are two of us and only one of him. Plus, it's not like we have a lot of money he could steal anyway."

The driver rolled down his window and asked where we were going.

Miguelito looked at me. We never figured out an answer to that question.

"Guatemala," I said. When you don't know what to say, I figure you might as well tell the truth.

The driver got a weird look on his face.

"Where are your parents?"

It was a weird question. I hadn't expected it. Why did he care where they were?

"En el Norte."

"You boys should go home," he said. "Get in and I'll drive you to La Entrada."

But that was where we just came from, why would we want to go back? I looked at Miguelito, then I looked back at the man and shook my head.

He just sighed, rolled up the window, and drove away.

When he left, me and Miguelito didn't say anything. We walked for a little bit longer because it was starting to get dark. Eventually we found a bridge over a ravine and decided it'd be a good place to sleep. It's fine. We had bad luck getting rides today, but hopefully we'll have better luck tomorrow. We're just getting started.

We're gonna eat some cookies, then go to sleep. We'll use our backpacks as pillows. It's a little noisy when cars drive over the bridge, but I think we'll be able to sleep okay.

Could you watch over us while we're here? I'll sleep better if you do.

Love,
D.

THE FOLLOWING DAY

Still under a bridge somewhere

Tía:

It's early in the morning, Miguelito is still sleeping, the sun is just rising. A car woke me up, and I started thinking about stuff. I figured I'd write to you to see if it helps me think straight. I'm trying to be positive, so Miguelito doesn't get discouraged. And so I don't get discouraged. But even though I haven't said anything to him, I think that if we can't get any rides today, it isn't too late to turn around. We've missed a few days of work and school, but other than that, we could just go back to our lives. What would be the point, though? Just go back to working nonstop so we can barely get by, even when we take money from my parents and Cami? When we left Naranjito, I got this thrilled feeling when I thought about how we were starting a new life. I can't imagine what it would be like to go back.

We'll see what happens.

—D.

A DAY LATER

Somewhere whose name I can't remember

Querida Tía:

So this morning we managed to flag down a car after a few hours. He said he could take us as far as some town I'd never heard of for fifty lempira. He said it was in the right direction. That was way cheaper than what the bus costs, so we got in.

I sat up front, and Miguelito sat in the back. I made sure he buckled his seat belt.

It smelled like cigarette smoke. The driver didn't talk very much. He looked about as old as Felipe, and he had a frizzy beard. I thought about starting a conversation, but in the end, I decided that if he was quiet, I should be quiet too.

When we got into the car, the clock on the dashboard said 3:32. At 6:50, we arrived in some town. Not a huge place, but way bigger than Naranjito. The driver pulled up to a bus station.

"This's it," he said.

I gave him fifty lempira and said gracias.

"Hey," he said when me and Miguelito reached for our doors. We looked back.

He thought about saying something. I was worried he was going to ask for more money. Were we supposed to give him fifty lempira *each*? But after a second, he got a sad sort of look on his face and just said, "Cuídense."

I smiled. Then me and Miguelito went into the bus station to see if there was a bathroom we could use. There was a sign that said PROHIBIDO BAÑARSE, but I splashed some water on my face and under my armpits anyway, because who knows when we'll have another chance.

Love,
D.

FOUR DAYS LATER

Not sure?

Querida Tía:

Things have gone pretty much the same for the past few days. We wake up, we walk, we try to flag down cars. They don't usually stop, but occasionally they do. When that happens, the drivers take us as far as they're willing to take us. Then Miguelito and I get out, figure out which direction Guatemala is in, and walk that way.

All the drivers who've picked us up have been men. Some of them talk a lot, some of them don't. They usually ask for money, but it's never very much. It can't be a lot of money for a grown-up who owns his own car, so I'm not totally sure what's in it for them. Maybe they just like having company. Or maybe they feel sorry for us and pick us up as a favor. It's hard for me to remember sometimes, but Miguelito is just eleven and I'm thirteen (I'm turning fourteen in a little over three weeks, though). People probably see two kids on the street and think they might as well help us.

One man who had a rosary hanging from his rearview mirror said, "Dios los guarde y los proteja," and I almost asked him if he knew you, because that was the last thing you said before you died. I took it as a sign that you're en el cielo looking out for us, like you promised you would be. Maybe you're reading these letters after all.

Love,
D.

TWO DAYS LATER

Outside Ocotepeque

Querida Tía:

We're almost at the border with Guatemala, I think. The landscape has been changing: it's way less mountainy here, and there are more rivers and valleys. Most of all, there are a *lot* more haciendas and farms. I didn't know that even within Honduras, the landscape could be so different. I thought it all looked like Naranjito, to be honest. I guess I never really thought about it.

It has been hard to know where to go. We've been traveling for nine days, even though I think that if there were a bus that went straight from Naranjito to Guatemala, we could've made it in one. Part of the problem is that we're walking part of the way, and that's so much slower than driving. Miguelito gets tired, and my foot hurts, so we need to rest a lot.

I think the bigger problem is that when we've gotten rides, we aren't necessarily taking the fastest route to Guatemala. But as we've gotten closer to the border, it has become easier, because everywhere we go, there have been migrantes like us, and we can ask them. They usually know exactly where we're supposed to go. It's easy to tell when someone's a migrante. Sometimes they're adults or kids or old people or mothers with babies. But somehow, they move in a way that makes it obvious.

I bet other people can tell me and Miguelito are migrantes, too, and thinking about that makes my stomach feel a little upset. It's a similar feeling to when Cami and Daniela and me were about to perform for the school talent show, and everyone had their eyes on me even before we started to sing.

Once we started asking other migrantes where to go, things got a lot easier. Yesterday, an old woman told us that to get into Guatemala, we needed to go to a town called Ocotepeque. From there, we should walk to a pueblo called Santa Fe. She says Santa Fe is right near the border. Then, in Santa Fe, we have a few options:

1) We can go through the official checkpoint and show the agentes de la Migra our passports (we don't have passports).
2) We can go through the official checkpoint and bribe the agentes de la Migra (we don't have enough money).
3) We can pay a pollero to bring us across the border (we don't have enough money).
4) We can try to sneak around the checkpoint without getting caught.

Obviously, the only real option is option four. So that's what we'll do.

Love,
D.

THE FOLLOWING DAY
Santa Fe

As soon as we got to Ocotepeque, men in cars kept driving up to us and asking if we needed a ride across the border. Almost all of them said it was just a forty-five-minute drive, nice and comfy in their cars, and then we'd be in Guatemala. They promised we won't get caught. They said they'd take us across for "just" twenty-five dólares each.

Miguelito thought this was funny: for the past week, we've been trying so hard to get cars to stop so we can ask them to give us rides. But in Ocotepeque, we can't walk anywhere for more than a few minutes without a driver *trying* to give us a ride. Obviously, we can't afford to pay them fifty dólares (that's almost all the money we have left, not to mention we don't even have dólares, only lempira). So, instead, we walked all the way to Sante Fe. It took about four hours, and now we're pretty much dead.

From here, the border is only like a three-hour walk away. All the other migrantes say we should keep going and cross the border at night, because it's easier to avoid getting caught that way. But there's no way we can walk for another three hours. Plus, I think Miguelito gets a little scared after dark. We've found some benches to sleep on. We'll cross the border into Guatemala tomorrow.

Before I started writing, Miguelito asked me what we'll do when we get to Guatemala.

"Are we just gonna keep going like this?"

I've been thinking about it. I can tell Miguelito doesn't like the idea of walking all the way across another country.

"Remember Tía Gloria?" I said. I reminded him that Tía Gloria is your daughter, and Papá and Felipe's sister, and that her sons Elías and Damián are our older cousins. Even though we've never met them in person, he remembered when I reminded him how you always made us call them durante la Navidad y en Semana Santa. "Remember how she lives in Guate? And that's why we can only talk to her on holidays, because it's expensive?" Miguelito noded. He was really tired. "I wrote down her phone number before we left," I said. "Once we're across, we can try and find a way to call her and see what she says to do." He nodded again, then closed his eyes.

I don't know what to expect tomorrow, but I'm kind of excited. I've never been to another country before. I'm curious if it'll be really different. But right now, I'm just grateful to be off my feet.

Love,
D.

THE NEXT DAY

On a bus! In Guatemala!!!!

Querida Tía:

Okay, so getting across was easy. Or, no, it wasn't easy at all, that's the most we've ever walked without stopping. We're exhausted and dirty, because we had to hike through a lot of mud and plants and stuff, and my ankle is killing me. But I'm glad we didn't spend fifty dólares for someone to smuggle us across.

We walked for like three hours, from Santa Fe to the pueblo right on the border. There were a lot of policías and agentes de la Migra guatemalteca there, and long lines of cars. And lots of big 18-wheeler trucks driving through the checkpoint. Wherever we went in the pueblo, the policías kept looking at us, so we walked away from the checkpoint and into the woods next to it.

For a while, there were still a lot of cameras and policías in the woods, and pieces of clothes and trash on the ground, I guess from other migrantes. Eventually, after about an hour, it just looked like an empty forest. There were a few fences we had to climb over, but that was it.

Finally, we started to see a few ads on the side of the road, and then buildings, and power lines, and soon we were at the edge of a town. We stopped at the first little tienda we saw. Outside, there was a pickup truck with its bed full of hundreds of oranges. I looked at Miguelito and, without saying so, we agreed that we should ask to use the tienda's telephone.

Inside, there was a señorita standing behind a counter, writing on a notepad. She was short, with skin darker than mine and really straight, really black hair. She looked like she was probably nineteen or twenty years old.

When we walked in, she said, "Hola, buenas," without looking up.

It occurred to me that we were in a different country, so maybe it's not normal to use the phone in a store here.

"Do you have a phone we can pay to use?" I asked either way.

She lifted her eyes from the notepad for the first time, and she was clearly surprised by what she saw: an eleven-year-old and a thirteen-year-old from Honduras, soaked with sweat, showing up in her tienda with school backpacks. I was embarrassed to be so dirty and gross. We probably smelled terrible. I'd never worried about smelling bad in my life, but suddenly, I was aware of how damp it was under my armpits. And I was doubly embarrassed, because even though I was standing by the entrance so I wouldn't get the floor dirty, Miguelito just walked right in and got mud everywhere.

"Pues . . . sí . . . " she said. "Let me guess. You don't have quetzales?"

I was even more embarrassed when I had to admit we didn't. "We only have lempira. Can we pay you with lempira?"

She smiled.

"Are you calling someone in Guate?" We nodded. She gave us a white plastic phone, with the cord trailing to somewhere behind her counter. "Llamadas gratis. My treat. Let me grab you some towels, too."

Miguelito picked up the phone with his grubby hand without saying anything. I was about to apologize for getting everything so dirty and thank her for letting us use her phone, but she was already gone. Miguelito and me started dialing the number, leaving dirty smudges on the buttons.

It rang. We huddled together, holding the receiver between our two ears so we could both hear. Then, after a few seconds: "¿Aló?"

"¿Tía Gloria?"

"Who is this?"

"It's D. and Miguelito. Your sobrinos."

"¡Chicos! Why are you calling now? What's happening?"

Before I could say anything, Miguelito explained it all with one of his trademark run-on sentences:

"After Tía died we were working too hard and we're going to el Norte to live with D.'s parents, and we just crossed into Guatemala, and it was scary, and it started raining, and we don't have quetzales, and we want to see if we can get your help getting to México, so we can keep going, and we wanted to know where you live, so we can stay with you for a night and rest and . . . "

I held my hand up to signal for Miguelito to stop. Tía Gloria was quiet for a second.

"D., do your parents know?"

Why hadn't I expected her to ask this? Why hadn't I figured out what I was going to say before dialing the phone?

"Um . . . " I said. "Yeah. Yeah, no, they do. It was their idea. We've been talking to them, and they're gonna meet up with us in los Estados Unidos to help us do the . . . paperwork and everything." I hoped it sounded believable.

"Well!" she said. "Where are you now? Ciudad de Guatemala? Can you catch a bus to Quetzaltenango?"

She gave us her address in Quetzaltenango and said she'd be waiting for us the next day. Then she hung up.

The señorita reappeared behind the counter and handed us some clean white towels. "You boys have no idea where you're going, do you?" Before we could say anything, she called out: "¡Antonio! Aquí hay dos chicos que quieren un aventón al bus."

Antonio appeared from the back of the tienda, looked at us, and smirked. He looked the same age as her, but he was tall and strong and looked like he hadn't shaved in a few days.

"They're going to Quetzaltenango."

"Oh yeah?" he said, already heading out the door. "Perfect, c'mon. Leave the towels on the floor. I got oranges to move."

He led us to his truck, and we all crammed into the cab. He drove us through the town, which was actually pretty big—bigger than any of the towns we went through in Honduras. There was reggaetón playing on the radio.

"You guys like Drake?" he asked.

I don't know who Drake is, but the song playing on the radio was "Mía" by Bad Bunny. I've heard it on the radio a million times. I didn't want to tell him he was wrong about the singer, so I didn't say anything.

After a short drive, we arrived in what looked like the middle of town, outside a bus station. Antonio parked, told us to wait in the car, and disappeared.

He came back a few minutes later, opened my door, and handed me a bunch of papers and told me where to go, what buses to get on, what tickets to buy to get to Quetzaltenango. He said that when we got off the first bus, we should ask the driver which bus to get on next. "Ask *the driver*, okay? Not just any adult. You got quetzales?"

I shook my head. He asked me to give him all of our lempira, then he gave us a bunch of quetzales. I couldn't remember how the conversion worked, but he gave us a lot of bills.

I didn't totally process what was happening. I didn't know why he was saying and doing so many things to help us. I was a little scared for some reason. Miguelito kept looking at me and waiting for me to say something, but I didn't know what to say.

"Now, get your muddy butts out of my truck," Antonio said. "Come around to the back, there's something I've got to do before you go."

We got out and stood behind the bed of the truck.

"Turn around," he said.

We were too confused to do anything except obey him. If he'd told me to do a headstand right then and there, I would have. But I was scared. We were facing the bus station, and he was behind us, facing our backsides. I grabbed Miguelito's hand and squeezed it tight.

He touched my backpack. I heard it jostling around, then a zipping noise. The straps got tighter on my shoulders, and I felt the bag get heavier. Then I heard him unzip Miguelito's backpack and do the same thing.

"I hope you like oranges," he said. "You're lucky Sara thought you were cute. Now, go, your bus leaves in twenty."

And that's how we ended up on this bus, heading for Quetzaltenango.

Love,
D.

A DAY LATER

Quetzaltenango

Querida Tía:

We spent all night and most of today on crowded buses. They weren't comfortable at all. They were basically school buses, but they were a billion times better than a park bench, and we slept almost the whole way. I was nervous when we needed to make connections, and I was nervous about asking the drivers to tell us where to go, and I was nervous about buying tickets. But Antonio said to do it, so I did it.

One of the bus drivers was a little rude to me: I asked him where we should go to get our next bus, and when I didn't understand and asked him to repeat himself, he got angry. I guess we don't look like very responsible travelers. We were pretty dirty and stinky, plus we're kids. And it's my fault I didn't understand him, because I don't talk the same way people here do—their accent is different from ours.

We got here, to Quetzaltenango, in the afternoon. It's a really big town, with big, beautiful buildings that look like they're at least as old as the church in Naranjito. To be honest, I'm pretty proud of myself for figuring out how to travel this far in a new country. Tía Gloria gave us her address, but she didn't explain how to get to her house from the bus stop. Antonio said not to ask for directions from anyone except the bus drivers, but he didn't say what to do after the bus trip was over. Eventually I figured out that the best people to ask were mothers with kids. They were the most likely to stop and help us. Most other people just walked past or said no, even though we weren't asking them for anything.

The closer we got, the scarier the barrios seemed. There were tons of people on the street who were watching us and, I don't know, just giving bad vibes. Today was the first time in my life I've felt unsafe walking down the street. I wondered if this was what Naranjito would've felt like once the gangs showed up. I kept Miguelito close. I didn't want him to notice that I was scared, but silently, I prayed that we would find the house before the sun went down, because I know all the worst things happen at night.

Finally, after navigating that way for like two hours—and after getting bad directions from a few people—we finally arrived at Tía Gloria's house as the sun was beginning to set.

"What the hell happened to you two!" was the first thing she said when she saw us. Which was funny, because she'd never seen us before. For all she knew, we could be muddy and smelly like that all the time. "I couldn't wait to hug you, but . . . now I think I'm going to wait a little longer!" She was smiling wide.

We met our cousins, Elías and Damián, too (and unlike Tía Gloria, they hugged us even though we were gross). Meeting for the first time didn't feel like meeting them at all, because we've talked to them on the phone on holidays for our whole lives. The only difference was that, on the phone, we never saw what they looked like. I always pictured them looking more or less like me and Miguelito, but they're more muscly than I imagined, and their skin is darker. Elías is a little bit taller than Damián, but they're both shorter than we are.

For me and Miguelito, it always seemed exotic that our cousins lived so far away, in a place as different as Guatemala. It's crazy to me that now we're here, with them in that exotic place. It feels like everything that has happened in the past week has been a dream.

Love,
D.

THE NEXT DAY

Quetzaltenango

Querida Tía:

Being clean, and wearing completely clean clothes for the first time in a week, is the best feeling in the world. And there's an incredible smell that's still lingering in the house because Tía Gloria made a tasty red stew that she calls pepián de pollo. After eating nothing except cookies and oranges for the past week, I was ready for something hot.

Last night, at dinner, we spent a few minutes talking about our trip. Tía Gloria seemed especially interested in how safe we've been, who we've been getting rides from, and whether anyone has tried to hurt or rob us on the way. We said no—the worst parts of the trip so far have been sleeping on benches, walking for hours, getting stuck in the rain, and dealing with a rude bus driver. And being confused a lot. I told her no one has tried to hurt us, most people have actually been really nice, like the guy who told us which buses to take to get here. The trip has been hard, but we're doing okay. It beats working on a hacienda for the rest of my life. I didn't want her to get worried and call my parents, so I downplayed some of the harder parts of the trip.

After we talked all about the trip, she looked down at her plate and thought about something for a few seconds. When she looked up, there were tears in her eyes. "I'm glad to hear that. Because Damián and Elías have something they want to say."

I turned to my cousins. Damián is fourteen years old, and he and Miguelito have identical senses of humor. Within a few minutes of getting here, they were basically best friends. They're like Naruto and Sasuke. Actually, no—Sasuke is too serious. They're like two Narutos. They both keep doing goofy stuff to try to make the rest of us laugh. At dinner, they kept cracking up, because they've invented a game where they switch the first sounds of words. So "Tía Gloria" has become "Glía Toria," and "Guatemala y México" have become "Muatemala y Géxico." At one point, they were laughing so hard they almost cried because they tried doing it with "pipián de pollo," but then they realized that both words already begin with a *p* sound. They've started calling each other "Oamián" and "Miguelito."

If anyone is more like Sasuke, it's Elías—he's a year older and a lot more serious than Damián. He laughs when someone else tells a joke, but he doesn't joke around himself. When he talks, he uses as few words as possible. When Tía Gloria said they had something to tell us, he's the one who started speaking. He got right to the point:

"Okay. Mamá está enferma. Me and my brother have been working hard, but we still can't afford her medicamentos. We can't keep going like this. We've been trying to convince her to let us go to el Norte. I've been researching how to get across México. When you called yesterday, she finally said we can go, as long as we go with you. Once we're there, we can send back money for her medicamentos and, eventually, send money for her to come join us."

I hadn't been expecting anything like that. Miguelito looked at me, like he wanted me to say something. I just turned and looked at Tía Gloria. She sighed.

"That's their reason," she said. "It isn't my reason. If it were just the money, I wouldn't let them go. ¡Al carajo con mis medicamentos! But I have my own reasons. It isn't safe here." She explained how crime has been getting worse, and boys younger than us keep getting mixed up with the Maras. She said she knows it's not the safest trip, but that staying in Quetzaltenango can't be an option, and that if we all go together, at least we'll have each other.

She paused for a second. "I'm not going to get any sleep until you make it," she said, "but I'll feel a little better if I know you're staying together."

Obviously, we said they could come.

She's right, it'll be better to be a group of four, and it'll be helpful to have Elías with us, since he knows where to go. Not to mention, I love Miguelito, but I think if he was the only person I got to talk to for the next few days, I might go a little crazy.

So tomorrow, we're going to set out for the Bexican Morder.

Love,
D.

THE FOLLOWING DAY

La frontera mexicana

Querida Tía:

I had no idea the border was so close to my cousins' house. It's just one more three-hour bus ride away. We're pretty much there, we're just taking a few minutes to rest before we cross. Me and Miguelito crossed half of Honduras and all of Guatemala in a little over a week. I know México is bigger than Guatemala, but still, I figure that at this rate, we can make it to Nashville in another week, and my parents will only have missed me for one Sunday phone call.

When we left Quetzaltenango, Damián and Elías said a long, emotional goodbye to their mamá. When we were walking out the door, she called out, "And, Elías, make sure Damián and your cousins are safe, okay?"

He waved back in a way that said, *Yeah, yeah, I know, Mamá.*

We still had a lot of oranges, and they were making our bags too heavy, so we left some behind for Tía Gloria. Elías led us to the bus. He knew exactly which one to get on and everything. On the way, we traded our last few quetzales for 490 pesos mexicanos ("mesos pexicanos," Miguelito and Damián keep saying). Our cousins also traded some of their quetzales for pesos. It'd feel weird to ask how much they have, but I don't think it's a lot.

On the bus, I came clean to Elías and told him my parents weren't in México waiting for us.

"That's okay," he said, "I thought that sounded kind of fishy anyway. We'll cross ourselves, it'll be fine. I've been reading about it online at the locutorio."

Once we got off the bus, Elías asked a woman with kids which way we should go. Immediately, she said she didn't know anything about migration, didn't get involved in migration, had nothing to do with migration. Then she told us that even though she had no idea how to get to México, she *thought* there was a house a few blocks away where they'd be able to help us out. It was just a five-minute walk away.

At the house, two nice, smiley ladies gave us plastic bags with a bunch of stuff in them. They fed us tamales and put cookies and granola bars and juices in our backpacks. They also gave me pills to make my ankle hurt less and a pink liquid that they said we should drink if our stomachs started hurting really badly or if we got diarrhea. Miguelito and Damián started giggling when the ladies said that, but they tried to keep it down because they knew they were embarrassing me and Elías.

"And don't worry if, a few hours after you take it, your poop turns dark black, like the color of charcoal. That's normal," one of the ladies said.

That was too much for Miguelito, and he burst out laughing. The ladies didn't seem to mind. They laughed a little too.

Elías asked them where we had to go to get into México.

"México is on the other side of the river," the other lady said. We hadn't seen a river yet, but I guessed that it must be nearby. She said she couldn't help us cross, but if we wanted to rest that night in the pueblo, they could find us somewhere to sleep. They also said that if we wanted to go back home, they could help us with that, too.

Me and Elías shook our heads. Why would we go back now?

Before we left, they hung a plastic rosary around each of our necks, put their hands on our foreheads, and said an Avemaría.

We walked a little ways away, and now we're resting here for a minute before we go where she told us to go. I'll let you know what happens when we try to cross.

Love,
D.

A FEW HOURS LATER

¡México!

Querida Tía:

The ladies were right—all we had to do was walk for fifteen minutes and we came to the longest river I've ever been to. It stretched as far as I could see in both directions. We weren't the only migrantes. There were a lot of them on the Guatemala side of the river, and a few people crossing the river on rafts. The other side, I figured, was México.

On our side, a bunch of men kept asking if we needed help crossing the river. I was worried they'd be mean, but they were all nice to us. We told the first few, "No, gracias," and they just smiled and said to come back if we changed our minds. They all gave us the same price: thirty quetzales per person to cross. It was a lot, but since they were all charging the same amount, we figured that we didn't have much of a choice, so we hired a guy in a red baseball cap to take us across. He looked as trustworthy as anyone else.

The raft was just two inflatable tubes with a bunch of wood planks on top. It didn't make me feel super safe, but all the other migrantes' rafts looked exactly the same, and nobody was drowning or freaking out. And even though it was the longest river I've ever seen, it wasn't super wide. If something went wrong, someone on the bank would've seen and hopefully paddled out to save us.

Paddle might not be the right word—the guy in the red baseball cap just had a long pole he plunged into the water, and he pushed us across with it. We were silent the whole way across—I looked left and right to try to see how far the river went, but it seemed endless. The river was calm, and even though the raft didn't look particularly well built, after the first few minutes, I wasn't scared. Getting across was fast. It only took around fifteen minutes.

When we got to the other side, Miguelito said, "Melcome to Wéxico."

Damián burst out laughing. Then me and Elías started laughing too. I'm glad our cousins joined us.

I asked them if we could stop for a minute so I could write to you about crossing on the raft—it was so cool that I didn't want to forget any of the details.

Love,
D.

A COUPLE HOURS LATER

A little farther into México, waiting for the train

Querida Tía:

Ever since we crossed the river, we've been surrounded by all kinds of people—old people, young people, mothers with babies, groups of adolescentes like us. Lots of solo men. I can tell from the accents that some people are hondureños and salvadoreños, but there's also people who speak Spanish in ways I haven't heard before, so I guess they're venezolanos or other kinds of sudamericanos. And there are a few people who don't speak Spanish at all. I don't know where they're from or how they got here.

With so many other migrantes around, it's easy to know where to go. After we crossed the river, we just followed the crowd. We walked for around an hour, and even though we should've been tired, we were so excited to be in a new country that we were full of energy, at least at first. We're not in a city or even a town, but the area is pretty built up, and there are tons of cars.

While we walked, we talked about what our lives were like back home. Elías and Damián already knew that you and Felipe had died, but they hadn't known all the details. They told us about their mamá's sickness, how she was tired all the time. They said that when we were at her house, she made an effort to cook and seem lively, but most of the time, she can't do a lot and has to stay in bed for most of the day. They're hoping that when she can afford her medicamentos, she'll be better.

I feel bad for them, because I remember how hard you tried to stay positive for me and Miguelito during the last weeks you were alive. Like, you even kept trying to cook elaborate meals and made new kinds of foods you hadn't cooked before. It was like you were trying to prove you could still do all the stuff you always did. But eventually, you had to admit you were too weak. I hope that won't be what happens to Tía Gloria.

Damián and Miguelito did most of the talking, but I joined in sometimes, too. Elías was quieter, but I can tell he's still happy to have our company. He's the one who has researched how to get to los Estados Unidos, so he pays more attention to his surroundings than we do. I guess he was too distracted to talk.

When the sun was getting low, we stopped near here, with other migrantes, on either side of some train tracks. Elías went up to a woman about Mamá's age who was sitting on the ground with two kids. He talked to her for a minute and came back.

We asked him what was going on. He explained in his usual, serious way.

"We're waiting for a train called La Bestia," he says.

I've heard people talking about La Bestia before, but I was never sure exactly what it was. Elías kept explaining. The conversation went something like this:

ELÍAS: It'll take us to el Norte. When it gets here, we'll have to run next to it and grab on and climb onto the roof. First, we take a few trains to Ciudad de México. Then, from there, I think we can jump on one that goes to Juárez. And Juárez is right on the other side of los Estados Unidos. (*Me and Miguelito were a little surprised by this. But Elías knows what he's talking about, and he described La Bestia like it isn't that big of a deal.*)

MIGUELITO: Does it stop?

ELÍAS: I don't think so. But I think it'll go slow enough that we can grab on. I hope it will, anyway.

ME: Is it dangerous?

ELÍAS: A little. But we're all young and in good shape. I don't really know. But, like, all these people are gonna get on, right? (*He pointed at everyone around us: kids, women holding babies, old people. He stopped to think for a few seconds. He seemed unsure.*) But if it's too scary, we don't have to get on, we can just let the train pass, and we'll figure something else out. Or we could go back.

ME: No way.

If Elías thinks we can do it, we can do it. For now, we just have to wait. I'll write more once we catch the train.

Love,
D.

THE NEXT DAY

Casa del immigrante, Villahermosa

Querida Tía:

Okay, oh my God. You won't believe what happened. I didn't know what I was getting into.

After I wrote to you yesterday, we waited for a few more hours. Then, once it was completely dark out, we saw a light coming down the train tracks. The rails began to vibrate. Then there was the sound of a train whistle. The whole crowd of migrantes tensed: people stood, tightened their backpacks, and grabbed their kids' hands or put them in slings around their chests. As the train got closer, the gravel underneath the tracks started to bounce. I realized that I'd never seen a train up close before. It was way—*way*—bigger than I expected. It was tall and dark and metal, and so loud I wanted to cover my ears. It was moving so fast that I had no idea how in the world I was supposed to climb up onto it. It was so powerful and terrifying that it looked like it could crush my bones into powder.

My instinct was to run *away* from the tracks, not toward them. My legs were shaking, my stomach suddenly hurt, and I had a sour taste in my mouth. My armpits and hands felt cold and tingly and wet. Elías looked at me and my cousins to make sure we were ready to run.

Before I knew it, the train engine whooshed past us, and a massive crowd of migrantes started sprinting past me. It felt like more people had appeared out of nowhere, trying to keep up with the train. But how were we supposed to keep up with it if it's a train and we're just humans?! My cousins all broke into a sprint, and a second later, I did too. I felt like Simba trying to keep up with the stampede of ñus in *El rey león*. On the sides of most of the cars, there were rungs that formed a sort of ladder, and there were also a few handles and small ledges and pieces of metal that stuck out. I saw person after person grab hold and climb onto the top of the train. I didn't understand how they were fast enough and strong enough—they looked like el Hombre Araña.

Miguelito was the first of my cousins to get on—he just kind of flung himself at the side of the train like a wild animal and grabbed on to the metal rungs. He thwacked himself against the train pretty hard, and I was worried he was hurt. I figured I'd never know if I didn't make it onto the train.

Damián was next. He grabbed the same rung as Miguelito did, but a little more carefully, so he wouldn't body-slam the train. At almost exactly the same time, Elías gripped a handle on the same car and found some small ledge he could stand on, right next to the rungs. All three of them looked back at me: I was running as fast as I could, but my ankle was killing me, and the harder I pressed my right foot against the ground, the more it hurt. I wasn't running on hard ground, it was gravel, so no matter how much power I put into my legs, they just sank instead of making me run faster. But by then I had no choice. I had to get on—all three of my cousins had made it, and if I was left behind, I'd have no way of contacting them, I'd just be alone, in that town where I didn't know anyone, with no money and no idea what I was doing. Miguelito and Damián were watching me from on top of the train, looking terrified. Elías wasn't up yet, he was still standing on his ledge and gripping a handle like a garbage man. He kept yelling for me to *jump, jump, jump now!*

I gave one last push and hurled myself at the train car. I grabbed on to one of the rungs, but only with a few fingers of each hand, not with my whole palm. And I didn't jump far enough to get my legs onto the rungs, so they were dangling behind me, just a few inches from the ground that was speeding past underneath me. I clenched my fingers as tightly as I could. My knuckles were supporting all of my body weight, and they felt like they were going to explode. I only had a second before the joints in my hand would give out, two seconds at most. My fingers weren't strong enough to pull me any closer. In a flash, I pictured myself falling from the car, hitting my head, tumbling under the train's wheels, breaking my neck. I imagined Miguelito telling Tía Gloria, and Tía Gloria telling my parents. I closed my eyes tight and braced for the end.

Suddenly, miraculously, I was lifted by the chest. For half a second, I could've sworn that la Virgen or you or mi ángel de la guarda had flown to my rescue. I opened my eyes. Elías had grabbed me under my armpits, and he was pulling me up.

When I tried to climb the ladder, my legs felt like old bananas, and I thought that instead of helping me climb, they'd just compress into mush. But they didn't. Somehow, I made it to the top of the train. Miguelito grabbed my hand and showed me how to hold a metal grate, so I wouldn't fall.

My heart felt like it was going to jump out of my throat. My stomach felt like I'd just chugged a gallon of lime juice. Elías climbed up behind me, and with my free arm I hugged him and buried my head in his chest. I started to cry harder than I've ever cried before. When I could catch a breath between sobs, all I could say was "Gracias, gracias, gracias." Elías hugged me back and said "Sorry, sorry, sorry." With their free arms, Miguelito and Damián joined. I was weeping on the top of a train, in a foreign country, with the wind rushing past my head and my three cousins holding me.

Then, suddenly, something felt wrong.

Quickly, but gently so I wouldn't accidentally push my cousins off the train, I broke free from the group hug. With one arm still firmly holding on to the grate, I climbed up to the edge of the car.

I know that if you were still alive, you'd be horrified to hear that me and Miguelito did something so dangerous. But I guess my thinking was that . . . Like, you can see everything that's happening anyway, and maybe you even can see what's going to happen in the future. I don't know how things work en el cielo. But maybe you were watching out for me that day.

The train moved really fast for most of the time we were up there. Way faster than a car on the highway. The wind was so strong that all I could hear was the air rushing past my ears. It was cold and scary and loud and dark. Whenever the train passed through a pueblo, it went a lot slower. Occasionally it stopped fully, and we would either climb off to stretch our legs or we stay up here. When La Bestia went fast, we turned our backs to the wind. I held on to the metal grate with one arm and hugged Miguelito with the other.

We didn't talk, even when the train went slow through a pueblo and the wind died down. There were lights in these pueblos, so we could actually see each other. In these towns, more migrantes scrambled onto the roof. It kept getting more and more crowded up there. After a few hours, each train car felt like Felipe's microbus used to get when he was driving more passengers than the micro was meant to hold. It got so packed that I worried someone might accidentally get pushed off.

A lot of the people who got on were parents with small kids, and I have no idea how the kids can put up with this for so long. When me and Miguelito were that little, we couldn't even sit through church for a whole hour.

Eventually, in the middle of the night last night, we got off La Bestia. It didn't stop all the way, but it was moving really slowly by the time we had to jump off, so it wasn't too dangerous. Now we're in a city called Villahermosa—it's big, with roads made of cement and bricks instead of dirt. But as soon as we were off the train, Elías said we were not going into the city, we were going to a place that he'd heard about from other migrantes. It's called Casa del Migrante. He said he didn't know a lot about it, but he knew it was a place where we could rest and eat before getting on the next train. It didn't take us very long to find it: it was right next to the train tracks. It's where I'm writing to you from now.

As soon as we showed up, a nice señora lets us in and started explaining what this place is.

"We offer migrantes from all over the world a safe place where they can sleep, eat, and recover before . . . "

She kept talking, but I had a hard time focusing because I kept looking around. I had no idea that a place like this existed. It's a big set of buildings with a courtyard in the middle, and every inch of the walls is covered in murals. There's a big mural I saw immediately: it's a painting of hands holding a heart, and on the heart, it says *We are humans, we have dignity, we deserve respect.* Behind the heart there are a whole bunch of different flags. Honduras's flag is right underneath one for some other country that I've never seen before, with arcoiris-colored stripes stacked on top of each other, but no stars or words or anything.

And there's another mural with a map of los Estados Unidos and Latinoamérica. In front of the map, there's a picture of a person who I think is supposed to be Donel Tromp, and a brick wall and the bandera de los Estados Unidos. Tromp's hair is on fire, and above him there are lots of people who I think are supposed to be migrantes, and the words *You will light the flame of the people's resistance.* I don't really get it.

On the rest of the walls, there are paintings of butterflies and sunflowers and migrantes hugging their families. There's a corner with a big crucifix on the wall that looks like it's supposed to be a chapel.

I got so distracted by everything around me that I forget to listen to what the señora was telling us, so I tried to tune back in.

" . . . only one shower. And you can stay for three days, and then, unfortunately you have to leave to make room for new arrivals. Do any of you have any allergies?"

I told her that if I eat bananas my throat gets itchy.

The señora showed us to a big room with lots of cots, where there were a few other men and boys either sleeping or resting. She told us to go to the courtyard at a specific time for breakfast, and then she left.

"Elías?" I said, whispering so I wouldn't wake anyone up.

"Yeah?"

"This place is free?"

"Yeah."

"And they're gonna give us food for free?"

"Yeah."

"And we're allowed to stay three days?"

"Yeah."

It seemed too good to be true. I looked at Miguelito and Damián, who had already taken off their backpacks and shoes.

"So we're gonna stay here for all three days, right?"

"Yeah," all three of my cousins replied at the same time.

Thanks for looking out for us, Tía.

Love,
D.

A DAY LATER

Casa del Migrante, Villahermosa

Querida Tía:

Just woke up. I feel a thousand percent better than I did when we got here. You don't really appreciate a good bed until you spend a week sleeping on bus station benches. We don't have real beds here either, just sleeping pads with blankets, but I swear it's like sleeping on a cloud. I think somehow the park benches messed up the bones in my back, because when I lay down on the soft pad for the first time, it hurt for the first few minutes.

I think I slept for fourteen hours, even though there were guys all around me getting up and making noise. I only woke up once, to go to the bathroom. When I did, I looked around to make sure my cousins were still here. Elías and Damián were out like La Bella Durmiente. Miguelito was sleeping, too, but he was crinkling his eyebrows, and it seemed like he was having a bad dream. He looked so unhappy that I almost woke him up . . . but then his face relaxed, and he seemed to calm down.

Once I'm in Nashville, and for the rest of my life, no matter what other bad things are going on, I want to take a second before falling asleep to remember how wonderful it is to have a bed.

I might sleep for another few hours. Good night, Tía.

Buenas noches,
D.

THE NEXT DAY

Casa del Migrante, Villahermosa

Querida Tía:

This is the best place. There are ten or twelve people who work here, or maybe they're volunteers, I'm not sure, but in any case, they're really friendly. They cook the food and make sure we're in good enough shape to leave after three days. Most of them are mexicanos, but there are hispanos from other parts of the world, too. There's one woman here from Colombia named Sierra. I was a little scared of her at first because she has lots of tattoos all over her body, and I always associate that kind of stuff with gangs. She also has piercings, not just in her ears, but in her eyebrow, too, and one in the middle of her nose like a bull. But she's super nice—she's the friendliest person I've met here. When I told her that me and Miguelito left Naranjito because you and Felipe died, she asked lots of questions about how we survived alone, and she gave me a big hug.

We don't have to stay in the Casa del Migrante, we're allowed to leave, but none of us do—we just want to stay here and rest. Except for Miguelito, he has tons of energy. Earlier today, he went into town and bought . . . an aluminum pot.

"Why?" I asked.

"So we can cook food with it!"

"But you're gonna have to carry it on La Bestia and everything. All the way to Nashville."

He just shrugged. He's always been such a weirdo, but I love him.

At mealtimes, everyone comes together around big tables, and the people who work here bring out big pots of beans and rice and tortillas, and pitchers of water and juice. Everyone talks about where they're from and where they're going in el Norte, and we talk about the best way to get there. At dinner tonight, I talked to a man from El Salvador named Luis, who's making the journey for the second time. He got deported after the first time. He says he has a daughter my age in a city called Tucson, and he's hoping to get there in time for her eighth-grade graduation. It's only January, so that's a long time from now, but he's going to stop in Ciudad de México to make some money first.

He told me to stay away from la Migra as much as possible, but most of all, to steer clear of the Maras and the carteles. "La Migra won't just deport you," he said. "They'll beat you, and rob you, and sell you out to the Maras, and stick you in a cell so nasty you'll wish you were dead." I assume he means la Migra mexicana, because when we get across the border, we can just tell la Migra de los Estados Unidos our parents are here and they can just call them. That's what everyone says, at least.

After that, he said pretty much the same thing about the carteles: "They won't just beat you up. They'll kidnap you, call up your papá, and tell him to pay them five thousand dólares if he ever wants to see you alive again." He made me promise to be careful, and to trust my instincts if I ever got a bad feeling about something.

Since Luis has done all this before, I wanted to ask him if there's a better way to climb onto La Bestia. I told him how I would've died last time if Elías hadn't saved me. I need to figure out a safer way to do it, because we have to leave the Casa del Migrante tomorrow morning, and I'm a little scared to try again. Luis said it's important to know when to give up. I shouldn't get on if I think it's impossible. He said that even if it means getting separated from my cousins, that's better than getting killed. He recommended that next time, before we jump on, we should talk about where we're going, so we can meet up later if one of us doesn't make it onto the train. He also gave me some tips on safer ways to try to get on: staying calm, making sure my shoes are tied and my backpack straps are tight. Stuff like that.

I hope the tips are useful. I'm really nervous to get on La Bestia again, but we don't really have much of a choice. Hopefully I'll be in Nashville in a few days, with Mamá and Papá and my baby sister, sleeping on a real bed . . . That sounds even better than the sleeping pad I get here.

Love,
D.

A DAY LATER

Not exactly sure . . .

Querida Tía:

I had to really psyche myself up to get on La Bestia again. I prayed to God that it wouldn't be as scary this time, and when it finally showed up . . . it was going much slower. An answer to my prayers. But it was still scary to jump on—there's nothing easy about climbing on top of a massive moving train.

I lay on the roof and watch the clouds go by. The train sped up once we were out of town and in the middle of nowhere, but it still didn't go nearly as fast as the last one. It wasn't as crowded as the last one either—there were only maybe two dozen people up there. Almost all of them were adults, plus a few babies. We were the only adolescentes. I hope all the rest of the trains we take will be as easy to ride as that one. Maybe it was unusual for the first one to be so fast and crowded. On this train, we went so slowly that a man on our car was even napping: he looped his belt through the holes in the grate so he wouldn't fall, then he lay down and closed his eyes. I wasn't brave enough to do that, but it was a smart idea.

Then things got weird.

After around two hours, we heard a screeching sound, and the train started to brake. Something was happening a few cars ahead. People were starting to jump off. The man in front of us—the one who was napping—unhooked his belt from the train and looked up. Elías asked him if he knew what was going on.

"La Migra," he said. He looked scared.

We squinted into the sun and looked ahead. A few hundred meters down the train tracks, we could see pickup trucks.

"You mean it's like a checkpoint?" Elías asked.

"Looks like."

"So we have to jump off the train now?"

"That or get deported. Or get put in jail or something, I don't know. I just know I'm getting the hell off," he said. Then he climbed down and hopped onto the ground.

We looked at each other. We looked around. We were in the middle of nowhere—there were no pueblos, no buildings, not even any power lines—but if everyone else was getting off the train, we weren't going to stick around. We didn't want to find out what would happen at the checkpoint.

A few people said there was another way to get to the next pueblo after the checkpoint, and we could get back on La Bestia there. Right near us, there was a mountain with a path around it, and they said the pueblo was on the other side.

"We have to go over the mountain?" Elías asked a woman with a kid who looked about three years old. I knew Elías was asking because he was worried Miguelito might not be up to it.

"Not over it," the woman said, "just around it."

All the adults started to walk toward the mountain. It seemed like we didn't have much of a choice, so we started heading in that direction, too.

It took us a lot longer than we expected to reach the path at the foot of the mountain, because it's hot and it's the middle of the day, and there's no shade between the train tracks and the path. Now we're exhausted. But there are lots of trees by the mountain, so we're sitting down to cool off for a minute before starting down the path. We're eating our last sleeve of cookies. We'll have to buy more food when we get to the pueblo, even though we're running out of money fast.

When we sat down, Miguelito asked if we should have tried to keep up with the other people ahead of us. He's always the most eager to jump into an adventure (he was the only one of us who was excited to leave the Casa del Migrante), but he's also the first one to get nervous and worry things will go wrong.

"It'll be all right, Miguelito," Damián said. "I bet people walk here all the time—look how beat down the path is. And look at all the trash people have left. Plus, we're so much smaller, we couldn't keep up with everybody else anyway."

This is something Damián is good at: he always says "we" to Miguelito when he really means "you." The three of us could keep up with the adults if we wanted to, but Miguelito couldn't. He won't even turn twelve until April.

It doesn't matter, though, because Damián is right. It looks like people walk on this path all the time. I bet la Migra always sets up their checkpoint at that part of the train tracks. They probably hope people will think their only option is to go over the mountain, not around it. They must catch lots of people that way. But not us!

Love,
D.

THE NEXT DAY

Still walking . . .

Tía:

The walk is taking longer than I expected. I can't sleep. I'm not sure I've managed to fall asleep at all. It's too cold, and I keep jolting awake because I think I feel a snake slithering under my leg. And because my stomach keeps growling. My cousins' stomachs are growling, too. I can hear it, since we're all lying so close together on the ground. As soon as it's a tiny bit light out, we'll stand up and start walking. The sooner we start, the sooner we'll get there, the sooner we can eat. I hope the sun rises soon.

—D.

THE FOLLOWING DAY

Still in the middle of nowhere . . .

Querida Tía:

I slept even less than the night before last night. Even though I'm exhausted, I can't relax, it's like my body needs to be alert at every second. The pain in my stomach won't go away. We haven't eaten anything in forty-eight hours. I don't think I've ever gone this long without food before. And my mouth tastes like metal, like I have a 10-centavo coin on my tongue, and I can't spit it out. Maybe it's because I haven't brushed my teeth since we left the Casa del Migrante.

We're about to start walking. Again. Day three. At this point, I don't know how long it'll take before we get to the pueblo. I hope it'll be today.

But I have no idea. It was dumb of us to think this would be a short walk. How long can you live without eating? I know you can't survive without water for more than a few days, but all four of us are carrying full plastic gallons, thank God. I don't know if you can go longer than that without food.

Love,
D.

A COUPLE HOURS LATER

Still don't know . . .

Querida Tía:

Today, our stomachs have been the only things making noise. We walk silently. Everywhere we go, the path is still really well beaten down, and occasionally we still see trash on either side of it, so it must be a popular way to walk. I can see lots of trash from where we're sitting now, taking a rest while the sun is at its highest. But we haven't seen any other people.

My right foot has been aching ever since the first day we left Naranjito. It's more painful now than ever before. I think the last two days pushed it over the edge. When I put my full weight on it, I get this sharp needly feeling, and I can feel my heart beating *in my foot.* I can't keep all my weight on it for more than a second, and that makes it hard to walk. I've tried to adjust the way I move my legs so I don't have to press down on my right foot too much—I've been hobbling around the mountain like you used to hobble around the kitchen (no offense). But now, weirdly, my left foot hurts in a completely different way. When I step on my left heel, it's super painful. If we have to stop for the night again tonight—and I've been praying nonstop that we don't have to, that we make it to the pueblo today—I'll take off my shoe to see what's wrong. For now, I have to find a way to walk that doesn't involve putting too much weight on either my right ankle or my left heel.

Love,
D.

A FEW MORE HOURS LATER

Still don't know . . .

Querida Tía:

Another night out here in the wilderness. I guess I'll have to live with my foot like this for at least another day.

I'll never forget what Miguelito said to me earlier today. He called out my name from behind. I stopped, turned around, and looked at him. He looked dirtier than I'd ever seen him, even dirtier than when we walked through that rainstorm by the border between Honduras and Guatemala. The skin on his face was a different color than usual, it looked more yellow, and around his eyes it was way darker. And it was peeling on his ears and neck. He said he didn't expect the walk to take this long. "I'm scared we . . . if we don't . . . I'm so hungry . . . This is . . . It's really," he started to tear up. "It's too hard."

I tried to think what Felipe would say. He was always repeating little proverbs. He usually said them to try to teach us life lessons. But sometimes it was like he was saying them for himself, not for us. There was one he used to say all the time after he had a bad day at work, or if something else bad was going on. You said it to me and Miguelito a lot too, after Felipe died, when we were really depressed. You'd say it before you made us say the Rosary at night, to remind us that Felipe would've wanted us to stay strong and that God has a plan.

I wrapped Miguelito in a big hug and gave it a try. I said: "Dios aprieta, pero no ahoga." God might squeeze, but he doesn't strangle.

Miguelito pressed his head into my shoulder. He cried for a minute or two. He tried to say something, but I couldn't understand it because his mouth was against my shirt.

"What'd you say?"

He lifted his head just a little.

"I miss . . . " He could barely get the words out. "I want Papá so . . . so much."

"I know," I said. "I miss him too."

He pressed his face back into my shoulder and cried some more.

Then, after another few seconds, he suddenly stopped. He pulled his face away from my shirt and even though his eyes were still bloodshot, and the tears turned the dirt on his face into mud, he squinted and gave me a suspicious look, like he thought I was playing a trick on him.

"You're not going to make me say the Rosary now, are you?"

I lightly slapped him on the back of the head, like you used to do to both of us when we were annoying you, and we started walking so we could catch up with Elías and Damián.

I didn't want to tell him how much I miss my papá, too. I would do anything to hear his deep voice on the other end of the phone, saying that everything was going to be okay. That we would be together soon.

And I'd do anything to see you again, too, Tía.

Love you,
D.

THE FOLLOWING DAY

Still don't know...

Querida Tía:

Well, we didn't make it today, either. We're not even going to try to walk through any part of the night this time. We need to lie down. It's a little warmer tonight, for whatever reason, so we don't need to huddle together, we can sleep separately.

When we lay down for the night, I tried to take off my left shoe to see why it's so hard to walk. When I pulled off the sock, the smell was so horrible I had to turn my face for a second to let it dissipate. And then I looked at the damage: Half my foot was covered in blisters. The blister on the back of my foot, where my heel rubs up against my shoe, was torn open, and there was sticky skin hanging loose. Another blister covered the entire bottom of my heel. It was just a dark purple circle, with no regular-colored skin at all. There was another big one behind my big toe, too, in the shape of a comma. I wish there were something I could do to take care of it, but we don't have any bandages or first-aid stuff.

I was just about to close my notebook, but just now, Miguelito said something. I'd thought he was asleep. He said, "Hey, D.," but when I asked what was up, he said nothing. I kept writing here, and then five minutes later it happened again.

"Hey, D.?"

"Yeah?"

"Happy birthday."

I was hoping he'd forget. I couldn't bring myself to stand up after seeing what my foot looks like, but I scooted over to where he was lying and, even though it's not too cold, we huddled together for a minute.

Love,
D.

THE NEXT DAY

Somewhere?

Tía:

Morning. I haven't eaten anything. But my stomach hurts less. My body feels lighter. My head feels lighter. I keep getting dizzy. I try to drink water to fill my stomach, but I can't keep it down. My lips are dry. My head is hot. I keep forgetting how many days it's been. Four. This is day four. I can barely walk, but I'm going to keep trying. Right after I rest here for a minute.

A FEW HOURS LATER

Somewhere?

Querida Tía:

I guess I passed out. When I woke up, my face was wet. I think my cousins rubbed some water on it. By then, it was already dark, and I wasn't sure if it was still the same day. (It is. It's still the day after my birthday, just way later . . . I guess I was passed out for a while.)

After I'd been awake for a few minutes, Damián asked me if I was able to stand up. "We want to show you something," he said. He looked worried, but he also looked excited.

I managed to get onto my feet. Elías and Miguelito helped steady me while I stood up. Damián pointed in front of him.

"Look over there," he said, "Look what I noticed. Do you see the lights?"

I saw the lights.

"Do you know what lights mean?"

"They mean . . . we're there?"

"Almost!" Elías said, jumping in. "We just have to make it the rest of the way. I don't think you should walk any more today though. It was really scary when we found you . . . We thought you were right behind us, but after we didn't see you for a while, we walked back and found you collapsed on the ground. Do you remember passing out?"

I didn't.

"We're all gonna sleep as well as we can tonight, and then tomorrow we'll go into the pueblo and spend all our pesos on food. Okay?"

I nodded. I even smiled a little bit. If those lights really do mean that tomorrow we'll get to the pueblo . . . then we can eat and recover, and then we can get back on La Bestia, and we'll be at the border and then in Nashville in no time.

* * *

I just took off my shoe, and it made a sticky sound when I pulled it off. My sock was soaked with blood and pus. When I peeled it off my foot, loose skin peeled off with it. It's getting worse. Elías helped me wash it as well as he could, but all we have is water. We can't decide if it's a good idea to wrap it up, because the only thing we have is clothes, and all the clothes we have are filthy. We don't want it to get infected, so we decided to leave it uncovered for tonight, then wrap it up before we start walking tomorrow.

Tomorrow . . . tomorrow we finally make it!

Love,
D.

A DAY LATER

The pueblo! We're in the pueblo!

Querida Tía:

Oh my God! We made it!! There's finally food back in my belly. I really thought that we weren't going to make it. We had walked for I don't know how long, hours and hours, because we really wanted to make it to the pueblo today. I don't think we could've survived another night without eating. And my foot didn't make it any easier. This morning, Elías tore off a strip of his T-shirt and wrapped it around my foot like a bandage. When I stood up, I gave it a try: every time I leaned on my left foot, it hurt. Every time I leaned on my right foot, it also hurt, but less, and in a different way. So I tried to walk on my right leg as much as possible.

Once we started walking, I was way slower than my cousins. I was really lightheaded. Everything had a light gray halo around it. And everything seemed too bright. The reflection of the sun on the ground hurts my eyes, and I had to squint to see where I was walking.

But finally, after hours, Damián spotted train tracks in the distance. He called out to tell us that we were almost there! He was so excited that I thought he was going to cry.

We followed the train tracks for about half an hour, then we came to a very small pueblo. Once we were there, we came to a tienda almost immediately.

It was a small tienda, with a few shelves of food and a señor sitting in a chair listening to the radio. He was stunned when we walked in. He'd never seen four boys looking as filthy and bloody and exhausted as us just burst into his shop before. I think that for a second—just for a second—he thought about kicking us out. He might've thought we were up to no good. His face got really worried and tense, but a second later, it relaxed. He gave us a kind, confused smile.

"What can I help you boys with?"

All of a sudden, I had no idea what to eat. I could have eaten anything and everything. Miguelito and Elías and Damián were silent. I could barely even get words out. I just said the word *food*, which probably sounded super rude. But the man just kept looking confused, even though he was also smiling.

"Any . . . particular kind?" he asked.

All four of us were still incapable of speech.

"Well . . . " he said, "my wife just made these . . . maybe you'd like to try them?"

He held out a tray of something that looked like empanadas. All four of us reached out and grabbed one. We weren't even thinking about money. We would spend all our money there, it didn't matter, what mattered was getting those empanadas into my mouth immediately.

It was still warm. When my mouth touched the pastry, the very thin outer layer shattered, then my teeth pressed into dough that was soft like a pillow. I was expecting it to be filled with beans or maybe chicken, but instead my mouth flooded with a sweet juice . . . They were filled with *pineapple*. When I swallowed and I felt food going down my throat for the first time in five days, my lips automatically pressed into a smile so wide it hurt the muscles in my face. The tears on my cheeks mingled with the warm pineapple juice that was trickling down my neck.

I looked at my cousins. Miguelito was closing his eyes tight and shaking his head back and forth while he chewed. Elías and Damián were laughing like crazy people and looking at each other with an expression on their faces like *Can you believe it?*

After we each finished our first pastry, we looked up at the man. At some point while we were eating, a woman had appeared behind him. I assumed it was his wife. She was smiling really wide while she watched us devour the food she made.

Elías took all the pesos we had left, fanned them out in front of the señor, and asked how many of those pastries he would give us for however much money we had.

The man plucked out only one of the bills, then grabbed the entire tray of pastries and handed it to Elías.

"Buen provecho," he said.

Tía, I don't remember the last time I ate so much. He let us eat as much as we needed. I'm not saying it was as good as your cooking, but there's something special about filling your stomach for the first time in days. But I still miss you cooking, Tía. And you. Every day.

Love,
D.

TWO WEEKS LATER

Somewhere in Oaxaca, I think.

Querida Tía:

So, I'm going to miss a few of my parents' phone calls.

I'm going to miss a *lot* of my parents' phone calls, actually.

This trip to el Norte is taking a lot longer than I thought.

Ever since we survived our trip around the mountain, my foot hasn't been doing too well. It's not healing at all, because it doesn't have the chance. That makes it hard for me to jump onto moving trains. Most of the time I can't run as fast as I need to to grab on. This is an especially big problem, because a lot of the train conductors don't like it when we ride on the roof of the trains, so when they see us waiting to jump on, they actually go *faster*. They say some people die trying to get on. We haven't seen that happen yet, but I believe it.

Other times, though, there are nice conductors who slow the train down when they're driving past crowds so that we don't get hurt climbing on. Because of my foot, Elías says that from now on, we can only get on trains going really slowly, so that even with my messed-up feet, I'll be able to get on. And we agree that since I'm the most likely to miss the train, I'll be the first one up. That way, there's no risk of me getting left behind.

It's a smart plan, but it means it takes us a lot longer to get anywhere, because sometimes the trains only come once every five hours. And sometimes we have to wait for three or four trains to pass before there's one going slowly enough for me to get on. Sometimes, we spend days in the same pueblo, waiting for a train. I feel bad, because my cousins are basically making their own journey longer for my sake. Once, I tried to tell Elías and Damián that they should go on without me and

Miguelito, but they wouldn't even let me finish the sentence. I think Damián would be sad to be separated from Miguelito. Whenever we're not on La Bestia, the two of them spend a lot of their time inventing more and more complicated and elaborate word games whose rules I can't even understand.

Love,
D.

A WEEK LATER

By the train tracks in the middle of nowhere

Querida Tía:

We've completely run out of money. We ran out fast. We didn't have nearly enough pesos to feed ourselves for this whole trip.

That means we're hungry. Not starving like when we went around the mountain. But very, very hungry. We haven't eaten much since the last time I wrote to you, and what we have eaten has just been cookies, fruits we find, whatever nice people in pueblos give us . . . nothing really filling.

But that's about to change.

* * *

We couldn't get on the last train, and the next one won't be here for a few hours, so we went out to see if we could find any food. There are a few houses scattered around the countryside here, and we spotted a dark yellow one with a chicken yard. There were at least two dozen chickens fenced in. I decided I'd ask if they had any food they'd share with us. People share food more than you'd expect if you just ask nicely! And since they had all those chickens, I was hoping they'd have something to spare.

I went up to the door alone. We've figured out that for whatever reason, people are scared of a group of four dirty teenage boys, but they're less scared of one dirty teenage boy.

I knocked on the door and put a big smile on my face. A señora opened. She looked confused. I went into my usual speech, which I've rehearsed a lot by now. It's usually something like: "Hola, señora, buenas tardes. Me and my cousins are very hungry and we wondered if you have any spare food you'd be nice enough to give us? We could also do some work for you in exchange if you want. I've worked with animals a lot before on—"

Her face got angry-looking really quickly.

"¿Me estás chingando?" she said. "You people are literally knocking on my door now? Véte al carajo. I don't even have food to spare for street dogs, I'm sure as hell not giving limosnas to every dirty prieto de la calle who shows up here."

She was so mean I kind of stepped away and held my hands in front of my face. I opened my mouth to say *Okay, I'm sorry*, but before I could get the words out, she started yelling again.

"¡Véte! ¡Lárgate ya!"

I ran—as fast as my swollen, messed-up feet would let me—back to my cousins, who had been sitting on a log a few meters away, out of the woman's sight. I was a little flustered. She didn't have to give us anything, but why did she have to say it like that?

I told my cousins everything that happened, except I left out that she called me a *dirty prieto de la calle*—a dirty dark kid from the street—because it made me feel weird to think about.

It didn't even make sense for her to say that—my skin is barely any darker than hers. Unless it's gotten darker from being in the sun so much in the past few weeks. I wouldn't know, I haven't looked in a mirror.

My cousins could tell I felt weird about what happened, and Damián tried to cheer me up by making fun of the lady: "Forget about her! She's the one who has to live in that ugly, pee-colored house. She's probably just in a bad mood because her whole house smells like chickenshit, so her friends never want to come over. You're probably the first person who's knocked on her door in months."

Miguelito and Elías laughed. I smiled. If I'd been alone, I would've thought about how horrible that interaction was for days. I would've worried that everyone who ever saw me was secretly thinking I was a *dirty prieto*. But with my cousins, it's easy to get over stuff. By the time Damián was done teasing the woman, I actually felt bad for her.

I spotted something moving just a few meters away. It was three of the woman's chickens. They must have escaped her chicken yard.

Cluck, cluck, cluck.

"Miguelito, do you still have that stupid pot you bought near the Casa del Migrante?"

Zip.

"Yep, right here!"

I elbowed Elías. I pointed at the chickens.

He looked at the chickens, then back at me.

I pointed at the small rocks on the ground.

"Nooooo, no, no, no, no," he said.

But I already had a rock in my hand.

Cluck, cluck, cluck.

Whoosh.

Thwack.

Lunchtime.

Love,
D.

A FEW HOURS LATER

Back on La Bestia, baby!

Querida Tía:

Everything feels so different now that my belly is full.

Preparing our chicken feast took a lot of work. The grossest part was plucking out all the feathers and then cutting the chicken into pieces small enough to fit in the pot. Only Elías had done it before, at home with Tía Gloria, and the rest of us were happy to let him do it all. I hate touching raw chicken. We ate our fill. When you're as hungry as we were, there's something really magical about the moment when you finally eat. It's not just that your belly gets full. It's more like, you feel life coming back into your body. You realize that when you were half-starved, you had disconnected your brain from your body so you wouldn't be miserable. Then, when you feel your stomach digesting the food, all this energy and joy rushes through you. I could tell my cousins were experiencing something similar. All four of us were so happy to be eating that food.

I'm so grateful to be sharing these moments with them. Even on this terrible, painful journey north, moments like this with Miguelito, Elías, and Damián feel special.

We agreed to make the leftover chicken last for another two days. We put the leftovers in my backpack, in the pot. I told Miguelito that it was only fair for me to carry it for a while.

We got back to the tracks just as the next train was passing, nice and slow.

Love,
D.

A FEW WEEKS LATER

The middle of México somewhere

Querida Tía:

Sorry about all the silence. I've been too exhausted to write, especially because there hasn't been anything that eventful to tell you about. Plus, when I was on top of the train, it didn't stop long enough for me to think or write. But you haven't missed all that much: it has just been more weeks on La Bestia. The landscape changed around us: it got hotter and dryer, and the plants looked different from how they looked when we were farther south, and way different from how they looked in Naranjito.

Sometimes we were on La Bestia for two whole days and nights at a time. We never really knew for sure which train to take: we ask the other migrantes, but sometimes they're wrong. Sometimes the trains went super fast between two cities, but other times they went slow and stopped at a million little pueblos in between. Even though my foot isn't healing, I'm getting better at stepping on it by shifting my weight when I walk. And I'm getting better at jumping on La Bestia, as long as it's not going too fast.

At one point, a little over a week ago, there was a massive rainstorm while we were on board. It was in the middle of the night. We didn't know what to do. Most of the other migrantes had tarps or blankets they covered themselves with, but we didn't, we hadn't thought to prepare for rain. The train was going pretty fast too, so every drop felt like getting slapped across the face with a cold towel. At first, we tried just hiding our heads under our shirts, but they just got soaked through almost immediately. And besides, it was dangerous, because we couldn't see.

A few minutes after the storm began, another man on our same car called us over. He said to get under his tarp, that it was big enough for us all. At first, we weren't sure, because we're learning that you can't necessarily trust everyone. But we had no choice. We would've gotten sick if we'd stayed in the rain. Something else I'm learning on this trip is that sometimes, even if it's a risk, you have to trust people. Sure, there was the woman who yelled at me outside her house, and the agentes de la Migra who set up a checkpoint so we had to walk around that mountain. There have been lots of mean people, but I think there are way more kind, generous people in the world. You just have to notice them.

Anyway, my stuff got wet, including my notebook. It was in my bag so it wasn't totally soaked, but I was worried that if I didn't let it dry completely, I'd rip the pages. So I guess that's also part of why I haven't written in a while.

Love you,
D.

ABOUT A MONTH LATER—EARLY MORNING, SUN ISN'T UP YET

Literally at the bottom of a ditch

Querida Tía:

Oh my God. I'm okay. I think. I kind of am still stunned from everything that just happened. I don't know what I'm going to do. I'm going to write to you, Tía, because you're sometimes the only person who can help me calm down. I'm literally writing to you from the bottom of a ditch. We'd been on La Bestia for maybe seven hours, and I thought we would have been getting close to the pueblo with the Casa del Migrante, but the train suddenly started braking. There was a loud screech, and I got jolted forward. I had to hold on to the metal grate on top of the train to keep from flying off the car. I thought it was la Migra again. Me and my cousins looked at each other. At the time, we thought the worst thing that could happen was having to take another five-day detour around another mountain. We didn't know how bad it was gonna get.

I peeked over the side of the car and . . . it wasn't la Migra. On each side of the train, there were around twenty men holding big clubs. Hombres del cartel. They were on the ground, fourteen or fifteen cars ahead of us. But even though the train was braking (I guess they had some way of forcing the conductor to stop it), the train was still moving pretty fast, and we were getting closer every second.

Elías looked at the three of us and whispered: "We have to run. Now!"

We climbed down the metal rungs on the side of the car. We'd never gotten off a train when it was moving that fast, but we had no choice. Elías, Miguelito, and Damián jumped first, then me. I landed hard on my right foot, then tumbled onto my stomach. Damián pulled me up off the ground by my backpack straps. There was a sharp pain shooting up my right leg, but I forced myself to run anyway.

I heard two gunshots. I heard a woman screaming. The pain in my foot vanished.

I felt pure adrenaline. My body was so hot that I swear even my bones were burning up. I feel like I'm still coming down from the adrenaline rush. I was running faster than I ever had. So fast that my legs must have looked like a blur, like el Correcaminos running from el Coyote de Looney Tunes. I followed my cousins. We jumped over a barbed-wire fence. I made it over, somehow. I think that's what cut me; I could see the spikes drag against my chest and my stomach, but I felt nothing. Now I can see the scrapes. They're still bleeding a little. Anyway, back to what happened . . . We dashed into a thicket of trees.

A male voice behind me yelled *stop*. I turned my head and saw three adult men behind us. They were fifteen meters away, maybe, and they were still on the other side of the barbed-wire fence. Two of them were chasing us, but the third, a tall man with a face tattoo, wasn't running anymore. He was standing with one leg in front of the other, lifting his gun.

He fired.
I had to—

A FEW MINUTES LATER

Still in the ditch

Sorry, Tía, I heard something and I was scared it was the hombres del cartel, so I stopped writing because I was scared that even the sound of my pen on paper would be the end of everything. But I don't think it was them, I think it was just some animal walking around. But I'm not sure . . . I'm so scared, still. Please keep me safe, Tía. I'm going to keep writing, even though I can barely read my own handwriting because my hand is shaking so much.

The first thing I can remember hearing, after the sound of the gunshot, was the leaves on the trees rustling. I turned and yelled "Go, go" to my cousins. I'm so much slower than they are, I didn't want them to get caught too just because they were trying to stay with me.

I wasn't going to turn around to look behind me again, I couldn't lose the time. I was going to run until I couldn't run anymore.

I heard branches snapping on the ground as the men got closer. I could barely see Damián a few meters in front of me, dodging trees, trying to get away. Two more shots. I didn't think either of them hit me, but I'm not sure I would have felt them if they did.

A cloud covered the moon and, for a few seconds, there was total darkness. I kept running blindly. I was worried I was going to hit a tree. That was when I started praying, to God and to you: *Señor, guíame a salvo. Tía, protégeme.*

There was a fast flash of light and a loud *bang* when they fired one more time, from closer than before. In the darkness, the flash was so bright that I got dazed.

Suddenly, I was tumbling.

I landed on something soft.

The moon reappeared, and I could see again, a little bit anyway. I looked down. I was on top of Damián. He was on top of Miguelito, and Miguelito was on top of Elías.

We'd fallen into a ditch.

Elías was on the bottom of our pile. I knew he was alive because he was holding a finger over his lips to show that we should be quiet.

Miguelito was alive. I knew because I saw him trembling.

Damián was alive. I knew because I felt him breathing underneath me.

And I was alive too. I remember thinking that I was pretty sure since I could see the blood from a new gash on my chest trickling onto Damián's neck.

We lay there, trying to breathe as quietly as possible, even though we were so scared, we were basically hyperventilating.

We heard the men who were chasing us walking around. I think they must have been ten meters away, or even closer.

There were voices, but we couldn't tell what they were saying. Then there was the sound of a car door opening, and a car door closing, and a car speeding away.

Elías was still holding his finger over his lips. Very, very quietly, he whispered, "Wait, they might still be here."

I shifted my weight so I wasn't crushing Damián. I touched Miguelito on the shoulder to make sure he really was okay. Silently, I thanked God for keeping us safe. Silently, I thanked him for putting this ditch in our path.

And thank you, Tía, for protecting us.

But we're not safe yet. We're waiting a few hours to make sure it's clear for us to leave the ditch. I hope that if they are still here, they'll eventually get tired of waiting and leave.

So, in the meantime, please don't go anywhere, Tía. I might need your help again.

Love,
D.

A COUPLE HOURS LATER

Alone

Querida Tía:

I can't believe it. I'm alone. Miguelito and Elías and Damián are gone. I'm scared. I'm trying to understand, trying just to breathe and not freak out.

I will be okay. Will I? Will I be okay, Tía? Will you keep me safe? You put that ditch in my path to protect me—will you bring my cousins back, too?

Let me tell you what happened. We were sitting silently in the ditch. My cousins were trying to relax, and I was writing to you. From in the ditch, we heard the train—our train, the one that got held up—start moving again. We didn't move. Around two hours later, another train passed by. After it was gone, Elías broke the silence:

"If they're still here, they'll definitely find us when the sun comes up," he whispered. "The next time we hear a train, we should run for it."

We all agreed.

An hour later, we heard a train whistle in the distance.

We climbed out of our ditch and sprinted for the same barbed-wire fence we jumped earlier. My cousins all climbed it pretty easily, but my foot was still throbbing, and it was hard for me to climb over. By the time I did, my cousins were already at the train tracks. I saw the train rushing towards them. A few other migrantes were getting ready to jump on, too. The train wasn't going at full speed, but it was definitely not a slow one either. I sprinted. By the time I reached the tracks, my cousins were already running alongside the train. Damián got on. Miguelito got on. Elías got on.

I struggled to get a hold of the train. It was just moving too fast. It was exactly like the first time I tried to jump onto La Bestia, I couldn't get traction on the gravelly ground, and every time I took a step, pain shot through my foot and even up my leg. Plus, I was weighed down by all that leftover chicken and Miguelito's pot.

I made a final push and leaped towards the rungs of the last train car.

I grazed it with my fingers, then fell flat on my face.

Gravel in my mouth. Pebbles pressed into my eye sockets. At least I didn't fall under the wheels.

The train sped forward, taking my cousins with it.

Please keep me safe, Tía, I'm so scared.

Love,
D.

AN HOUR LATER

Still alone by the tracks

Querida Tía:

Being alone is scary. I've never been alone like this, not for real. In Naranjito, even after you and Felipe died, me and Miguelito still had each other. And we left together. Crossed two borders together. Met up with Elías and Damián together. Survived five days of starvation together. Rode train after train together. Will he be okay? At least he has Elías and Damián. Especially Damián. He will make sure Miguelito isn't too scared, and Elías will take care of practical stuff, like finding food and making sure they get to the next Casa del Migrante.

The Casa del Migrante: that's where I have to go. Elías said it was the stop after the next one on the train. They'll know to wait for me there. I'll wait for the next train. No matter what, I'll get on it. No matter how fast it's moving, no matter how bad it hurts my feet, I'll climb on the next train and ride it to the Casa del Migrante and my cousins will be there and everything will be fine. Then we can just keep going and we'll make it to Nashville.

Everything will be fine then. Right, Tía?

Love,
D.

A COUPLE HOURS LATER

Stillllllll heeeeere

Querida Tía:

I decided I should take off my shoes to make sure my feet are okay. The sole of my right shoe is fully split in two. I could bend it down the middle if I wanted. Underneath, on my foot, there are bruises in long black-and-blue lines. When I try to move my ankle in a circle, the pain is terrible.

The right foot hurts, but it's my left foot that's killing me. That's the one with all the burst blisters. The scrap of Elías's T-shirt we used as a bandage is soaking wet, and dark red. It used to be white. I took off the shoe, then peeled back the bandage. A whole lot of dead skin came off with it. My foot is a slimy mess of red and purple and yellow. On my heel, there was an especially bruised, inflamed area with a long, broken thorn sticking out. I grabbed the thorn and pulled. The pain was excruciating, but I got it out. It was at least half an inch long. I have no idea how it got there. But at this point, I'm not questioning pain and injury. It's just part of life now.

After pulling out the thorn, I crawled around barefoot and found two big, cleanish leaves. Once the leaves were stuck to my feet, I carefully, painfully slid my shoes back on. The shoes are so gross that I'll probably get an infection, but I need to wear them if I'm going to make it onto the next train.

And now I'm sitting by the tracks.

And waiting.

And waiting.

And eating chicken.

And waiting.

I hope a train comes. A train has to come.

Another one of Felipe's proverbs was *A mal tiempo, buena cara.* In bad times, keep a good face. In just a few hours, I'll be at the Casa del Migrante. I'll be able to eat and sleep. Maybe they'll give me medicine for my feet. And my cousins will be there. I swear that the instant I see Elías, Damián, and Miguelito again, I'm giving each of them a big kiss. I'll give them another one for you.

Love,
D.

A FEW HOURS LATER

Just off La Bestia

Querida Tía:

This has got to be the most eventful day of my life. A few hours after my last letter, a train finally did show up. It was going fast, but I didn't care.

I was too scared and lonely to let it pass by. Even if that train were going a thousand miles an hour, I was determined to get on it.

I broke into a sprint. The pain in my feet was agonizing as I ran, but I dealt with it. After just a few seconds, I flung myself against the train.

My head slammed against one of the rungs, hard. It hit just above my right eyebrow. But my left hand grabbed a rung and I made it to the top of the train.

The noise from the wind and the train were muffled, and there was gray closing in everywhere. I must've really hit my head hard. The last thing I saw was a man with a face tattoo crawling toward me. As everything went black, I thought that for sure he must've been the same hombre del cartel who was chasing me earlier, and I felt my heart start to race even as I passed out . . .

I woke up with the wind rushing past my ears. The sun was shining hard on my face. I don't know how long I was out. My head was killing me—and it still is, it feels like someone threw a baseball straight at my head. This must be how the chicken felt after I hit it with that rock.

When I woke up, something was holding me down at the waist. There was a belt looped through my pants and through the metal grate on top of the train.

The man with the face tattoo had tethered me to the train. If he hadn't, I would've fallen off. I freaked out when I saw him, but there was nothing to be afraid of. While I was waking up, he appeared in front of me with a big smile on his face.

I was beginning to freak out when he got close, but there was nothing to be scared of.

"Man, I was worried about you! You took a hit!" he yelled. He unfastened the belt. "Hope you don't mind I looped you in. Thought you'd roll right off."

I could barely keep up with what was happening. I remembered my cousins and asked the man if we had passed the Casa del Migrante.

"Nah, that's coming up! You were really knocked out!"

He was very upbeat. He said the Casa del Migrante was in the next town we were going to stop at. Eventually, we got here.

I've been sitting here by the tracks ever since then, rereading my letters to you and trying to remember everything that happened this morning: the cartel guys, the chase, the gunshots, the ditch. Getting separated from my cousins. Sprinting to jump onto that train. Passing out. It'll be okay. I just got off a few minutes' walk, I think, from the Casa del Migrante. I'm sitting here, too nervous to move, praying that Miguelito and Elías and Damián will be there waiting for me. Please just help me get up. Please just help me get there.

Love,
D.

MORE HOURS LATER

Casa del Migrante

Querida Tía:

Okay, I'm at the Casa del Migrante. I haven't met up with my cousins yet, but I'm about to. There's no reason they shouldn't be here. They'll be here. Why wouldn't they be here? I have to wait for another twenty minutes before I can go and look for them. It'll be such a relief to be back together with them . . . It'll feel like I can finally exhale. Ever since we got separated, everything has felt kind of unreal, and I'm just looking forward to things feeling normal again. As normal as a journey like this one can feel, anyway. The Casa del Migrante seems to be set up similar to the one in Villahermosa, except with fewer murals. As soon as I showed up, a woman who works here looked at my feet and gasped. I guess I look like I'm in pretty bad shape.

I asked if my cousins were here, and I told her their names.

"Oh, querido, I can check, but first we need to fix you up," she said.

So she took me to a room in the building with cotton pads and pill bottles and bandages. I said one more time that I wanted to see my cousins, but I was too weak to put up a fight. I figured that I've waited this long, I can deal with a few more minutes without them.

The woman started treating my injuries. I don't know if she's a nurse or what, but she's really nice. She told me to take off all my clothes except my underwear. I was embarrassed, but I did it. She frowned when she saw the bloody leaves inside my shoes, but she didn't say anything. She just rubbed alcohol wipes all over my chest and stomach and feet, and above my eyebrow where I hit my head. It really stung. Then she applied some kind of cream on my feet and bandaged them up with real bandages—way better than Elías's dirty T-shirt. Finally, she gave me two plastic baggies full of different pills.

"These," she said, holding up one baggie, "are for the pain. Your feet probably hurt, right?"

I nodded.

She gave me pills to make them hurt less and told me I have to always eat something before I take them, or else I'll get sick. Then she shook the other baggie with pills to make sure all my scrapes and blisters don't get infected.

She stepped out for a minute, then came back with all new clothes for me: new underwear, new shirt, new pants, new shoes. Not *new,* new shoes—they actually look pretty old—but they're clean, and not cracked and blood-soaked like my old ones.

"So, I checked," she said, "an Elías and a Miguelito showed up here together yesterday. I don't know where they are, but if you just look around the bunks and courtyard, I'm sure you'll find them. Unless they already left. People are supposed to tell us when they leave, but sometimes they forget."

I wanted to go look for my cousins immediately, but she says I have to wait here for twenty minutes with my legs up after she applied that ointment and those bandages to my feet. So I'm waiting. And writing to you, Tía. But I can't wait—*can't wait, can't wait, can't wait*—to finally see my cousins again. They're definitely here, right? Promise me they are?

Love,
D.

SOMEHOW STILL THE SAME DAY
LONGEST DAY OF MY LIFE
Casa del Migrante

Querida Tía:

This letter is hard to write. I know you already know what's going on and you can see everything from up there. But I still feel like I should tell you.

When the nurse person let me go, I started looking around the Casa del Migrante for my cousins. After a few minutes, I went into a kitchen-type area, and I spotted Elías.

I called out to him. He turned around and looked at me, put his hand on his chest with relief, and then ran up and hugged me. I was a little panicked when he reacted like that. He said everyone was okay, but there was something he had to tell me about Damián. Apparently, the same cartel guys who we thought were waiting for us to climb out of the ditch weren't waiting for us there . . . they'd moved a few kilometers down the tracks, and they'd stopped the train my cousins got on. They chased them, again, and caught Damián. They didn't kill him or kidnap him or anything, but they beat him up pretty bad. They asked him for money they said he owed them, but obviously he didn't have any money or anything valuable to give him. They threatened to kidnap him and use him to extort his family, but he said he didn't know anyone's phone numbers, he couldn't contact family if he wanted to. And I guess they believed him, because they let him go.

It was horrible to imagine that all this happened to my cousins. And horrible to think that missing that train might have actually been what saved me. I wanted to see Damián, to see with my own eyes that he was okay. I asked Elías where he was. But Damián wasn't at the Casa del Migrante. He was so beat up that he gave up on going north. He turned himself in to la Migra. Elías wasn't sure if that meant they'd put him in jail or something, or if they'd just send him back to Quetzaltenango. He said he asked some of the adults at the Casa del Migrante, and they said the most likely thing was that he'd been sent back home, since he's just a kid. But there's no way to know until someone hears from him.

I can't believe this is happening. Has already happened. I thought my cousins would be safe from the cartel guys. I thought that nightmare was over. While I was safely sitting by the train tracks eating chicken, this was happening to Damián . . .

I was just starting to process this information when I saw Miguelito walk up behind Elías. I rushed over to give him a huge hug. I held on to him for at least a minute. Then I pulled back.

"You're okay?" I asked. "I was so so so worried about you."

"I'm okay. Elías took good care of me."

And he is okay, it's true, at least physically, even though when I first saw him, his eyes were red and swollen. I can't imagine how scary it must have been for him to see Damián like that . . . I don't know what he'll do without Damián.

It must have been heartbreaking for Elías, too, to see his brother like that. After he promised Tía Gloria that he'd look after him . . . Elías feels guilty all the time anyway, I can't imagine how he's feeling now. I'll have to remember to be extra nice to both of them.

I thought of something I could say that might cheer Miguelito up, at least for a second.

"Miguelito, I was worried we wouldn't be together for—"

"No, D., don't say it," Miguelito interrupted me.

"But you said it to me."

"You can say it in Nashville."

"Happ—"

"I said don't!" Miguelito snapped.

He never lashes out at me like that. Even when he was exhausted and hungry, and dealing with so much more than an eleven-year-old should ever have to, he never yelled at me once.

Dealing with more than a *twelve*-year-old should ever have to. Today is the first time in twelve years that I haven't wished Miguelito a happy birthday.

Love,
D.

THREE DAYS LATER
Casa del Migrante

Querida Tía:

When you spend so much time with someone, and then they're suddenly gone, it's like a part of you is gone too. Or like you're a different person. When I lost you and Felipe—and now that I've lost Damián in a different way—it feels like I'm not the same D. Esperanza as I was before. Does that make sense? You lost your parents, and you saw your kids leave Naranjito and go to los Estados Unidos, and you lost Felipe . . . How did you deal with it?

I think I'm going to try not to think about Damián until I'm in Nashville. We're leaving the Casa del Migrante tomorrow, and I hope we make it to Juárez before too long. The three of us. Sorry if I write a little less for a little bit. I'm just worried that if I write too much, I'll think about my feelings too much, and it'll make it harder to do the things I have to do to make it to el Norte. I don't want to be tempted to give up. I don't even know what giving up would look like.

I know I'm fourteen and I should be able to deal with hard stuff like this. You and Papá and Mamá and Felipe never gave up. But sometimes when everything changes all of the sudden, it feels like I'm still a kid.

Love,
D.

A WEEK LATER

Ciudad Juárez

Querida Tía:

Since we left the Casa del Migrante, it has been more of everything: more of La Bestia, more hunger, more rain, more sleeping by railroad tracks, more dodging la Migra. I know I said I wasn't going to write about Damián, but all of us are heartbroken that he's not here. It's different without him. Our family balance is off. Miguelito doesn't have Damián to joke with. Elías is worried about his brother and feels guilty. And me, I just miss him. I feel bad that I wasn't there to convince him to stay strong.

The journey has been taking us all over. It's hard to always know which train to get on. We ride one train for two days, thinking it's going the right way . . . and we end up in Piedras Negras, 800 kilometers in exactly the wrong direction. We bicker over whose mistake it was. We take a slow, three-day train back.

Without Damián, and after over two months away from home, this journey is wearing us down. So it's a good thing—an incredible thing, a magical thing, a beautiful thing—that this morning, as our train sped down the tracks alongside a highway, it passed right by a big sign that said BIENVENIDOS A LA HEROICA CIUDAD JUÁREZ.

Love,
D.

THE FOLLOWING DAY

Ciudad Juárez

Tía:

We got off the train last night, then slept. Now it's daytime and it's *hot.* The farther north we've traveled, the hotter and drier it has become. It feels like at least thirty-five degrees Celsius. It's so hot, and I'm so nervous and excited, that I think I might throw up. For the past few days, I've been worrying about what I'll say to Papá when we call. He and Mamá will have been so worried for the past . . . almost three months, when we weren't there to pick up their calls. And we didn't tell anyone in Naranjito that we were leaving. I know they'll be relieved to hear from me at first, but after that, they might be really, really mad . . . It's not the best way to start our relationship in a new country. I hope they're not so mad that they don't want me anymore. I don't think they will be, but it's hard not to worry.

We're out of food. We've been out of money for over a month. The pills the woman at the Casa del Migrante gave me ran out. My mouth is dry, my foot hurts, and my stomach is empty. We could probably find a way to scrounge some food, and we could definitely find a way to fill our water bottles. But we're so close, we decided that we'll just get across the border, then figure it out from there.

It turns out, Juárez is a big city. Walking through it takes hours, and there are buildings that shoot up taller than anything I've seen in any of the cities we've passed through so far. Every once in a while, we've been stopping to ask someone which direction we should go to get to the border. But a lot of the time, we can see the wall separating the city from los Estados Unidos, so we just walk in that direction. But we have to be careful, because we see la Migra everywhere in this city. On almost every street, there are cops in uniforms looking tough. They haven't paid very much attention to us. They probably just think we're homeless kids from the city. We've seen lots of those, too, and a lot of them look like they could be from Honduras or Guatemala, too.

After sunset, we started to see more scary people around. We're a lot tougher than we were when we started this journey, but we're not stupid: we know that three dark-skinned migrante kids are vulnerable after dark in a place like this. Even though we're eager to make it across the border, Elías thinks it would be more responsible to sleep someplace safe for the night. So we decided to spend the night under this bridge. It's by a small ravine that's kind of pretty.

I'll write more soon.

Love,
D.

THE NEXT DAY
Ciudad Juárez

Querida Tía:

I just wanted to write to tell you about what I'm eating right now. It's the most delicious food I've ever tasted. Apart from yours, obviously.

After I woke Miguelito and Elías up, we walked for a few hours. I say *walk*, but I should really say *hobble*. We'd probably move faster if they carried me. Anyway, we still can't see the border wall, so a few minutes ago, we asked a very short lady with a food cart which way to go. She was nice and gave us directions. Elías thanked her and we started walking away, but she wanted to keep talking.

"Where are you from?" she asked.

"I'm from Guatemala," Elías said. "These are my cousins. They're from Honduras."

"Are you hungry?"

"We . . . "

Of course we were hungry, but we don't have any money.

". . . We can't afford any of this," Elías said, gesturing to the pictures of food on her cart.

"My treat. What would you boys like?"

We've come across so many mean, unhappy people on this journey, but there have also been so many generous, kind souls. It would be so easy to only remember the selfish people, but I hope I never forget this lady.

I pointed to a picture of corn on her menu. She handed me something absolutely spectacular: it's corn—regular corn—but on top of it, she put some kind of crema, and some kind of cheese, and some kind of spices and some kind of herb. I was salivating just watching her put it together. And then, besides giving me the corn, *she gave me a cold Coke in a glass bottle.*

I don't know what Elías and Miguelito got. I was too absorbed in my corn. Why has this been kept from me my whole life? It's salty and sweet and creamy and crispy and tangy, and then I washed it down with the cold, bubbly Coke.

I asked the lady what this food is called.

"Elotes. Elotes con chile."

"Do they sell it in Nashville?"

She laughed.

"Of course! You can buy anything up there!"

We've been thanking her over and over. If I were a millionaire, I'd give her all my money so she could give elotes con chile away for free all day, as a service to the world.

I feel myself coming back to life. I swear the food is even making my feet feel better.

Love,
D.

PART II

DETAINED

MAY 8, 2018

La Perrera, Texas, Estados Unidos

Querida Tía:

I guess the last time I wrote to you was yesterday? Yeah, it was, after that nice lady gave us something to eat. That feels like a hundred years ago now. I think she was the last nice person we encountered.

So, big news: we're in los Estados Unidos. We . . . made it?

But things haven't gone like I expected.

Now I'm alone. I'm not totally sure where Miguelito and Elías are, but I think they're still in this building. I think I might have been arrested, I don't really know. I'm so scared. I'm standing against a wall because this cell they put me in is so crowded that I have no place to sit. They call this place "La Perrera," the dog kennel.

I guess I should catch you up on everything that has happened in the last twenty-four hours. It has been a lot. I probably won't be able to tell it all in one letter, it's too much. But I'll catch you up. Hopefully by the time I've told it all, they will have let me out of here, and I'll be back with my cousins, and we'll be on our way to Nashville.

Here's what you missed:

* * *

After eating in Juárez, we kept walking in the same direction for a few hours. We passed through a really nice-looking barrio, with the streets made completely out of stone. Some of the houses looked regular, but a lot of them looked like they must belong to rich people, they were so big and beautiful and clean. I wondered if the houses would just get even nicer as we got closer to los Estados Unidos (now that we're here, it's weird, the few houses we drove past were actually way less nice-looking than those houses in Juárez). Eventually, we made it to the bridge. We turned left to walk along the Río Bravo for a while, then finally saw a canal in the distance. I'm not sure if canal is the right word—it was like a riachuelo that branched off from the Río Bravo. It looked like it probably floods when it rains. All we had to do was walk along the river until we got to that canal. Then we just had to cross, and we'd be in los Estados Unidos.

We were just about to cross the last street before the river when I spotted la Migra mexicana in a cop car. And they spotted us, too: the car turned on its lights and began to drive toward us.

We did not make it this far just to get caught now, was all I could think.

We sprinted. My cousins were way faster than me, but I pushed through the pain and tried to keep up. After about a minute, my cousins ran down a residential street. I followed just a few seconds behind, but when I turned, I didn't see them anywhere. I started to worry. Where did they go? What if la Migra caught me but not them? The thought of being separated from Miguelito and Elías was unbearable.

I heard Miguelito's voice.

"D.!"

They were hiding behind some trash bins in an alley.

I limped over to my cousins as fast as I could. Just a few seconds after I joined them, la Migra drove past slowly. They'd turned off their lights. We sat and waited. The canal was a twenty-meter dash from there, at most. We were just about to make a run for it when another cop car drove past.

We waited . . . and then a few minutes later, a car drove past again. This kept happening every few minutes. Over a dozen times. We weren't sure if it was the same car or different ones, but it didn't really make a difference. We couldn't risk bolting toward the canal if they were just going to catch us. After about an hour, I had an idea: we'd see how much time passed between their drive-bys. Maybe they were passing through at regular intervals.

After a few minutes, they appeared again. We didn't have a watch or anything, so I started counting the intervals: "Uno, dos, tres, cuatro, cinco . . . "

" . . . quinientos sesenta y seis, quinientos sesenta y cuatro, quinientos ses—there they are! So five hundred and sixty-four seconds. Let's check again? Can someone else count this time?"

Elías took over. The second time, it was five hundred and ninety-eight seconds.

So, they drove past once every six hundred seconds, more or less. Once every ten minutes.

We decided that the next time they drove by, we'd count to sixty, and then sprint toward the canal.

Almost ten minutes later, we saw the car drive past again. Miguelito began:

"Uno, dos, tres, cuatro . . . "

The wait was excruciating. My heart was pounding a mile a minute. I could feel it throbbing in my neck.

"Cincuenta y tres, cincuenta y cuatro, cincuenta y cinco . . . "

I took a deep breath. I braced for the agonizing pain I knew would shoot through my foot as soon as we started running.

"Cincuenta y seis . . . "

I thought about Damián, beaten up by the cartel, and probably on a bus back to Guatemala. Or in a cárcel de la Migra mexicana.

"Cincuenta y siete . . . "

I though about how you told me to take care of Miguelito. I hoped I was doing the right thing. I hoped I was doing what you and Felipe would want.

"Cincuenta y ocho . . . "

I thought about the past two and a half years: the micro accident, you getting sick, then the haciendas and the poverty and the threat of violence that brought us here. Causa y efecto.

"Cincuenta y nueve . . . "

I said a prayer. *Señor, protégeme solo una vez más.*

"¡Sesenta!"

* * *

I'm getting kind of tired, even though the lights are still on. I'm going to try to sleep. For a while, I didn't know how I could possibly sleep, because there are so many people in this tiny cell, and when they put me in here like two hours ago, there wasn't even any place I could sit down. I didn't think I could make it across the room without stepping on someone. But after I'd been standing for a while, I heard someone say "Hey" in a soft voice. I looked down and saw a woman with a toddler on her lap. I was confused for a second, but then I noticed she had scrunched up close against the woman to her left to make a small space on her right that was just barely big enough for me to sit down against the wall. She already barely has any room for herself—especially considering she's holding a kid—but she was offering some of her limited space to me. I narrowed my shoulders to make myself as compact as possible, then sat down. I tried to thank her, but before I could even turn my head to say something, she was asleep. She's been sleeping almost the whole time I've been writing to you.

I'm going to sleep now, too. I'll keep going with the story when I wake up.

Love,
D.

STILL MAY 8, 2018, I THINK

Still in La Perrera, Texas, Estados Unidos

Querida Tía:

I'm not actually totally sure if it's the 8th or the 9th. There are no windows or clocks in here, and time has been moving strangely. When you have no way to measure the time, and you just have to trust your body to keep track of how many hours it feels like have passed, it's a little confusing. The lights are still on: there are five or six fluorescent fixtures on the ceiling that fill the room with bright white light. It's not so bright that it hurts your eyes, exactly, but it's too bright to be comfortable. It reminds me of when you've been in the dark for a long time and then look at the TV or some other backlit screen: you have to squint slightly or else your eyes will water a little. A lot of the other people in here are holding a hand over their eyebrows like a visor, or they've covered their eyes with a hat or some other piece of clothing.

I was a little nervous to talk to anyone, and I still am—no one seems to talk much in here—but I wanted to know when they were going to turn off the lights. The woman with the toddler is still sitting next to me, and she seems nice, so I turned to ask her: "When do they turn off the lights?"

She hesitated for a second; maybe she thought I was still asleep and she was surprised by the question. But then her eyes got wide: "They're always on."

"They never turn them off?"

"¡Cállense! No talking!" yelled the agente de la Migra who's watching us. He has a very bad accent, and I wonder if he knows the Spanish word for anything besides "shut up."

I really want to tell you more about this place, because it's so like . . . it's really unpleasant. It's cramped and gross and sad. But it'll make more sense after I keep filling you in on what happened when we crossed the frontera.

* * *

After Miguelito finished counting to sixty, we ran. He and Elías were much faster, but I pushed through the pain in my foot.

My cousins were just getting to the other end of the canal as I was entering it. The soil at the bottom was slimy and covered in greenish mushrooms. When I was almost all the way across, I slipped and landed on my elbow. I could hear Miguelito and Elías laughing. That was how I started my new life in los Estados Unidos: covered in green slime.

Miguelito and Elías came back into the canal, lifted me to my feet, and helped me get to the other side. So we were . . . there? Here? We couldn't tell at first. We hadn't climbed over any fences, and there weren't any signs saying we were in a different country or anything.

I turned to Elías and asked if he thought we made it.

"¿Yo qué se? Everything looks the same."

We'd only been across the canal for about five minutes when we saw two cars speeding in our direction. Clearly, someone had spotted us. One of them was coming from the left and the other was coming from the right, so we had nowhere to run except back into México. Were they drug traffickers or the cartel or something? I glanced at my cousins, and we got ready to run if we had to.

They got closer and we saw they were white trucks with a green stripe down the middle. So not the cartel, good. I figured it had to be la Migra. But was it la Migra mexicana or la migra de los Estados Unidos? If they were from México, we were screwed. They'd deport us right away. But if they were from los Estados Unidos, it would mean we'd made it. We could tell them we were trying to get back to our families.

The trucks parked and a tall white guy stepped out. He was speaking English—Dios, we made it, we really were in los Estados Unidos. I looked at my cousins and smiled, even though I could feel my lips splitting in the heat. My foot was oozing blood and pus, and I still couldn't feel the elbow I fell on in the canal, but all I felt was relief. Miguelito gave me a thumbs-up.

For the previous few weeks, I hadn't let myself think about seeing Mamá and Papá in person. I knew there was a pretty good chance I wouldn't make it here, and I didn't want to be disappointed. But once we were across, I finally imagined hugging them for the first time, and I think I felt something streaming down my cheeks, but I couldn't tell if it was tears or sweat or slime.

The white guy from the truck was yelling at us. I tried to remember the tiny amount of English I learned in school and from playing Call of Duty, but I could barely catch anything:

"*English english* fucking trash *english* cholos *english english*?" I didn't understand what he was saying, but I couldn't understand why he was calling us cholos. Did that mean he could speak Spanish? Or was that a word in English, too, and I just don't know it? Because we aren't cholos, we're not in a gang. We're here because we're trying to get as far away from gangs as possible.

I didn't get why he was so upset. He talked to the guy from the other truck for a minute. The only word I could pick out was *trash*. I wondered what was happening. The man came over to us and yelled something in English. I kept looking at Elías and Miguelito, but they didn't understand any better than I did. We didn't need to speak fluent English to tell that man was in a bad mood. We'd really pissed him off somehow. I just wished I knew what we'd done.

If he knew any Spanish, he didn't want to speak it. We kept saying "No English, no entendemos, solo hablamos español," but he just yelled louder. Finally, he took off his sunglasses, spat on the ground, grabbed me by my backpack straps, and started screaming right in my face. I still didn't know what he was saying—the only word I could pick out was *deport*. But why would he deport us?

"Señor, por favor, solo estamos acá para estar con nuestras familias," Elías said, trying to explain that we weren't doing anything wrong, that we were just trying to join our parents. "No somos cholos ni del cartel ni nada."

That just seemed to piss the agente off even more: "*English english* América, trash. *English! english* trash *english english*."

None of us knew what to make of him. He was literally the first person from los Estados Unidos we'd ever met, and it felt like he could barely hold himself back from beating us up.

The whole journey to el Norte was uncertain. The whole way, we didn't know where we were going to sleep, or how we were going to eat. But I never expected this. I thought I'd be safe in los Estados Unidos. And now I have no idea what to think. That guy was so angry, it went against everything I thought I knew about coming here. I wondered if he was confused and thought we were drug smugglers or something. But how could that have been possible when we were just kids? Miguelito is only twelve! Were we accidentally breaking some law or doing something people think is super disrespectful? There was no reason for him to treat us like we were disgusting. I mean, we were sweaty and dirty and slimy, and I was bleeding through my sock, but I feel like that wasn't the thing he was so repulsed by.

I'd never been screamed at by a grown-up that way. It was nothing like when you used to scold me and Miguelito in Naranjito. The agente in the other truck wasn't doing anything to help. I started to feel like maybe I wasn't safe in los Estados Unidos, at least not by the frontera. Like, I was an injured, exhausted kid alone in the desert with a pissed-off white guy, who was yelling at me and calling me *trash*. And he had a gun. If he could be this hostile toward us even though we were just kids, I'm afraid of what else he might do. I'd expected that in los Estados Unidos, la Migra would be welcoming, unlike in México. Maybe we were just unlucky we ran into this one mean agente. But why wasn't the one in the other truck doing anything to stop him?

I got this weird, sharp feeling between my ribs. I didn't know what to do about feeling unsafe, and I wanted to cry, but I was afraid that'd just make things worse. I was worried about what this man might do to me or my cousins.

He yanked me toward his truck and grunted: "Get in."

* * *

There's a new guard in la perrera who just got here like ten minutes ago, and he keeps looking at me. I'm worried he's going to yell at me for writing to you. No one ever told me writing in here was against the rules, but nobody told me anything, really. They didn't let us bring any of our stuff in here, but I didn't want to lose my notebook, so I managed to slip it under my shirt before they took my backpack away and brought me here. Some of the guards probably noticed, but I think they were too lazy to care. I don't want to test my luck. I'd be heartbroken if he took away all my letters to you, so I'm going to stop writing, just in case. More soon.

Love,
D.

PROBABLY MAY 9, 2018, BY NOW, I THINK

Still in La Perrera

Querida Tía:

I don't remember falling asleep, but I guess I did. They took us to get oatmeal, and then I fell asleep. I have no idea how long I was out—the woman who was up against the wall next to me is gone. I'm guessing that I slept for part of the night, and now it's the 9th, but honestly, I really don't know. There's literally nothing for me to do here except for write to you. So, now that that one agente who kept looking at my notebook is gone, I guess I can go back to filling you in:

* * *

Okay, so we'd just gotten across the frontera and the agente had put us in his truck. It was crowded in there with the three of us inside; there was a mesh net between the back seat, where we were pressed against each other, and the front. The seats were covered in crumbs, and the whole cabin smelled like sweat and dirt. But it was air-conditioned, at least, and after spending so long in the heat, the cool air felt nice on my sweaty skin.

At that point, I couldn't think of anything to say to the pissed-off gringo. He had stopped talking, and me and Miguelito and Elías were too nervous to talk to each other. I think if we'd tried to say anything, the agente would have started yelling again. I was worried he might get so mad that he'd deport me back to Honduras, or at least make me go back into México. But he was driving away from the border—I was pretty sure, anyway, because he was driving away from the direction we came from. I hoped he was just having a bad day. I figured that must be it. I thought he would bring us to someone who understood we were trying just trying to join our families, because then I'd at least be able to call Papá and ask him to come get me.

That was before they brought me here, before they'd called my parents. I wondered what seeing Papá would be like. Would he be really, *really* mad? Or would the relief that I'm okay and in los Estados Unidos make him so happy that he'd forget to be mad? I knew he'd be surprised, but he'd still pick me up. When I left Honduras, I assumed that when I got to the border, it would be easy for him to get me. I figured that Texas and Nashville weren't that far away from each other. But México turned out to be way bigger than I thought, so maybe I'm wrong about the size of los Estados Unidos, too.

The agente de la Migra wasn't driving for very long. For the first minute or two of the drive, we were on a dirt road. But soon the agente pulled onto a paved road and started driving really fast through a small town. The truck windows were tinted, and I couldn't see much, but I could tell it wasn't exactly a busy city, nothing compared to Juárez. There was just a gas station, ranches, some trailers with old people in folding chairs outside who remind me of the abuelitos who sit around in Naranjito. We'd only been in the truck for five or ten minutes before he pulled into a driveway, then braked for a second. The property we were turning onto was surrounded by a tall fence with razor wire on top. He parked in front of a gate and sat there for a few seconds. I wasn't really sure what he was waiting for, but then suddenly, the gate began pulling back all by itself. He didn't have to get out to open it or even push a button or anything. After he drove through, the gate closed again. He pulled into the parking lot and turned off the engine.

"Out" was all he said.

The parking lot was big, and there was no shade anywhere, it was just baking in the sun. Behind us, two green helicopters were sitting on a helipad. It was the first time I'd seen helicopters up close, outside of a movie or video game (they're actually way smaller than I expected). We followed the pissed-off agente across the parking lot toward a flat building with almost no windows. It stretched on so long that I couldn't even see the end of it. We walked past a tall flagpole with the flag of los Estados Unidos at the top, then we went into the lobby. It just looked like a regular building inside—there were phones and desks, and other men in the same green uniform walking around.

One of them was walking out the door as we entered. He looked us up and down with this confused look on his face, then turned to the pissed-off gringo, pinched his nose with his fingers, and waved his hand in front of his face.

The agente who drove us lifted his eyebrows, made an expression like he was really frustrated, and said: "*English english english english english english.*"

The second man made a sound like he was pretending to throw up, then both of them burst out laughing. The agente who drove us slapped the other guy on the back, then we went the rest of the way inside.

* * *

I keep wanting to skip ahead to tell you about how horrible it is in this place, but I think it'll make more sense if I catch you up on the last few days first. I think that if I didn't have this notebook with me, I'd go insane. But my hand is starting to cramp. So, sorry, Tía, if my handwriting gets hard to read. Okay, back to the story.

* * *

The agente told Miguelito and Elías to wait on some chair, then he took me to a desk where a woman was sitting behind a computer. I didn't like being separated from my cousins—staying close to them is the only way I've survived the past few months—but I could still see them from where I was sitting. The woman at the desk was typing something. When I sat down, she quickly glanced up from the monitor and made a motion for me to wait. She didn't look angry or annoyed like the agente who brought me there. Honestly, she just looked bored, even though she was typing faster than I'd seen anyone type before. She wasn't wearing a green uniform like most of the other grown-ups there, she was just in black pants and a green blouse, a different kind of green from the rest. There was so much happening that it was hard for me to keep up. I figured that that woman probably wasn't a cop. Would she speak Spanish? The pissed-off gringo didn't, and I guess it might not be realistic to expect people here to understand me when I talk. When I was still with Miguelito and Elías, it didn't matter as much that I didn't speak English: even though I couldn't understand what the adults were saying, I could talk to my cousins in Spanish and it made me feel less alone. But with everyone around me speaking English, I got this weird disoriented feeling. It's hard to describe the dizziness of not being able to speak to anyone. It almost feels like you're not a real person. Once my parents get me, I'll have to learn English fast.

The woman sighed and looked up from her computer. "Bueno, vamos a empezar," she said with no accent at all.

"¡Hablas español!" I said. I was instantly relieved. I should've known, because even though she worked for la Migra, she was more morena than most of the other people in this building. She smiled a tiny bit when she saw how excited I was, but she still barely looked less bored than she did just a second earlier. I still felt like it was a good sign that she spoke Spanish, and bored was better than angry. I was nervous and exhausted and overwhelmed, but I felt a little more comfortable around her than I did around the other agentes. I wanted to explain that I came to los Estados Unidos to be with my parents. I tried to explain that I came here with my cousins and I needed to call Papá so he could come pick me up, but I was so nervous that I mumbled, and I'm not sure she understood. She didn't seem to be listening very closely in any case.

"One thing at a time," she said before I was finished, still speaking Spanish. She hadn't looked me straight in the eyes the whole time, but I felt like she was the closest thing I had to a friend there. "Birth certificate?" she said.

"What?"

She exhaled. "Do you have your birth certificate? It makes it easier for me."

I don't even really know what a birth certificate is, exactly. I'm not sure I ever had one. I guess they gave one to Mamá when I was born. Did you have mine, Tiá? Did you keep it under your mattress with all the other important papers? If you did, you never told me about it. I couldn't figure out anything to say, and I was scared of saying the wrong thing—I was worried that you're supposed to bring your birth certificate to los Estados Unidos, or else they send you back to go get it. I just kept looking at her, silent.

"Okay." She started to speak more slowly, and she looked me in the eye for the first time. "When you left, did they give you any papers to take with you?"

"Who?"

"Whoever sent you here."

"I don't . . . No one sent me here, I just came with Miguelito . . . He's my cousin . . . He's over there somewhere . . . I don't think anyone gave him any papers either."

"Or whoever told you to come. Any papers at all."

I didn't know what to say, because no one told me to come. I tried to think if I had anything to give her. Even though she wasn't being friendly or anything, she wasn't being mean, and I didn't want to disappoint her. I remembered copying down Papá's number before we left Naranjito. "Is this okay?" I asked, pulling the paper out of my pocket. It was crumpled, and the blue ink was smeared somehow. I guess it got wet in the rain while we were on La Bestia, but it was still readable. It was the only piece of paper I had to give her.

She squinted at it for a second. "Phone numbers?"

I nodged. "My papá's number is on there."

"Which one is it?"

"The first one." I forgot that Tía Gloria's number and Cami's number were on there too.

She immediately picked up a landline on the desk and began dialing the number. While it was ringing, she seemed to have a sudden thought, and turned to me:

"What's your father's name? His full name?"

"Víctor Esperanza," I said. I got a knot in my throat almost immediately, thinking that I'd be able to talk to him. I'd have to come clean about traveling north. I prayed he'd just be surprised and relieved, not mad. He'd ask why I didn't tell him, and to be honest, I didn't even know the answer to that question myself. Me and Miguelito talked about telling my parents we were coming, but they would have told us to stay put.

And I was worried about making a bad first impression. I haven't ever really known my parents, they've just been voices on the phone. What if he thinks I'm a disappointment?

"Right, okay," the woman said. She waited for him to pick up. "Hola, ¿Señor Esperanza? I'm calling from Customs and Border Patrol in El Paso, Texas. We have an underaged migrant here who says he's your kid—" She stopped abruptly, looked up at me, and mouthed the words *¿Cómo te llamas?*, and I told her my name. "Says his name is D. Esperanza."

I reached for the phone—I had assumed she would let me talk to him right away—but she made a gesture for me to sit back down, and I obeyed. I didn't want to push my luck, I knew the pissed-off gringo who found us was still somewhere in the building, and I didn't want her to call him over. But it was torture to know Papá was on the line and I couldn't talk to him. Was he upset? I tried to watch her facial expressions, how she reacted, in case that gave me some clue into whether he was mad or disappointed in me for coming. I strained to hear his voice, but I couldn't.

"Yes, it's really him. D. Esperanza, from—" she looked up again and mouthed *¿De dónde eres?* "—from Naranjito, Honduras . . . No, sir, we aren't asking for money . . . Not a kidnapping . . . Not a scam either . . . Well, he's here all the same. He'll be transferred from CBP to HHS custody and . . ."

She started explaining a lot of stuff I didn't understand, talking fast. I couldn't keep track of what this lady was saying. To me, it was just a bunch of acronyms I'd never heard before. Even though she was speaking Spanish, it was like it was another language. But I'm just a kid. I hoped Papá understood what she was saying. I'm sure he did. Still, I wanted her to let me talk to him, and I felt my heart drop in my chest when she put down the receiver.

She asked me for a few more pieces of information, then she waved the same angry-looking agente over.

* * *

Okay, I think that's all my hand can write in a day. I'll finish catching you up tomorrow. ("Tomorrow," whatever that means in this place where time doesn't exist.)

Love,
D.

PROBABLY MAY 10, 2018, I GUESS

Still in La Perrera

Querida Tía:

There's a baby in here that hasn't stopped crying today. The mother keeps shushing, but it's no use. Everyone is obviously kind of annoyed by the sound, but also, what's she supposed to do? What's the baby supposed to do? Isn't it messed up that they keep a baby in this place? Isn't it messed up that they keep *anyone* in this place? I hope they let me out soon.

Okay, picking back up where we left off, with the angry-looking agente:

* * *

I was relieved when I saw the angry-looking agente was walking with Elías and Miguelito. We were too confused and frightened to say anything, but I could tell they were as happy to see me as I was to see them. The agente got distracted talking to his friend—the same guy who held his nose when we came in—and we had a few minutes to whisper. I told them about the woman calling Papá, and they said something similar happened to them. But our conversation got cut short when the agente turned back to us. He led us to a small, empty room with concrete floors, fluorescent lights, and no windows. There were a few people in there already, some of them huddling together. The agente opened the door, and I gave Elías a look, like, does he expect us to go in there, or . . . ? When the agente saw us hesitating, he got mad again:

"Go! Vamos!" So I guess besides *cholos*, he knew at least one other Spanish word.

This is one of the hardest things to write about.

The agente closed the door behind us and almost right away we realized it was really cold in there. That was why the people inside were all huddled together. Miguelito said he was really cold, and really scared. I have to remember that he's not even a teenager yet, so this is a lot for him.

I don't understand why it was so cold. It didn't make any sense. It was a normal temperature when we were walking through the building to get to this little cell. After a few minutes, the temperature started to get really unpleasant. Before we came in, our clothes were damp with sweat (sweat and blood in my case), and they were getting really cold really fast. But there was nothing we could do, we didn't have a change of clothes or blankets or anything. There weren't beds, or even any cots or sleeping pads like they had at the Casa del Migrante, just a hard concrete floor. There wasn't a toilet either, and I was hoping that meant they weren't going to leave us in there for too long. But I wasn't sure, because they haven't given us any food or water, so maybe they weren't expecting us to need a toilet.

After maybe five minutes, we huddled together like we did at night when we were stuck walking around that mountain for five days. We were starting to shiver. The blood around my foot started to change consistency—it wasn't freezing, but it was kind of getting thicker. And my toes started to go numb.

Miguelito looked at me, and I could tell he was trying not to cry. He looked terrified. "¿Van a abrir la puerta?" he asked.

"No sé, Miguelito. It's gonna be okay, though." I had no idea how long we'd be in there, but I was really worried about Miguelito. He's smaller than me, so he was getting cold faster. I held him tight—the three of us were already holding each other for warmth, but this was more like a hug, and I hoped he understood that I wasn't just trying to keep warm, I was trying to show that I cared about him, and I was going to be there for him no matter what. After standing like that for a minute, his shoulders started moving up and down. He wasn't making any noise, but I could tell he was crying. Other people's tears always make me get emotional, too, but right then I had to push down whatever I was feeling. I didn't know how long we were going to be in there, and I couldn't get distracted. I needed to stay focused on surviving, just like I have since we left Naranjito. Just like I have since you and Felipe died, really. Just like I'm doing now.

* * *

They're taking us to eat more of their gross oatmeal. (I've almost got you caught up, don't worry!) I'll write more when I'm back.

Love,
D.

STILL MAY 10, 2018

Still in La Perrera

Querida Tía:

Okay, it wasn't gross oatmeal this time. We got apples and sandwiches instead. I'd thought it was the morning, but if they're not giving us oatmeal, maybe it's the afternoon, or the evening? There's no way to tell. Anyway, I'm glad they didn't give us that oatmeal, because I always get so sleepy after I eat it.

Thanks for reading my letters, Tía. Writing about all the stuff that has happened has been the only way I've stayed sane in here. So, let's keep going:

* * *

When we were in La Hielera—the icebox, I learned later that that's what it's called—I wanted to call out for help. Did the agentes on the other side of the door know it was so cold in there? (They did know, I now know.) At the time, I thought that maybe it was just a mistake and the air-conditioning was on really high, and maybe they'd want to know. I thought about asking the other people in the cell, but after what we went through on La Bestia, I'm nervous about talking to strangers. And asking the agentes was even scarier. But I felt Miguelito crying against me, and I decided I had to do something. I couldn't stand to see him falling apart like that.

I walked up to the windowless door and knocked on it softly. The instant I let go of Miguelito and Elías, I felt the cold air slipping down my sleeves and creeping up my pant legs. "¿Disculpe?" I called. I was too nervous to yell loudly.

No response. I knocked again, harder, and yelled: "¿Hay alguien ahí? Es que hace mucho frío aquí."

I went back to my huddle with Elías and Miguelito. I didn't want to be away from their body heat for more than a few seconds. We stood like that for another ten minutes or so. Miguelito was still crying, and Elías was just standing very still and silent, trying to focus on conserving as much warmth as possible. Every few minutes, I went up to bang on the door and call for help again. The longer we waited, the louder I yelled. I was still scared of what the officers would do if they showed up, but by that point, I was even more nervous about staying in that cell longer. After the third time I knocked, I gave up. I preferred to save my energy and warmth.

In my head, I was praying the whole time, asking God to give me the strength to make it through.

This is when I started talking to you. Do you remember? Did you hear me? While I felt my brain slowing down in the cold, I wished you were still alive and there with us. Or better yet, I wished I were back home with you. I started asking you to keep me warm, moving my lips very slightly: *Por favor, Tía, ayúdame como hiciste esas noches.*

And, anyway, I should say thank you, because you came through. Just when my eyelids were falling shut, we heard the sound of a metal latch, and the door opened. It only took a few seconds for the cell to get warmer as the outside air rushed in. All three of us stood up. I can't speak for Elías or Miguelito, but my mind had gotten so slow and foggy that I forgot to be scared of whoever was coming in. I just scrambled toward the door to get as close to the source of warmth as possible.

That time it was a different agente who opened the door. He gave me a dirty look and said something in English. "N-n-no entiendo," I replied. I could barely move my lips.

He rolled his eyes, ran his arm across his face like he was wiping his nose, then pointed to my face. I made the same motion and felt something wet against the back of my hand—my face had gone numb, so I hadn't noticed, but there was a line of cold, thick snot running from my nose down my upper lip, over my mouth, and onto my chin.

* * *

That guard who looks at me funny when I'm writing just got back, so I'm going to sign off for now. We're almost caught up, I promise.

Love,
D.

STILL MAY 10, 2018, I'M PRETTY SURE

Still in La Perrera

Querida Tía:

The thing is, I know I've been writing a lot, and maybe with more detail than I need to give you. But I'm in here all day, every day, anyway, and the last few days were probably the most eventful days of my life . . . So I might as well tell you everything, right? You're not in a hurry?

* * *

The agente led us to a room with a table and some chairs, where another man in a uniform was waiting for us. Unlike the agente who picked us up at the border, this one spoke to us in Spanish, even though he had a really thick gringo accent that made him hard to understand:

"¿Quiénes son? What are you here for?"

"I'm D. Esperanza, these are my cousins Miguelito and Elías. I'm fourteen yea—"

"Who sent you?"

"¿Mande? What?"

"Any Mara connection?" he was yelling almost immediately all of the sudden. "Drugs, yeah? MS-Thirteen or what?"

I was too confused to say anything. I just shook my head no. My body was only just beginning to warm up from La Hielera, and it felt like my brain needed to thaw a little bit before I'd be able to understand what was going on.

"¿Qué?" he asked, "¿No sabes hablar? Talk!" He slammed his palms down on the table, and I started to feel tears in my eyes. "Oh, mi niña pequeña, don't cry!" he said sarcastically.

He asked Elías more or less the same set of questions, but Elías was better prepared. He watched me get overwhelmed when I tried to answer, so he had time to get his answer ready. "No, señor, we're not in a gang. We don't have drugs or anything. We're here to be with our families. We didn't mean to do anything wrong. When can we see our families?"

"Always the same shit." He opened the door and told someone to escort Elías and Miguelito away, but he kept me in the room. Elías gave me a look, and I knew he was trying to communicate that he was sorry to leave me alone with that man, but we both knew he had no choice.

When Miguelito and Elías walked out the door, it felt the same as when I couldn't manage to climb onto La Bestia a few weeks ago, when I saw them vanishing in the distance, while I stood crying on the train tracks. As soon as they were gone, I felt suddenly lost. Without them to give me strength, and with this angry man yelling questions I didn't even understand, it felt like I was in a dream, or a nightmare.

"All right, mi niña pequeña, what's really going on? How many times have you crossed the border? Tell me if you don't want to go back to La Hielera."

That's when I learned what they called the cold room: *La Hielera*—the icebox. That was also when I realized that room was cold on purpose.

I was still crying, and even more confused. I tried to explain that I wasn't a bad guy: "I'm sorry, I haven't . . . This is my first time crossing ever. We don't do drugs or anything, I promise. You can check our stuff."

"Never trust a thug, kid. You think you can just wander over here and stink up my buddy's truck?" Then he said something that really scared me: "If you don't like it in Mexico, that's not my problem. But you're going back if I have anything to do with it."

I didn't understand then—and I still don't understand now—how can he send me back? I came to los Estados Unidos to be with my parents. I wanted to tell him that there was some kind of misunderstanding, that Papá was supposed to come pick me up. I wished the agente hadn't sent Elías and Miguelito away. At that point, we'd been together for months. They kept me safe. We kept each other safe. Once it was just me and the agente, I felt exposed. Was he really going to send me back? Without my cousins? I started crying even harder. He rolled his eyes and left the room.

* * *

When they took Elías and Miguelito away from me that time, I eventually got them back. So I'm holding on to hope that I'll get them back when they let me out of la perrera soon. If they ever let me out.

Love,
D.

STILL MAY 10, 2018

La Perrera

Querida Tía:

I think all this time in here is starting to mess with my head. It's hard for me to process what's happening. I'm disoriented, and all the shapes seem to be blurring together. I can't focus on anyone's face. Ever since we were picked up on the Estados Unidos side of the border, it has felt like there's a fog in my brain. I keep having emotions that don't make sense together: I'm relieved to finally be in los Estados Unidos, where I should be safe, but I'm nervous because I haven't felt safe at all since I've been here. I'm excited to finally be back with my parents, but I'm terrified that they might just keep me here forever, and I'll never see my parents. All these contradictory feelings are crashing into each other in my head and making it hard to keep up. It's like my brain is on overdrive and there's no room for it to take in any new information.

It feels like writing is the only thing that's helping, so I'll keep catching you up:

* * *

A few minutes after that angry gringo guy interrogated me, the same lady who called Papá on the telephone came in and told me to follow her. There were eight or nine people in there, and some of them were the same kids from that freezing cold room. As I scanned the room, I realized that Elías and Miguelito were in there, too.

Even though we had only been apart for a few minutes, it felt like when we ate those pineapple empanadas after starving halfway to death for five days. It felt the same as when we were reunited at the Casa de Migrante after I missed that train. They were like two bright flashlights shining through the fog in my brain. I hurried over to them. Elías seemed kind of numb, but he looked me straight in the eyes, and I know that meant he was mostly okay. Miguelito seemed paler than usual, and he was mostly just staring at the ground. I was worried about him, but he smiled slightly, and that made me feel a little better. We were all too nervous to say anything—if we said the wrong thing, we could make the grown-ups so mad, they'd deport us or stick us back in La Hielera. But even without talking, I could tell that my cousins were relieved to see me, too.

The woman told us to follow her. She wasn't unfriendly, but she definitely wasn't worried about making us feel comfortable, either. She said we were going "somewhere else," and I didn't feel brave enough to ask where, or how long it'd be before we saw our families.

We walked past windows, and I saw that it was the middle of the afternoon—the sun was lower, but it was still shining, and I felt it warming my skin through the glass. After all that time half-freezing to death in La Hielera, the warm air felt amazing. I made a mental note to be grateful for warmth. I'm never going to complain about being too hot again.

The lady took us to a room, and Miguelito, Elías, and I all sat next to each other on the floor. The lady gave each of us a cookie wrapped in plastic and a juice box—that small kind with a plastic straw that doesn't always pierce the top of the box on the first try. It had probably been twelve hours since we got in that agent's truck, but that was the first time they'd given us any kind of food. After handing out the cookies and juice, the lady left us in the room with the same bored-looking Migra guy.

El agente de la Migra made a noise, said something in English, and motioned for everyone to get up. Miguelito was sleeping, and Elías and I figured that we had to wake him up, because we never knew if something would get us in trouble or not. If Miguelito was sleeping and the Migra guy had to wake him up, they might get mad. The things that piss them off seem so random. I never have any idea what the rules are. The best approach is to draw as little attention to yourself as possible.

Waking Miguelito up made me sad, though, because he looked totally peaceful. He was sleeping really deeply, leaning against the wall with his mouth open. He was drooling a little bit, and if we weren't so worried, Elías and I would have (lovingly) made fun of him. I touched his shoulder and shook him a little. "Miguelito," I whispered. "Hey, levántate—we're moving."

He opened his eyes halfway. He was still mostly asleep. Something happened on his face that I'd never seen before: For a few seconds he kept looking peaceful, but then all of a sudden his whole face darkened in a way I can't describe. He didn't frown or cry, but it was like the skin on his face was suddenly stretched tighter, like when you pull plastic wrap tight over the top of a bowl. I could see him remembering where he was and everything that had happened today. It was like watching the past five months hit him all at once.

Elías watched this transformation on Miguelito's face, too, and I knew he understood it just as well as I did. After all our time together, we learned how to read each other's reactions. It's a different kind of closeness that I've never experienced before. Obviously, I loved you and Felipe more than anything, but I never had to pay attention to what you needed, exactly. You wanted me to feel like I could rely on you, but you didn't rely on me in the same way. I know you and Felipe were trying hard to be like parents for me. I could only pick up on the most basic stuff: when you wanted a hug or when you wanted to be left alone or when you were annoyed at me for being messy or for staying out playing fútbol too long. But with my cousins, I'm always tuned in to what their needs are. I can tell when Miguelito is nervous about something before he even realizes he's nervous, and I can see when Elías is acting tough even though he's scared. They can read me the same way, too. It's like I have a superpower. I've never experienced anything like it before.

They separated us into three or four groups, then led each group down a different hallway. I got sorted into a different group than Miguelito and Elías, but there was so much going on all of a sudden that I didn't even think to say anything. They were trying to make us go fast. The agente sorting us kept saying, "Come on, hurry up, over there, go." I just went where they told me. I somehow thought that they couldn't possibly keep us apart for long. We'd been separated a few times by that point, and I was trying not to fear the worst. But maybe I should have.

The agents hurried my group through a blue door and then closed it behind us. I've been here ever since.

I'll fill you in on what it's like in here next time. Now I'm going to try to sleep, I guess.

Love,
D.

MAYBE MAY 11, 2018, NOW I GUESS, I DON'T KNOW

La Perrera

Querida Tía:

The first thing you'd learn about this place is how many people are crowded in here. The room is about eight feet long and fifteen or eighteen feet across, with no windows. They've crammed at least twenty people in here, maybe twenty-five, and everyone is trying to take up as little square footage as possible. But honestly, there's barely space to move. Trying to get from one end of the room to the other is like walking from the very front of a packed city bus to the very back. It's technically possible, but you have to maneuver your way around every single person, sliding your torso across everyone's backs and trying not to press your butt into anybody. But even with so many people in here, not a single person ever talks, so it's eerily quiet.

I said there are no windows, but that's not exactly right—there are no windows to the outside, but there is a window with a metal grate instead of glass, and it opens to an office where another Migra guy is sitting in front of a computer.

In a place this crowded, I'm never even sure how to arrange my body so I'm not taking up somebody else's space. There literally isn't enough surface area for everyone to sit on the floor, so about a third of the people here are standing at any given moment. Some shift their weight from one foot to the other, and others lean shoulder-to-shoulder against the wall. Of the people on their feet, most look about as old as my teacher back in Naranjito, who was maybe in her twenties. There are also some older adults about the same age as my parents, and a few teenagers who look slightly older than me. Most of the people standing are men, and almost all of them have an empty look in their eyes, like they're trying hard not to think about anything at all. It seems like most of them are traveling alone, because none ever talk or even look at each other. I wonder if they crossed the border by themselves or if, like me, they crossed with family members but got separated. Maybe they have their own Miguelitos and Elíases in other crowded rooms of this same building.

The hardest thing for me to believe is how young the kids in here are. A few feet away, a woman who looks four or five years older than me is holding a toddler who can't be older than three, and scattered across the room, there are six or seven other kids. A few of them who look like they're seven or eight years old are sitting on the floor with their mothers. Most of the moms are sitting with their backs against the wall, with their feet in front of them and a kid perched on their legs. I guess that must be a way to save space in here: stacking kids on top of adults like I used to stack crates at the tiendita.

But most of the kids here don't seem to have any parents. They're not here with any adults at all, they're just sitting alone on the floor, cross-legged or hugging their knees.

There are five beds, though I'm not sure it's accurate to call them *beds*, because they're made of cement, and they don't have mattresses. There are some thin blankets and pillows, though, and people are sleeping on them, so I guess you have to call them beds. There are two or three people on each one, including a few moms with their kids. I can see why they get the beds: even though everyone in here looks sweaty and exhausted including me—I haven't showered or changed clothes since we left the

Casa del Migrante—most of these mothers and kids look like they couldn't stand if they wanted to.

There's a very old man on the edge of a bed right now, as I write, sitting up and sharing the space with a woman and her daughter. They've given him the bed's only pillow. He looks even older than you, Tía. He's almost completely bald, and he has bristly white hairs growing from his chin. He looks like he hasn't moved for years. Something about looking at him makes my heart drop. He reminds me of the abuelitos I used to see sitting around Naranjito. You know who I'm talking about. You always used to say that after a life of working and raising families, they had earned the right to sit outside, chatting and laughing, reading days-old newspapers, sometimes listening to the radio. It feels messed up that a man that old has ended up in a place like this, with no friends, no family, no community—not even any old newspaper to read. I try to square the scene in front of me with everything my parents told me about life in los Estados Unidos. If they ever passed through any place this depressing, they never mentioned it on the phone.

Love,
D.

MAY 11, 2018, MORE OR LESS

La Perrera

Querida Tía:

Every now and then—I'm guessing two or three times a day—they take us out of the cell to get some food. We line up, and they take us to a table with napkins, paper bowls, plastic spoons, and usually a big pot of something. Last time, there was a line of people coming from the opposite direction, too, toward the same table. I assumed they were from another room that's more or less the same as where we're being held, and as I got closer to the table, it occurred to me that Miguelito and Elías might be on that other line. I quickly looked across, and they were almost the first people I saw. They were standing right next to each other in line, and they'd already spotted me: both of them were sending huge, ear-to-ear smiles in my direction, and even though their skin looked pale and sick under the white lights, it was the most excited I've seen them since we stole that chicken and cooked it in Miguelito's pot. I was so happy, I nearly jumped onto the back of the guy in front of me—I've never experienced an emotion so strong that it was practically lifting me off the ground. They're safe, and they're still here, in the same building as me, thank God. It feels like the answer to a prayer.

I could tell they were giddy, too, and when we reached opposite ends of the table, I could see them trying to contain themselves and stand still, the same as me. There were a bunch of Migra guys standing around, so we couldn't talk, but I mouthed *¿Están bien?*, and they nodded enthusiastically. They pointed to me to ask the same question, to ask whether I was okay, and I nodded up and down with a big grin of my own.

It's funny, because I'm not sure if I actually *am* okay. I could be in really bad shape. If you'd asked me before we ate, I would have said that I desperately need to know what time it is, I need a shower and a change of clothes, I need a bandage for my foot or at least the chance to wash it. I need someone to explain to me what the hell is happening and why I'm here and why these gringos with guns keep yelling at me. I need to know why they won't let me talk to Papá on the phone. I need them to please, for the love of God, turn off those stupid white lights. But more than any of this, the most pressing thing I needed to know was that my cousins were okay. And there they were, and they were okay. Knowing that makes me feel like I'm doing okay, too.

What *isn't* okay is the food they give us here. They feed us some kind of wet, mushy oatmeal, but it doesn't taste normal, it has kind of a bitter flavor I've never tasted in oatmeal before. I guess that's what oatmeal here tastes like—gross.

Whenever we get back from the food table, fitting everyone back into this cell is like playing Tetris. People don't go back to their previous positions—when we come back, everyone just stakes out a few square feet for themselves. I think the families with small kids have a system for who gets the "beds." Other than that, you just have to find a patch of floor and keep it.

All the small kids are sleeping now. Before we ate, the kids were doing what you'd expect them to be doing (at least as much as you can expect anything in a place like this): they were whispering, crying. They make me think of my own little sister, who's in this country, who's so close now. The kids in here without any family cry more, and then the guards tell them to shut up. Sometimes some of the other mamás who are here try to comfort them, but they're also busy trying to soothe their own kids. The kids in here get more restless than the adults do, because they don't have any toys or crayons or anything to keep them busy. But now none of them are on their feet.

Everyone else is getting sleepy, too, including me. There's this heaviness in my body I never felt before I got here. Staying on my feet takes tons of effort, like when I had to hoist myself onto the top of La Bestia.

I can't keep my eyes open.

Love,
D.

LATER

La Perrera

Tía:

It's an unknown number of hours later—one, five, fifteen, who knows—and I have a headache, but the heaviness has mostly left my body. Some of the others are awake now, too. There aren't as many people lying on top of each other.

I woke up because I needed to use the bathroom. There's a toilet in here . . . but I try to use it as little as possible. It's in the corner of the room, concealed on three sides by a low wall that anyone could see over, and then on the fourth side, there's just a plastic curtain. Everyone uses the same toilet: men, women, kids. It's gross, it's humiliating. Whenever anybody walks toward the "bathroom," stepping carefully over everyone on the floor, the other twenty-plus people in here turn the other way and pretend not to notice the sounds coming from behind the curtain. But the agents yell at us if we speak too loudly, so it's always quiet. The noises come through loud and clear.

But when you have to go, you have to go. My face is burning with embarrassment already.

—D.

MAY 12, 2018 – I ASKED SOMEONE FOR THE REAL DATE

Not in La Perrera! On a bus somewhere in Texas, Estados Unidos

Querida Tía:

I'm out! Thank you, Tía. This morning, they called my name and told me to "gather my things" (even though I have no things except for this notebook, no one has any "things" except the clothes on their back, I don't know why they even said this) and took me out of La Perrera. Now I'm sitting on a bus in a parking lot outside an airport, waiting to get on an airplane to Papá. They took me out of La Perrera along with a few other kids. They didn't call any adults, so I guess all these other kids crossed without their parents, too. They put us on this bus. It looks like a regular school bus except it's white, with official-looking markings on the side and metal grates over the windows. I'm guessing they put Miguelito and Elías on another bus. The driver is in some kind of cage in the front. There are locked metal grills all around his seat, so no one can bother him. I guess they're worried someone might distract him while he's driving, and he could get in an accident.

They told the boys to sit in the back and the girls to sit in the front. I'm sitting next to a boy who says he's from Guatemala, and I want to ask him what he thinks being on an airplane is going to be like, but it feels like we're not allowed to talk. We weren't allowed to talk in La Perrera, and on this bus we're being guarded by the same agentes de la Migra. They're up front with their guns on their belts. I don't want to risk getting in trouble (I don't want to do anything that might make them change their mind and take me back to La Perrera or deport me). It's okay, I'll find out what it's like on an airplane soon.

On the drive to the airport, I looked out the window and tried to relax. There wasn't really anything interesting to look at, but we definitely drove toward a more developed area—there started to be more houses and buildings, and they got bigger. After spending three days (I think) in La Perrera, even this seat on the bus feels comfortable. I tried to take a nap on the drive, but sometimes my body refuses to get rest when it needs it the most. Not to mention, I've never been able to sleep very well when I'm hungry, and we left before they gave us our daily gross oatmeal.

I think the fact that there were no windows or clocks in La Perrera really messed with my sense of time. I know it was just a few days ago that I crossed the border, but it feels like it was at least a month ago. If I hadn't been keeping track of how many meals they gave us and how often the agentes de la Migra changed shifts, I wouldn't have any idea.

Time was slippery on the bus ride, too. When we got to this airport, it felt like we'd only been driving for a few minutes, but that can't be true, because when we left when the sun was just rising, but now it's high in the sky, so it must be around noon. From this parking lot, we can watch the airplanes taking off and landing, and it's kind of cool. Before, I only ever saw airplanes in the sky, and I never really thought about them much. I never wondered before how they managed to stay in the air, but now I can't figure it out . . . They're so heavy and made of metal, but they take off so easily. I'm going to try to remember to ask Papá.

A few minutes ago, another agente came on board the bus and said they brought us to the airport so they can fly us to see our parents. "You see the airplanes out the windows? See how they're taking off and flying all around the country?" he said in Spanish. "Those are other kids we put on planes, going to join their families. Aren't you kids lucky? You lucky fucks, you get to go live the American Dream. What a treat." After he said that, he ignored us and started talking and laughing with the other agentes. I don't get why they're laughing, but it makes me feel a little uneasy, like, what's so funny?

Since then, I've been watching the airplanes and wondering if Elías and Miguelito are on board. Maybe they got transferred out of La Perrera before I did and they're already home. The excitement of seeing Papá and of being on an airplane for the first time is making me even hungrier. I hope I'm allowed to eat on the airplane.

Love,
D.

MAY 12, 2018
Different bus

Querida Tía:

We waited and waited, and I watched probably thirty airplanes take off and land. But when they finally took us off the bus, we didn't go into the airport. We just walked a few meters across the parking lot, where they told us to get onto a different bus.

This second bus is really different from the first one: the seats have padding, they aren't just hard plastic, and there aren't bars on the windows. It just feels nicer in general. The driver isn't in a cage. One of the other kids even found a little bathroom in the back. I didn't know it was possible to have a bathroom on a bus. Where does the water go when you flush the toilet, does it just drop it on the road? There are even TVs on the ceiling, but they're turned off and no one is going to ask the driver to turn them on. The agentes de la Migra didn't follow us onto this bus. I guess their job is done, and they're going home now. There are no adults except for the driver and a white woman sitting in the front, but she isn't in a uniform. When we got on board, she asked us if we were hungry (her Spanish is pretty bad, but we understood), and we all nodded. She said we'd get to eat in about an hour, and then the driver started the bus.

At first, I thought this bus would take us from the parking lot to the front door of the airport, and I was surprised when she said it could take an hour. But we've been driving in the opposite direction. I'm not exactly sure what's going on, and I don't think anyone else is either. We're all still too nervous to ask. We're even too nervous to talk to each other except a few whispers.

Being on this bus makes me feel weird, like I'm not supposed to be here. I'm worried I'm in the wrong place, even though this is where they told me to go. When they let me out of La Perrera, I was just relieved to be outside, to have personal space and see the sun again. But now I'm on this bus, where there are no bars on the windows and no men with guns at the front. There's even a seat belt I can buckle (and I do—after the micro accident, getting on buses always gives me a little bit of a sick feeling in my stomach). This bus is so nice that I'm worried I'm going to break something or get something dirty. I didn't realize it at the time, but the last bus made me feel like a prisoner being driven between jails. I hadn't really thought about how they've been treating me like a criminal. It's only now, on this bus—with the soft seats and the windows you can open so you feel the sunshine and the breeze—that I feel weird about it. When I think about the last few days, I get this uncomfortable feeling in my chest, and I feel embarrassed, even though I don't really know why.

Love,
D.

MAY 12, 2018
"El Albergue"

Querida Tía:

I'm writing to you from the floor of a place called "El Albergue" while I wait to talk to Mamá and Papá on the phone. The bus didn't take us to the airport, and I'm worried I might still have to wait even longer to go to Nashville. I'll fill you in.

That second bus drove for like an hour, then stopped in a parking lot outside a big building. Three women got on and told us that we're at a place called El Albergue, and that we're safe here. Safe from what? The agente had told us we were going to fly to see our families, so I wasn't sure why we were stopping here first.

This new place is enormous. It's a whole compound. There are a few buildings, and a lot of them are bigger than the building where La Perrera was. There's also a fenced-in field where I saw some kids playing fútbol and another group of kids walking in a straight line between two buildings. There must be hundreds of kids here. I hope Miguelito and Elías are here somewhere. I'm still nervous about asking questions, but if I find an adult who seems nice enough, I'm going to tell them Miguelito and Elías are my family so that they can bring us together. The women on the bus didn't seem especially friendly, but they were way nicer than the agentes in their uniforms. They wouldn't yell at me if I asked a question, anyway.

A woman pulled me away from the rest of the kids and told me to go with her. I was worried I was in trouble for some reason, but, actually, she just wanted to look at my feet. She cleaned them, then rubbed something on them that really stung. She wasn't very gentle about it. The woman who'd treated my foot at the Casa del Migrante had taken the time to explain everything she was doing. But this gringa just yanked my foot around, and she didn't seem to care when I winced. But I needed help, so I didn't complain. Finally, she rubbed some ointment on my foot and gave me a bottle of pills I'm supposed to take.

After that, she took me to a cafeteria. There were hundreds of seats and lots of tables, but me and the kids from my bus were the only ones in there. They gave us lunch—hot rice with beans, and tons of different vegetables: carrots, peppers, broccoli. I devoured every crumb. I hadn't eaten since last night. It wouldn't have been anything special in Naranjito—nothing compares to your baleadas—but even though I know it was just regular food, it tasted like the best thing I've ever put in my mouth.

While we were eating, one of the women who brought us here gave us a presentation. It was a little hard to focus on everything she said, mostly because I was distracted by the food. She spoke slowly and in short, simple sentences. It must have been because she thought we were just little kids who couldn't understand anything, because she had dark skin like most of us and she spoke Spanish the same as we do. She sounded bored, like she had given this same speech hundreds of times:

"Welcome to El Albergue. You are safe here," she said.

The woman on the bus said the same thing, and I don't really get it. People have been telling me I'm safe so much that it makes me feel less safe, honestly. What is it that I'm supposed to be safe from? Los Estados Unidos is supposed to be the safe place. I came here *to be safe*.

"We are working hard to reunite you with your families. This is very difficult and time-consuming. While we find them, you will stay here."

I don't understand what she meant by "find them." I gave Papá's phone number to los agentes de la Migra days ago, and I know exactly where he is—he's in Nashville. All they have to do is call him for the address.

"I do not know how long you will be here. Some children are here for only two or three weeks. Others are here for some time longer."

Obviously, this was horrible to hear. But I also sort of didn't believe it, and I'm still not sure I do. "Some time longer?" More than three weeks? Just today, when we were on the first bus, they told us we were going to go to our families. They said we were going to get on an airplane. Why would they keep me here for weeks when they could just send me to Papá today? Wouldn't that be easier for them? I looked at the other kids to see how they were reacting. I expected them to look confused or angry or sad, but most of them just had blank expressions on their faces.

The woman kept talking. She said our cases are "handled by agents of the U.S. government," and that El Albergue wasn't the government, just a "contractor," whatever that means. She said the adults who work here can't tell us when we will be released. I was bummed when I heard this, but I'm not sure I believed it. She said we'll get to call our parents soon, "and then you will be divided into your groups, and we will show you where you will sleep. You should all have been assigned a group: Alpha, Bravo, Charlie, or Delta, and so on. Did anyone not receive a group or bed number?"

She looked at all of us. But most of the kids still weren't showing any emotion at all, they were just dead-eyed. I wondered what kind of emotion my face was showing. She started talking a lot about the schedule, and how we had to follow the schedule all the time. She talked about where we're supposed to go, and at what time of day, and the things we're supposed to learn in school, and how we're supposed to line up for food in the cafeteria, but I couldn't focus. She kept calling us El Albergue's "clients," which was weird, I didn't get it. My mind kept returning to two questions: Will I really be here for a few weeks? And are Miguelito and Elías here? I barely heard the rest of what the woman said. I hope it wasn't anything important.

I snapped out of it when she stopped talking and the kids around me started standing and lining up. She must have told us to go somewhere. I joined the line and left the cafeteria with all the other kids.

They brought us here, to another room, to take turns calling our parents. It's going really slowly, so I figured I'd write to pass the time.

I can't wait to talk to Mamá and Papá. I hope come get me soon.

Love,
D.

MAY 12, 2018

El Albergue, cafeteria

Querida Tía:

It's dinnertime, and we're allowed to talk, but almost everybody is too shy, so I figure I might as well write to you. I'm starting to learn that people call this place *El Albergue* in Spanish, and all the adults here are called *tícher*, in English. So far, I haven't learned any of their names, they're all just *tícher*. Before the tíchers let us talk to our parents, they said we had to answer some questions. I figured that answering questions is no big deal, and once I got to talk to Papá, he would find a way to come get me. I don't want to spend six months alone here.

While I waited, after I finished writing to you, I planned what I was going to say to Papá. I was still worried he'd be mad that I left Naranjito without telling him. I figured I'd say that I'm okay, and then I'd ask him if he had to go through all this before he got to stay in los Estados Unidos, and how long it was before they let him go, and where he thought Miguelito and Elías were, and how far Tennessee is from Texas, and if they'd let me out if he drove here to pick me up.

After maybe forty-five minutes, one of the tíchers called my name from her desk, and I went to sit in the empty chair next to her. "So, you're D. Esperanza," she said in English without looking up from her computer. I'm not sure if she's asking me or telling me, so I didn't say anything.

After a second, she turned from her computer and looked at me, and I nodded yes.

She started asking a few basic questions, going back and forth between bad Spanish (that I could barely understand) and fast English (that I couldn't understand at all). The questions were simple, though: where I'm from, my birthday, my parents' names. She typed some of my answers into her computer, and checked other pieces of information on a piece of paper she had next to her. She took my picture with a little camera plugged into the computer, spent a few minutes clicking. Finally, she said it was time to talk to Papá.

"You'll have five minutes to talk, okay?" she said in English. I recognized the words she was saying, but I wonder if I was remembering the meaning of *five* correctly. I thought it meant "cinco," but I didn't think they'd only let me talk for five minutes, so it must have meant "quince." I guess I looked confused, because she switched to Spanish and almost yelled in my ear, "Sink-oh mee-new-toes. ¿Ehn-tee-en-days?" So I wasn't misunderstanding. I'd get cinco minutos. She held her hand up and stretched her fingers out, then switched back to English. "When you *english english english* five *english english* I will *english english english english* like this, okay?"

I nodded even though I didn't understand. I tried to ask if I could talk for a little longer, since I haven't spoken to Papá since before I left Naranjito, but she cut me off before I could finish the question. She answered in English, and she was clearly slightly annoyed, but she spoke slowly so I understood. "There are a lot of kids. Five minutes."

She dialed a landline telephone, and I heard Papá pick up. She talked to him in bad Spanish for a while, maybe ten minutes. She spoke really fast, and I couldn't understand anything except my own name.

Finally, she handed me the receiver and said: "Remember: *sink-oh mee-new-toes*." I thought she would just look at her phone or the time on her computer, but she had a stopwatch on her desk, and she started it as soon as I grabbed the phone.

I was so happy and nervous and terrified to talk to Papá that it's all kind of a blur. I'd never heard him with this combination of feelings in his voice, it was like he was worried and euphoric all at the same time. I could tell that he'd been anxious about me for months, and that he was terrified but relieved when la Migra called him and told him I was in los Estados Unidos. He asked me a thousand questions at once: Are you okay? Are you hurt? Did they take you to a doctor? Why did you leave? Why didn't you tell me? Did you go alone? How did you travel? Did you go on La Bestia? Why didn't you call? Where did you get food? Where did you get money? Have the grown-ups around you given you food? How are they treating you? What are they telling you? I answered these questions as fast as I could, and I could hear his relief when I told him I'm okay, I've eaten, and that I'm not hurt except for my foot. I'm glad he wasn't mad at me. Or at least not so mad that he doesn't love me anymore.

I had planned to ask him lots of my own questions about what's happening, but they all vanished from my head as soon as I heard his voice. It had been so many days of loneliness, and now, finally, a voice I recognized, someone who loved me. The last familiar faces I'd seen were Miguelito and Elías's, and I hadn't heard a familiar voice since I was separated from them outside La Hielera.

Papá was still asking me questions when the tícher held up her hand and stretched out her five fingers like she did before, and she mouthed some words that I didn't understand. I was trying to figure out what she was saying, but before I knew it, she had plucked the receiver out of my hand and disconnected the call.

"Sorry, kid," she said, "we have lots of calls to make."

So, that was it for the phone call.

They gave me a bag of toiletries, some clothes, a towel, and flip-flops, and then a male tícher walked with me and seven other boys to Bravo Dorm. It's a very basic, empty-looking central room, with four doors that open to four bedrooms. "All right, everybody take a shower. You get ten minutes. Then get dressed in your new clean clothes, and at five o'clock, I'll come get you for dinner," he said in English. He checked our bed numbers and showed us where we're supposed to sleep. "Kid," he said, pointing to a short boy with skin darker than mine, "this is gonna be your new roommie."

I was a little bit shy because everything is so unfamiliar and I'd barely spoken all day, but the boy didn't look mean at all, and he had a sort of smirk on his face. "Hola, Roomie," I said. "Soy D." Roomie is a weird name, but I guess he comes from a country where people have weird names.

He smiled a little and said ,"No, soy—" and then said a different name. The problem is, I had no idea what he said, and I still don't. I tried to repeat it, and he just giggled a little. "No, no, soy—" and he said it again, but I still didn't get it. He speaks Spanish in a weird way that I don't understand, and there are sounds in his name that I haven't heard before. We tried to talk for a few minutes, but it was hard, though not as hard as talking to the gringos in English. After a few more minutes, he managed to explain that even though he's from Guatemala, his first language isn't Spanish, it's a totally different language. I can't pronounce the name of the language either. I tried to say his name a few more times, but I couldn't get it right, and he kept giggling.

"Está bien," he said with his accent. "Llámame tu *roomie*."

So I started calling him Roomie.

Love,
D.

MAY 12, 2018

My own room

Querida Tía:

Each bedroom here has a bunk bed and a small bathroom. After La Perrera, I was expecting another cramped, uncomfortable place. But it isn't cramped at all. I've never been in a hotel, but this feels like a five-star hotel. My bed—the top bunk—has sheets and blankets on it, and it's all for me, I don't have to share it with anyone. And the blankets are real, made out of fabric, they aren't the crinkly foil kind. There's a shelf with games and books. This whole room is just for me and Roomie.

The most unbelievable thing of all is that we have a whole bathroom all to ourselves. There's a toilet and a sink and a shower, and they're clean and just for us. The bathroom has a door that closes—there's no lock, but I don't give a crap, there's a *door that closes*, not just a thin little plastic curtain that lets all the sounds and smells out. And I *only have to share it with Roomie*. There are even two little cups. Whenever we want to, we can just fill up our cups in the sink and drink water. As much as we want. We don't have to ask an agente for a plastic bottle. And if drinking all that water makes us have to pee, we can pee as much as we want. I know it sounds dumb, but when you've gone without something basic, even for just a few days, it feels so precious when you get it back. I hope I never forget how special it feels to have this clean, white, private bathroom just for me and Roomie.

And the bed, the blankets, I think I could crawl under them right now and sleep for a week. In any other life, I wouldn't have thought twice about this pillow. It's nothing like the fluffy, soft almohadas you always made sure I had growing up. It's thin and plasticky. But I don't care. In La Perrera, I slept with my head on the hard floor, or leaned up against the hard wall. For three days. Just like the private bathroom, the pillow feels like an incredible gift.

The tícher who brought us to dinner says he'll be awake all night in the common area just outside the rooms. I just walked into the bathroom to make sure that it's still there, and now I'm going to climb into my bunk.

Good night!
D.

MAY 13, 2018
El Albergue

Querida Tía:

And I slept, I slept, I slept, santo cielo, I slept like I have never slept before. I think I was asleep before my eyes were even all the way closed. It was a pitch-black sleep with no dreams, which is probably good, because I don't think I would dream about anything good. Blankets are miracles. I never appreciated before how they take the warmth from your body and trap it so it can't get away, it's like a second skin. My head fell into the pillow like that's what it was built for, like there's no other place a head should ever be except resting on a pillow. The mattress held my body up like I was floating on the air. I love to sleep, I have always loved to sleep, and I have never slept like that in my life.

They woke us up before eight o'clock. I could have slept the entire day. I swear, even with the sun shining in through the window (that's another thing we have here that I never want to take for granted: windows and a general sense of what time of day it is). Roomie was sleeping even deeper than me, but they made him get out of bed. He grumbled something in his language—I could tell it meant something like "Please, for the love of God don't make me get out of bed."

The tícher who woke us up and took us to breakfast looked like she should speak Spanish. She had darker skin and features like ours, but she didn't talk very much. I think she doesn't want us to know she speaks Spanish, so she doesn't have to talk to us. But after a good night's sleep—a glorious night's sleep, a night's sleep that made me feel like a human again—I'm feeling a little bit more confident and comfortable here, so I tried asking her about Miguelito and Elías:

"Disculpa, do you know if my primos Miguelito and Elías are here? I crossed the border with them and then la Migra separated us in La Perrera."

"Could be. Are they kids, too?" she replied in Spanish. Which was a relief, at least I can talk to this woman. "It's possible they're in another group, on a different schedule. There's hundreds of kids here. Even if they're here, you might never see them. They keep everyone with their group at all times."

"Can I get them into our group, since they're my family?"

"You said they're your cousins?"

"Yeah."

"Sorry, we can only try to do that for siblings. Family connections are too hard to prove."

"Mande? Prove what?"

"Don't worry. They're safe, wherever they are."

I'm starting to hate the word *safe*. What's the point in being safe if you can't see your family, can't talk to your parents, can't go home? At least on La Bestia I was with my cousins. And I hated how the tícher didn't answer my question. But I was also worried I might get punished if I pushed it. At least she speaks Spanish. I wanted to know her name in case I need to talk to someone who understands me again.

"Gracias. ¿Cómo te llamas?"

"Puedes llamarme 'Tícher.'"

So that was how my first full day here started. It was a whirlwind after that. We went to breakfast in that same cafeteria, and everyone was quiet while they ate. I think this was partly because everyone was focused on their food. Eating this real cafeteria food still feels like a blessing. But mainly, I think we were quiet because we're all kind of shy. None of us has talked much since we got here. I asked a few boys' names, and we had a couple of short conversations, but it feels weird and hard. I've tried to talk to Roomie more than anyone else, and we've been getting along (he seems to have a good sense of humor—he laughs whenever me or the other kids try to pronounce his name), but because he doesn't speak a lot of Spanish, it's hard to really get a conversation going.

After breakfast they took us to the schoolroom. Everywhere they go, they make us walk en fila, for whatever reason, this is really important to them. Even the gringo tíchers who don't speak Spanish keep saying "¡Fila, chicos, fila!" whenever we're in the hallway or walking between buildings.

The schoolroom is plain-looking just like everywhere else. There's a chalkboard and a TV on a rolling cart and a bunch of desks. They told us we're mostly going to have lessons on how to speak English, and we're also going to learn some historia de los Estados Unidos. I figure that at least by the time I leave here, I'll speak English and I'll be able to go to school and talk to people in Nashville. The tícher started by writing *My name is . . .* on the board, and we talked about making introductions. It's funny, in Naranjito, in school, they taught us some *reaaaaaally* basic English, and they taught us to say "My name is" there too, but our teacher was hondureño like us, and it sounds really different to hear this white lady say it. I guess this explains why the agentes de la Migra had such a hard time understanding me. Even when I tried to speak English, I must've still had an accent.

Most of the class was English, but there was a little history, too. The tícher said we're going to start with the "pre-Hispanic era," which she said meant the time before 1492, before Cristobal Colón came to América and white people started building stuff here. I know I learned similar stuff to this in Naranjito. I remember having history class and some of the dates and words the tícher is saying sound familiar. But I remember almost nothing about it. In some ways, it feels like my life before I migrated is a dream. Or no, not even my life before I migrated—my life before the first time I boarded La Bestia. I feel like I've been through so much that my experiences before kind of got buried. It makes me sad, sort of. It's a hard feeling to understand. I don't want to think about it too hard.

After school, they walked us back to the cafeteria for lunch—"¡Fila, chicos, siempre en fila!"—and it was the same deal, we mostly just focused on our food. There are just eight boys in Bravo Group, and it's not just us in the cafeteria, there are other groups here, too. I kept looking up from my food to see if I could find Elías and Miguelito, but I don't think they were in the cafeteria. I don't know if they're at this albergue. I asked a tícher who looked like she speaks Spanish if all the groups have lunch at the same time, or if it's possible my cousins are on a different schedule. But she pretended she didn't understand me.

After lunch, they took us outside, gave us a ball, and told us to play fútbol for an hour. I was too distracted to really play. A lot of other kids didn't really play either, they just stood around watching the game, and they only ran if a tícher told them to. My feet still hurt way too much for me to run around. The pills and ointments they gave me are helping, I guess, but not very fast.

Whenever I see other groups walking between buildings, I look for my cousins. They kept us outside for a long time, maybe four hours. Some of the other boys got tired after a while and said they don't want to play anymore. The tíchers didn't care as long as we stayed outside, on the campo de fútbol or close to it. I played the whole time, though.

Afterward, it was back to the cafeteria for an early dinner, around four thirty or five. No sign of Elías and Miguelito at lunch.

Then they took us back to Bravo Dorm and told us we had "rec time" until lights-out at nine. They said that at nine we didn't have to go to sleep, but we had to be in bed with the lights off. In the dorm there were a few games, and I played with Roomie and the other boys—there's Snakes and Ladders, checkers, chess, and a few other games I've never seen before. Most of them are missing pieces, and it seems like everybody knows slightly different rules to the different games. If I were playing against my friends in Naranjito, we'd fight about it and get really competitive with each other. But here, everyone is just quiet. No one seems to really care about winning, we're just playing games because the tíchers tell us to. And it feels like we should spend time with each other. The other boys are nice, but quiet. The only exception is Roomie—he's always making jokes and laughing. His Spanish is so hard to understand that most of the time we don't even get the joke, but it doesn't matter, because he laughs so hard that it spreads to the rest of us. I'm glad that out of all the guys here, Roomie is my roomie.

I climbed into bed before lights-out so I could write to you, but my brain isn't tired. I can't stop worrying about how long I might be here. Or about getting sent back to La Perrera. Or about Miguelito and Elías and Damián. My body is, but I feel like my brain is too busy to sleep.

Love,
D.

MAY 17, 2018
El Albergue

Querida Tía:

It's my fifth day here, and I'm beginning to wonder when something will change. That's why I haven't written in a while—there's really nothing new to say. We go through the same routine every day, no matter if it's a weekday or the weekend: breakfast, school, lunch, fútbol, dinner, rec time, lights out. I'm still grateful to have my own bed, real food, and a private bathroom (thank God), but living here is hard in its own way. I feel like I have a lifetime of sleep to catch up on, but they wake us up at seven thirty every morning, and even though I'm so tired, it has been taking me hours to fall asleep. Sometimes I wake up in the middle of the night and it's so dark that I think I'm back in La Perrera. Or I have nightmares about La Bestia, or about Miguelito or Elías getting hurt or killed or deported. There are books on the game shelf that me and the other boys have been ignoring, and last night I grabbed one before bed, hoping my eyes would get tired and I'd fall asleep. I think it helped, not because my eyes got tired, but because it filled my brain with something different right before I slept.

The other boys are also having a hard time, I think. Getting to know them is hard. I think we're all friends—we never fight or anything. At night we play games, but even after a few days together, none of us really care about winning. It's like we're all just waiting for the days to pass. And, I don't know, everyone just feels kind of broken. I can't sleep, because I'm thinking about La Bestia and my cousins and La Perrera and a million other things, and I bet the other kids here have things they're worried about too. I got separated from my cousins, and some of them probably got separated from their siblings or parents or other family members. I don't think I can ask them. It doesn't feel like it's my business, and none of them ever bring it up. All we talk about is the food they give us, fútbol, and the games we play.

A few times I've tried asking the tíchers about Elías and Miguelito, or about when I'll be able to leave here. But most of them either don't speak Spanish or pretend not to. The few who admit they speak Spanish give me generic answers that don't really help. I wish I could just talk to someone for real, not about Snakes and Ladders or English lessons, but about what's going to happen. Or even about our hometowns and stuff. It's funny, the only person I feel like I've really gotten to know is Roomie. He tries to teach me (and the other boys) his language, and we can never get it right, but he just laughs and laughs. Sometimes during rec time, me and him will play games in our room, instead of in the common space with the other boys.

Love,
D.

MAY 21, 2018
El Albergue

Querida Tía:

Since coming here, I've realized there are two things that I really like. The first one is history. In Naranjito, they never taught history like a story. It was always more about facts and dates, and like I said, I don't think I've retained much of what I learned when I was younger anyway. The journey north blew it all out of my mind. In school here, we spend at least half an hour learning the history of los Estados Unidos, and it's really exciting. The tícher told us about the civilizations that were in América before Cristobal Colón, and then talked a lot about the thirteen colonies and how they fought a war to get free from Inglaterra because they were being oppressed, but then they just turned around and oppressed the nativos and the people they kidnapped from África. I like how it feels like a story of good versus evil, except who's good and who's evil keeps changing.

We're supposed to just talk about Estados Unidos history in class, but sometimes the tícher tries to explain how something similar happened in Centroamérica. She says that just like the gringos speak English because the británicos were the ones who took over los Estados Unidos, hispanos like us speak Spanish because España took over Honduras and Guatemala and El Salvador and all of México, and they did bad things to the nativos there, too. It took me a few classes to realize that when she talks about the nativos, that includes Roomie. I wish there were a way I could talk to him about it.

The second thing I've realized is that I really like reading. I haven't noticed the other kids reading, and I'm not surprised, because the books on the shelf are old and ratty-looking. I wasn't drawn to them at first, and I only picked one up because I hoped it would help me fall asleep. But I started getting really into the stories, and I think I actually like them for the same reason as I like history class: you start off thinking that it's good versus evil, or that the main character is the good guy, but most of the time, it ends up being more complicated than that.

I also think about the authors who write the books, and I like to imagine them coming up with something to write about and then trying to find the right words to describe it. It makes me think of writing music in Naranjito with Cami. Or writing these letters to you. I know writing music or letters isn't the same as writing a book, but still, reading these books makes me want to write a song. I feel like I could write a rap about what it was like to cross the border. I sometimes come up with lyrics when I'm reading at night, or when I remember something interesting from history class. I try to write them down before I fall asleep. Once I have something good down, I'll write it here to show it to you.

Love,
D.

MAY 25, 2018

El Albergue

Querida Tía:

Just a quick note before we go play fútbol. Good news. I got to talk to my parents today, and they said a lady called them and told them that all they have to do to get me is go somewhere to get their fingerprints taken, and then the tíchers here will let me go be with them in Nashville. Mamá is a little bit worried that if they show up at like, the official office place where they need to get their fingerprints taken, they might get in trouble with their own immigration situation. Like she's worried they might even get deported. But the lady they talked to on the phone said it's the only way for them to get me. Papá says they're going to talk to other migrantes they know in Nashville, but he says not to worry, they're going to do everything they can to get me as soon as possible. I hope it only takes a few days. I'm getting tired of being here.

Love,
D.

JUNE 13, 2018

El Albergue

Querida Tía:

I still don't have a ton to say, but I didn't want to go too long without writing to you. I just haven't felt very motivated lately. A lot of the time, for the past few weeks, it has felt like my mind isn't really here. I'll be in class, or playing fútbol, or in the cafeteria, but it's like my brain is still in Honduras or on La Bestia or in La Perrera.

It's kind of funny, in a sad way, because when I actually *was* in Honduras, my mind was always drifting toward going to los Estados Unidos and being with my parents. And when I actually *was* on La Bestia and traveling north, I kept trying to think about being safe at home in Honduras. And when I actually *was* in La Perrera, I tried to think about being anyplace else. It's like I can't be present in the place where I really am, ever.

Things are mostly comfortable and safe here. In a lot of ways, technically, I'm more comfortable in El Albergue than I was back home, and I never have to worry about gangs or not having money for food. I've been drawing a little bit at night. When I draw, I like to do it on different paper outside my notebook, so that what I write here is only letters to you. But everything is different when someone is watching you. When they take us outside to play fútbol, I can breathe fresh air and run around like kids are supposed to, but it's not the same as breathing fresh air and running around in Naranjito. I don't really feel free, because I can't leave, and they're always monitoring me. And that gives me this feeling I don't know how to describe, it's just kind of a sad, alone sensation that makes me feel like I'm not important or valuable, or like my existence is just a burden for people. I don't really have the words to describe it, I just know it's the opposite of how I felt around you and Felipe. It's closer to how I felt in the weeks after you died.

During the day, things are usually okay. There are enough distractions that I feel okay. I'm bored and lonely a lot, but I like history class, and I like playing fútbol, and I like hanging out with Roomie. But at night, especially after lights-out, I start to feel a knot in my stomach, because I still don't have my books to distract me, and I just keep thinking about everything that happened: La Bestia, getting separated from my cousins, La Hielera, La Perrera. I've been crying a lot in bed. I don't know if Roomie can hear—if he can, he pretends not to. And I've thrown up a few times in our bathroom. I just hope Papá can come pick me up soon. Last time I talked to him on the phone, they got their fingerprints taken at the official office place, but they still haven't let me go. Staying here is making me sick.

Love,
D.

JUNE 17, 2018

En el borde de la frontera

Tía:

Aaaaaand I'm back on a bus. I think it's around six in the morning—it's still dark, but it feels like the sun is close to rising. I'm not going home though. They're taking me to another albergue.

One of the tíchers woke me up late last night, after I'd only been asleep for a few hours. She kept saying my bed number into my ear until I opened my eyes. Then she said to grab my clothes and go to the gym. "Don't make noise. You're leaving," she said in Spanish. For a minute, I thought, *Well, either Papá is finally here to pick me up or I'm about to get deported.* I asked the tícher which was it, but she just said they'd explain everything when I got to the gym.

"Am I going to come back here? Should I say goodbye to Roomie?" I was trying to understand what was going on, but I was still half-asleep.

"No, don't wake him up. Now, quiet, hurry up, brush your teeth and get your stuff. There's no time—in five minutes, we're going to the gym."

I didn't really have anything to gather, since they'd taken my books away a few days earlier. Just this notebook and my clothes, basically. I was scared. Nights are already hard for me, and half the time I wouldn't have even fallen asleep by then, I would've been up in bed, trying not to cry. I don't understand why they had to pull me out of bed in the middle of the night. Nothing good happens at night.

There were a bunch of other kids in the gym—lots of us, probably over a hundred. We were all still sleepy. We sat on the floor, and they gave us something small to eat, a granola bar or something, and told us other kids needed our beds, so they were taking us to a different, new campamento for migrante kids. They said *campamento*, not *albergue*.

I've been on this bus ever since. I've been trying to sleep, but I can't. It's frustrating, because I don't know where they're taking me. It might not even be true that we're going to a campamento, whatever that means. For a few hours, we've been driving right next to México, along the border wall, and I'm worried that they're really planning to deport us. Will they just drive to the other side of the border, open the door, and make us get out? But if they were going to deport us all along, why wouldn't they have done it weeks ago? I haven't misbehaved or anything since I got here. I don't think this can be a punishment.

I keep thinking about how I didn't get to say goodbye to any of my friends, not even to Roomie. How will he feel when he wakes up and I'm not there? The ticher just kept saying, *Come on, come on, we have to leave now*, so I just left. I feel bad. I got along so well with Roomie, and the other kids don't try very hard to hang out with him, because he doesn't really speak Spanish. They're not mean to him or anything, but I'm the only person who really makes an effort to talk to him. What'll happen to him now?

I have this sad thought that even if my story has a happy ending—even if they open the doors right now and my family is here waiting to take me to Nashville—I'll still never see Roomie again. I'll have no way of finding him. I don't even know his real name. It's like getting separated from Miguelito and Elías all over again.

Love,
D.

JUNE 17, 2018

Tornillo, Texas, Estados Unidos

Querida Tía:

Okay, finally, after God knows how many hours on that bus, I'm here.

Why did they bring me someplace so . . . ugly? I didn't think they were going to welcome me with fireworks or anything like that, but I was expecting something more or less like El Albergue I came from. This place is completely different. It's . . . crappier? The other place felt so official and organized, but this place looks like they haven't finished building it yet. There aren't even buildings, there's just a lot of big tents and one *really* big tent, and a few trailers and porta-potties. Everything is dusty. Everywhere I look, there are workers running around putting up tents, clearing areas, driving machinery around. There are muddy areas and holes in the ground and piles of equipment, and when we walked past the tents, we could see boys and girls sitting around looking bored. The expressions on their faces reminded me of how people looked in La Perrera.

A tícher took us off the bus and made us walk—¡en fila, still, always en fila!—to the really big tent. We sat in plastic chairs and they gave us something yellow to drink in plastic cups, juice or Gatorade or something. Then a man started talking to us in Spanish with a thick accent:

"Welcome to Tornillo. This is a new, temporary overflow facility where we will keep you safe as the government attempts to reunite you with your sponsors."

Attempts? *Sponsors*? Papá could pick me up any day. I didn't get it.

"Each of you will be assigned a tent and bed number. There will be three adult teachers in your tent at all times." He went on to explain the schedule: when we'll be allowed to make phone calls to our parents, when we have to be in bed, when we'll eat. "While you are here, you must meet certain behavioral expectations," he said, and then he basically listed all the same rules we had to follow at the last place, plus a few new ones: "You are not permitted to go anywhere without adult supervision. No one is allowed to sit or lie on your bunk except for you. No physical contact of any kind is allowed—that includes high-fives, handshakes, hugs. Brief fist bumps are permitted. If you violate any of these rules, the tíchers will include a report in your record, which we will pass along to the ORR and HHS as they make a determination regarding your immigration status."

I didn't understand.

"I know that many of you don't understand what I'm talking about. So let me be clear: if you don't follow the rules, you may end up staying here for longer, and you might even get deported."

Right away at this place, everything was hectic. A tícher gave me a tent number and a bed number, and led me and five other boys through the obstacle course of construction and trailers and equipment to our sand-colored tent. It's big, maybe thirty feet long and twelve feet across, and tall enough for an adult to stand up straight. I thought it'd be weird sharing the tent with those five other boys after I'd only had to share a room with Roomie for a few weeks, but I figured that at least there would be space for all of us. From the outside, I could see that somehow they've hooked up an air-conditioning unit, which is kind of cool, I guess. I didn't know you could have air-conditioning in a tent.

As soon as we got inside, I thought that with all the disorganization, there must have been some kind of mistake, because there were already boys in the tent—a lot of them. Fifteen, at least. For a second, I thought they'd meant to bring us to a different tent and there had been a mix-up. But then I saw that there were two rows of five bunk beds, meaning there were enough mattresses for twenty kids. And there are three tíchers assigned here, too. They expect all of us to live in here. Suddenly, when I realized this, the tent didn't seem so big. It seemed tiny. There's barely room to walk, and no personal space at all.

What did I do to deserve to be here, Tía? It's horrible. There are no tables, no chairs, just boys sitting either on the ground or on their beds, looking bored. When I first got here, a few of them said hi. They asked my name, where I came from, if I crossed the border with my parents. Apparently, here, at this campamento, we're still really close to the border.

After being woken up in the middle of the night and then driving for hours, I was a little disoriented, so I went to my bunk—I'm on the top bunk, above another boy from Honduras. I started writing, and now I think I'm going to close my eyes.

I miss Roomie. I miss Miguelito and Elías and Damián, but maybe I can find them here—I'll look for them tomorrow.

I miss you, too, Tía.

Love,
D.

JUNE 18, 2018

Tornillo, Texas, Estados Unidos

Querida Tía:

In Tornillo, it's all chaos, all the time. That's what everyone calls this place, *Tornillo*, or sometimes *camp* or *campamento* (I don't really know what that means, but it makes me think of campamentos de concentración). The tíchers never know anything, and half the time they contradict each other, or themselves. Apparently, they just opened this whole place a week or two ago. They say it's a "temporary facility," unlike the place I just came from, which was permanent. For the past few weeks, they've had to find somewhere to put all these niños migrantes who are here without their parents, so they're building this place. And there definitely do seem to be lots of kids—more are arriving all the time. They're constantly putting up new tents, driving around in trucks full of materials, so that those kids have a place to sleep.

I'm not sure how long I've been here, because every day is basically the same and I haven't done a great job keeping track. Though I just checked back to the last time I wrote to you, so I can see I've been here around a week. Every morning, they tell us what we're going to do during the day, but I don't think there has been a single day where we've followed the whole schedule. Sometimes we don't follow it at all. Some days, we never leave our tent except to go to meals. There are no classes like there were in the last albergue. Sometimes they take us to a different tent to watch a movie or to sing songs. Occasionally they bring us to a campo to play fútbol—there's supposed to be a schedule for when we go, but it's not reliable at all, they're always changing it. The tíchers are always running around, exchanging messages with each other in English. Sometimes we'll go to the campo de fútbol, but when we get there, there are already boys from another tent playing. Or we'll go to the cafeteria tent but there's no food, and they have to bring us back later.

Even on days where we mostly follow the schedule, we still spend most of our time in the tent. It's hot and smelly. So hot, and so smelly. Twenty teenage boys baking in a plastic enclosure. We're not allowed to leave without a tícher. There are no books, so nighttime is still hard for me. We spend most of the day sitting around on our bunks or talking. There are board games, and we're allowed to play them, but like I said, there are no chairs or tables, so we have to sit on the ground to play, and it gets uncomfortable really fast. We try playing in our bunks sometimes, but it's against the rules to have two boys on the same bed, and when the tíchers catch us, they threaten to report us. When they say that, we do what they say right away, because we know that if they report us, we might get deported.

Like I said, it's really cramped in the tent, but that's not the worst part. The worst part is that next to each tent there's a porta-potty, and that's the only place where we can go to the bathroom. It's made out of all plastic, and we're in the desert, and it's July, so it sits there baking in the sun all day, cooking everyone's stuff, mixed with whatever chemicals are inside. There's no windows or anything, so it's definitely over forty degrees Celsius in there. Then, on top of that, we're not allowed to go anywhere alone, so we have to ask the tíchers to walk outside with us, and half the time they say no. I've only used the porta-potty during the day once, and I almost got sick. As soon as I walked in, I felt the top of my forehead start to sweat like I'd been in a steamy bath for half an hour, and the inside of my nose started to burn. I felt like I couldn't even breath—the smell crept down my throat and into my stomach, and I almost threw up. I felt like a little kid sticking his finger down his throat. My body had that same kind of automatic reflex. I asked the boys who have been here longer how they deal with it. I thought that maybe there was a secret real bathroom somewhere, or that they snuck into the tíchers' bathroom—the tíchers have an air-conditioned trailer they go to, we see them going into it all the time. But the other boys don't have any kind of tricks. They say they just hold it all day and use the porta-potty at night, when it isn't as hot.

So that's what I've been doing for the past few days. I hold it and hold it until it's cool enough out that I can go in the porta-potty without barfing. Its still hot, stinky and gross, but it's tolerable. It's still hot, but not like an oven. The hardest part is holding it all day. It's like when I was in La Perrera, I just have to not think about going to the bathroom, try to distract myself. I decided that tomorrow, I'm going to try to eat and drink as little as possible, because otherwise it's too uncomfortable.

The tíchers here are stressed all the time. Every time they take us somewhere, they say *¡Rápido!* over and over, I think it's the only Spanish word they know. One of two, actually: In Tornillo, just like in El Albergue, they all know the word *fila*. Apart from those two words, they don't know anything. Whenever I try to say something to them, they don't understand me. They're not usually rude, exactly, but they just kind of stand there nodding until I give up and go away. Once or twice, they've understood me and tried to answer, but they act like they're doing you a big favor, like it's really annoying for me to need ask them for something, or for me to want to know when I'll get to talk to Papá. They're always running around or talking into walkie-talkies, trying to coordinate things like who gets to use the campo de fútbol. There are three tíchers who are with us all day, and three who are with us all night. But it's never the same three—every day, it's different ones. I keep hoping they'll send us a Spanish-speaker, but even if they did, they'd probably just pretend not to understand us anyway, like the tíchers at El Albergue.

There are kids here from all over: mostly Honduras, Guatemala, Nicaragua, and El Salvador, but also some places I haven't heard of. They say the names, and I'm not sure if the places are countries or cities. During my first few days here, I've mostly talked to kids from Honduras because we have the most in common. There are also some boys who don't speak Spanish—they're like Roomie, they speak their own languages. Talking to them reminds me of him, and it makes me sad. I get worried that he thinks I didn't bother saying goodbye to him. I probably should have woken him up to say goodbye, but I didn't want to make the tícher mad.

I've gotten along fine with all the kids I've met, but the thing is, every few days they assign me to a new tent anyway, with new boys and new tíchers. I have no idea why they do that, but it means I keep having to meet a whole different group of kids and tíchers.

I hope I won't be here long. I've been through so much by now, I'm starting to learn that I just have to control the things I can control and leave the rest to God. The tíchers here aren't nice, but they're nicer than the gangs and the cartels and the gringos at the border. I keep asking when I'll get to call Papá, and when the tíchers answer me at all, they say we'll be able to make phone calls soon. I bet that when I talk to him, he'll be able to help get me out of here.

Love,
D.

P.S. I haven't found Miguelito and Elías here. I hope that they're with each other, at least.

JUNE 20, 2018

Tornillo

Querida Tía:

We made phone calls today. I got my ten minutes. Both Mamá and Papá were there, which was lucky. Usually one of them, or both of them, are at work, because we don't get a super reliable schedule about when we'll be allowed to call.

But, Tía, talking to them almost feels worse than not talking to them. I think about the long phone conversations I used to have with them in Naranjito, when I could look at that photo of them holding a baby me in their arms. Those conversations had so much joy. We'd talk about family and cousins, and they'd tell me stories from el Norte and their jobs, and what life is like in Nashville. Even when our calls were sad, like the ones after you and Tío Felipe died, they still felt warm and alive. Now it just feels so robotic, and none of us feel like we can talk for real. We all know we're being monitored. The tícher sits there with a notebook in her hand. She doesn't usually write anything, and I can't even always tell if she speaks Spanish, but still. I'm scared to say anything bad about this prison camp, and my parents are scared of saying something that'll get them in trouble, because they're indocumentados, too. And I know they're worried too. We've been talking on the phone for almost fourteen years, and I've never heard them sound the way they do now.

When we talk, it's lifeless, monotonous.

I asked them if they could come get me. Papá said right away that they were trying, that they were doing everything they could. I don't want to push it more than that. I don't want to say anything that'll get me in trouble, and I don't want to push it with the parents I've never met. But it's painful. Even though me and my parents are in the same country for the first time ever, I have never felt more orphaned than I do now.

Love,
D.

JUNE 21, 2018
Tornillo

Querida Tía:

Things here are normal . . . or like, not normal, nothing about this is normal, but they're the same. I've been trying not to eat too much, so I don't have to go to the bathroom. The good news is that means I don't have to eat the food here. At breakfast they serve us eggs from a box, a fruit (usually a banana, but I'm allergic), and cereal and milk. The cereals are the only good part. They come in these cute little boxes that unfortunately have only one serving in them, and the best kind is called Frosted Flakes. It comes in a blue box, and it's almost always gone by the time I get there. But it's okay, because all the other kinds of cereal are delicious, too.

I'm trying to not go to the bathroom, so I only eat the one box of cereal I'm allowed to have, with as little milk as possible because I don't want to have to pee either. A lot of the other kids do the same. It's easy to give up the rest of the food when it's so gross, but I wouldn't pass up my cereal. Honestly, most days it's the best part of my day.

Lunch and dinner are a little bit better, but still kind of gross. They give us something they call chicken, but it doesn't look or smell or taste like any chicken I've ever eaten, it's just a brown shape. Or they give us sandwiches with a kind of wet meat slop on it. And most days they give us a mix of vegetables that have been boiled into a mush. On the best days, they give us frozen pizzas they warm up. The pizzas are everyone's favorite, but they're really small. It doesn't really matter though, because I've been eating as little as possible. So far it's going okay. The hard part is going without water, because we're in the middle of the desert. I haven't stopped drinking completely—when I do, my mouth gets dry, and I figure that, since it's so hot, I'm probably sweating it all out anyway. I just have a few sips with every meal, or maybe half a cup, and then I can hold it until nighttime, when the porta-potty isn't a nauseating sauna.

I know this isn't healthy, and I'm probably getting dehydrated. When we run around on el campo, I've been getting dizzy, but I haven't passed out like a few of the other boys have. When that happens, they take them to the nurse, but they're usually back in the tent in about an hour. Nothing bad ever happens to them, and I think the tíchers blame it on the heat.

I'll write to you again whenever something happens! If anything ever happens!

Love,
D.

JUNE 25, 2018

Tornillo

Querida Tía:

I'm worried about Miguelito and Elías, and also about Damián, though I'm hoping Damián is back home by now. I have no way of knowing.

I'm bored and hungry and lonely, and I was wondering if I could talk to you? I know you can't talk back, but it makes me feel like I'm not completely alone here.

I guess I'll say more about what our routines here are like. During the day, we mostly talk and sleep. The other kids are nice, but we can never really get a conversation going for two reasons: First, because the tíchers are always telling us to be quiet, even when we're not being that loud. We're allowed to talk during the day (unlike at night, when we have to be completely silent), but sometimes they get mad at us anyway. And second, because everyone's kind of . . . shy? Or like, dazed, I guess. I've been in los Estados Unidos for almost two months, but a lot of these kids came straight from crossing the border, in the same clothes they traveled in, and they don't know what they're doing here. They're confused (like I am) by all the chaos, and by how no one ever really tells us anything. So when we talk, we mostly just ask basic questions: what's your name, where are you from, that kind of stuff. We'd probably get to know each other better if they weren't moving us to different tents every few days.

We try to play games during the day to pass the time with the cards and checkers we have here. We play both. I'm not great at poker, but I'm as good as the other kids at checkers—Felipe used to play with me on his rare day off. Sooner or later, though, we have to stop, because, like I said, there are no tables to play in or chairs to sit on, and eventually our legs start to cramp and our backs hurt from sitting on the ground.

We're not in the tent literally *all* day. They always take us to get meals three times a day, and when another tent isn't using the field, they take us to the campo de fútbol to play. But it seems like we're doing that less frequently, only on days when it's less hot, probably because the kids who aren't drinking water keep passing out. Sometimes they also take us to a tent where an old man—Tícher Raul, one of the few tíchers whose name I know—sings us songs with his guitar, and tries to get us to sing along. He's really nice, and I can tell he's trying to cheer us up.

Every once in a while, they take us to a tent with a TV, where a tícher shows us this crazy movie about a dog who's really good at básquetbol, even better than people and professional athletes. I didn't know there were dogs that could do that—I've never heard of that breed before. All the dogs like Caramelo in Naranjito were scrappy, and they were the most loving, wonderful dogs ever, but they didn't look like that. We watch the movie with Spanish dubbing, and the characters keep saying the dog is a gólden. When I'm with Papá, I'm going to ask him if we can get a gólden, too, so I can practice fútbol with him.

The movie starts with the dog, whose name is Buddy, and a clown, and they go to a kid's birthday party, but the clown messes everything up when he's performing, slips on a banana peel, and ends up faceplanting into the birthday cake. The mom who hired the clown is mad and throws him out, and he takes it out on Buddy and locks him in a cage, and yells: *Te di una oportunidad, perro pulgoso. Te llevaré a la perrera.*

¿Me entendiste? ¡Te vas a la perrera! ¡Odio las fiestas de cumpleaños! ¡Odio a los niños! ¡Odio ser un payasoooooooo! It's a funny movie, but hearing this adult clown who hates kids say he's going to take the gólden to the dog pound—the perrera—makes me a feel a little weird, since that's also what they call the place where they locked me and my cousins up after we crossed the border. Like, it makes me think about how they were treating us like dogs. Like we did something to deserve to be locked up like animals.

We haven't made it through the whole movie yet—we're only allowed to watch for thirty minutes at a time, and sometimes the tícher forgets where we left off and we start from the beginning. That's why I know the first scene so well. But even if we only get to watch TV for half an hour, that's half an hour I can get out of my head. It's better than sitting in the tent with nothing to do except mentally relive La Bestia, La Hielera, La Perrera. And also, the tícher who shows the movies for us also has, like, the biggest butt any of us have ever seen, and sometimes we whisper about her when we're walking en fila back to our tent. It gives us something to talk about, anyway.

It's a small thing, but walking between tents is actually one of my favorite parts of the day. I'm used to spending lots of time outside, and when I was traveling north with Miguelito and Elías and Damián, we were barely ever indoors. But now I don't take it for granted. Feeling the sun on your face and the fresh air on your skin just seems more special when you're stuck in a tent all day.

Love,
D.

P.S. Is Caramelo with you? I guess I don't know how el cielo works for dogs. I'm surprised I never thought about it before. If he's there, would you please give him an avocado for me?

JUNE 27, 2018

Tornillo

Querida Tía:

I don't get to write to you as often as I want, because I never have any privacy, and I'm always slightly worried that if another kid saw me writing, they'd ask to read it and I'd be embarrassed. Or even worse, that a tícher would see me writing and take my notebook away for some reason. And I can't write to you from my bed at night, because it's too dark.

Which is too bad—I can't handle nighttime here. The days are whatever. I'm bored and hungry, but at least there are distractions: small talk, little cereal boxes, checkers, the tícher with the big butt, the dog movies. Nights are different. At night I kind of . . . suffer. Even when the sun is beginning to set, my whole body starts to feel, just . . . wrong, like it knows the night is going to be hard. I'm not sure I can explain it. It's like I can't sit still, because something in my body isn't the way it's supposed to be. Like, I want to climb out of my skin. I know that doesn't really make sense, but I can't think of another way to describe it.

I don't exactly know why I feel this way. There are three tíchers watching us all night, which is also weird. I don't like being watched while I sleep. At the last albergue, there was always a teacher in the hall, but me and Roomie got to sleep with privacy.

Actually, thinking about Roomie is one of the hardest things about nighttime. I always think about him when I'm lying in bed. When you spend, I don't know, maybe 75 percent of your time with a person, and then out of nowhere they take you away from him, without even giving you the chance to say goodbye, it's just . . . It's really, really hard. Even though we didn't have a shared language, I felt like I shared as much with him as I did with Miguelito. After you've gone through so much hard stuff with someone, separation feels like this terrible tugging in your throat. It's like there's a rope tied around my neck and his, and the farther apart we move, the tighter it gets. It feels like part of me is still with him, in our bedroom, and that part of me will be stuck there until I see him again. But I don't know how that will ever happen. It feels like they've taken part of my family away from me forever. I want to say that I'm up all night worrying about him, but I don't think *worrying* is the right word. It's closer to the feeling I felt when you died. It's more like grieving.

And then at night I'm also scared for Miguelito and Elías and Damián. I wonder if Damián is okay, if he's back in Quetzaltenango with Tía Gloria, and if Miguelito and Elías are still locked up somewhere. Like, they could have been set free by now, or they might still be in a prison like this one. What if they're still in La Perrera? If they kept them there for weeks and weeks? I think they'd go insane if they had to stay that long. I try praying to make sure they're safe and okay, and I hope God listens. But it feels like I've been saying so many prayers ever since leaving Naranjito, and I don't know, I wish it made me feel better.

Sometimes at night, I think about how long I've been held like a prisoner in these centers, and I think about how no one has told me when I'll get out. And even if they did tell me something, I wouldn't believe them—they've lied to me before. I could be here, with no family and no friends and no news about my cousins, if they are okay, for years. This fills me with a lonely feeling so strong that I wish that I could fall through the floor and disappear, that I could just cut out the part of my life where I'm here, skip it, even if that meant skipping ten years of my life. I can't handle feeling like this for much longer. It makes me feel so empty inside.

It seems like for most of the night, I'm up thinking about these things, trying not to cry, or at least not cry so loudly people can hear me. Every once in a while, the nighttime tíchers have to tell one of the other boys to be quiet, either because he's crying or because he woke up scared from a nightmare.

I have nightmares, too. They're usually about me being frozen when something is happening. Sometimes I dream that I'm with Damián when he's getting beaten by the gang, and I'm standing right next to him, but my feet are frozen, and I can't do anything to help. Or I'm lying on top of La Bestia, and it's raining, and Miguelito and Elías are telling me it's time for us to get off, but my body is glued to the top of the train, and there are snakes slithering up the legs of my pants. Other times I don't remember the dreams super well, but I wake up sweating and with my blanket all tangled up, with this feeling in my stomach like I'm about to throw up.

I don't know what would happen if I threw up in bed. The tíchers would probably write a report, and I'd end up staying here even longer. So whenever I wake up feeling nauseated, I put both my hands over my mouth and press really hard until the urge goes back down.

Love,
D.

JUNE 30, 2018
Tornillo

Querida Tía:

They just put up even more new tents. The camp keeps getting built bigger and bigger, and more kids show up every day, looking just as confused as I was when I got here. They change our tents up every few days, but other than that, it's amazing how little has happened in the three or four weeks since I got here. I didn't know I could be so anxious and so bored at the same time.

Every day the food is the same, or basically the same. I think that because we've been complaining about the bathrooms, they've started to see a connection between us not eating and all the kids who keep passing out. It's happening a lot more. Some of the kids are eating and drinking basically nothing, unlike me—I'm smart enough to eat and drink a little so I don't get sick, but not so much that I have to use the porta-potty while the sun is still up. I've been getting woozy more often, but I'm not sure if that's because I'm not eating much or because I'm barely sleeping. The tíchers have started watching us more closely during meals, and sometimes they try to make us eat and drink more. But there are too many of us for them to keep track of how much everyone is putting in their mouth and, honestly, I don't think they care enough to really keep track of who is eating and who isn't.

The tícher with the big butt is still showing us movies about Buddy. It turns out he doesn't just play básquetbol, he plays fútbol and fútbol americano, and even béisbol and voléibol too. But it's boring to watch the same movies over and over, and those movies are for really little kids anyway. We asked the tícher if we could watch something more exciting, like el Hombre Araña or something, but she says these are the only movies she's allowed to show, because other movies might be inappropriate.

I talked to Mamá and Papá yesterday. I used to really look forward to those calls, but they're starting to make me sad. Even though they did what the lady said and got their fingerprints taken weeks ago, I still can't leave. They say that they've called the lady back a million times since then to ask why I can't leave yet, and she says that their fingerprints are "processing." That's pretty much what the tíchers here tell me, too. Whenever we talk, my parents try to stay positive and tell me not to worry, but I can tell that they're feeling helpless. There's like, a strained sound in their voice that I never used to hear.

Anyway, they're taking us go to lunch now.

More soon.

Love,
D.

JULY 4, 2018

Tornillo

Querida Tía:

At El Albergue, reading was the only thing that made life bearable. It stopped me from thinking sad thoughts after dark. Sometimes it also set my mind on a track to dream of nice things. But there are no books in Tornillo. I've asked the tíchers over and over again, and every time they say "Ahorita, ahorita," but it's the same as with the porta-potties, nothing ever changes. I'd even take a book in English at this point. I'd take a book in Japanese.

So, what I've been doing instead, when I feel lonely, is writing in my notebook: I know you know I've been writing you letters, but besides that, I've been making drawings, and coming up with stories and poems and songs and raps. It's not the same as reading, but it keeps my brain busy and, to be honest, I'm starting to think I'm pretty good at writing. It feels nice to be good at something. When we get back from dinner, I go to my bunk and get straight to writing, so that the bad thoughts don't have space to creep in before lights out. I'm in a top bunk right now, so I figure nobody'll see me writing, so I won't have to worry about being embarrassed or getting my notebook taken away. And then, if I'm lucky, I can fall right asleep without my brain wandering too much.

I've been thinking a lot about how in the dog movies, some characters are always threatening to put Buddy in the perrera, but la Migra put me, a human being, into a perrera without thinking twice. And even since letting me out of that place, they've still treated me like a criminal even though I haven't done anything wrong. I wanted to write about that, so I came up with a rap about it in Spanish.

I started with this line:

I'm an undocumented immigrant, not a thief.

I liked the idea, but it didn't feel exactly right. I didn't want to write it from my own perspective, or not just mine anyway. Since I was little, you and Felipe taught me that especially when you don't have a lot, it's important to include people. I know that writing raps isn't exactly what you were talking about, but I didn't want my song to be just about me, I wanted it to include Damián and Miguelito and Elías and Roomie and, really, in a way, everyone who was in the same situation as me. Like, clearly lots of kids aren't doing any better than I am. Writing it from just my perspective felt wrong, so I decided to change "soy" to "somos":

We are undocumented immigrants, not a thieves.

I liked it better this way, because it expressed how we're all a family and we're all suffering through the same experience. So I kept the shared perspective. But then I started to think it needed to rhyme more, like raps usually do, so I rewrote it a little bit and came up with this:

We are undocumented immigrants
Not even Donald Trump has found
United we are many and we are
In all states
Some praying
And me rhyming

Writing it that way cuts out the part about not being thieves, but I'm going to add that idea in later, I think. I want it to be a long rap, one I could perform someday. I've written more lines, but I'm still rewriting them. It's fun to reorganize the lines or change the words so they rhyme or sound better. I'm excited to keep writing it. I'll show you more when it's ready.

Love,
D.

JULY 5, 2018
Tornillo

Querida Tía:

Today is a great day. A wonderful day. I don't want to exaggerate, but it might be one of the best days of my life.

Is it because they're letting me out of here? No.

Is it because they've brought me books to read? No.

Is it because they've started serving baleadas and ice cream in the cafeteria? No.

Is it because they've finally given us tíchers who speak Spanish? Also no.

But it's the next best thing.

It's because they have replaced the porta-potties. After three weeks of half starving myself and holding it until nighttime, they have given us kids real toilet trailers, exactly the same kind that the tíchers use.

It took me a few days to realize they were setting them up, because there's always so much construction going on here. They're still putting up new tents every day, and hauling truckloads of equipment and materials in and crazy mountains of trash out. It makes sense that this place creates a lot of trash because they keep calling the campamento a "temporary shelter," and I guess temporary means disposable. Everything we use, we throw out. For example, in the cafeteria, everything goes in foam plates and bowls, and we eat with plastic forks and spoons. When you throw out your dishes, the trash can is full of just scraps and plastic. I've never seen so much foam in my life. I would've thought it'd be easier to wash dishes than to drive a truck all the way out here in the desert, but maybe they're trying to save water.

I guess they finally decided it was time to throw out the porta-potties, just like they throw out everything else. I don't know exactly what made them finally get rid of them. We kept telling the tíchers how gross they are, and I think they believed us but I don't think the people who run this place really care. They've never changed anything else we complain about.

Maybe they finally decided to buy us toilet trailers because more and more kids keep showing up, and it seems like this temporary shelter isn't actually going to be very temporary.

Or maybe it's because they finally figured out a connection between the toilets and all the kids that have been passing out. It's been happening more and more often. And kids aren't just passing out from not eating—a lot of the kids who are eating are getting sick in a different way. The food here isn't very good, but the bigger problem is that it's really unfamiliar to a lot of us from Honduras, Nicaragua, El Salvador, Guatemala. We're used to baleadas, tamales, rice, papaya. But here, half the food they feed us comes out of bags and boxes, and most of it is either some kind of bread or it has been cooked in a lot of oil. It's causing problems for a lot of kids' stomachs, and they've been trying to hold it during the day, but their bodies have been trying to, um . . . to get rid of that unfamiliar food. I don't know a lot about health or anything, but I think that has been making a lot of kids sick. Maybe there weren't enough nurses here to take care of all the sick kids, so they finally had to do something.

We're still going to have to hold it sometimes, since we're only allowed to use the trailers during specific bathroom breaks after meals. We go up by tent, and sometimes three or four tents go at once, so there's a line of sixty or eighty kids waiting to use the trailer, and just like always, the tíchers are telling us to hurry up—*Rápido, rápido, rápido.*

It's nice of them to give us real toilets, but the fact that we're only allowed to use them at certain times doesn't seem right. I've been thinking about it, and I think that everyone, everywhere—even really terrible people, even a monster who eats people like Shuu Tsukiyama from *Tokyo Ghoul*—should always be allowed to go to the bathroom when they need to. And they shouldn't have to hurry. It's messed up that we don't have the freedom to do that. Plus, they have a male tícher hold the door open and stand there when while we're using the bathroom, and it makes me feel weird. But ever since getting here, I've been trying not to get too upset about the way they treat us. I don't think it's okay for them to treat us this badly, but I'm stuck here, and there's no way out. There's nothing I can do to make my time here shorter, but if I misbehave, they'll report me and I might have to stay longer. So I've been trying to just accept things the way they are. I try to remember how much worse it was in La Perrera. And I try not to think about how much better it was to share a room (with a private toilet!) with Roomie.

Anyway, today it was really nice to use the bathroom without feeling like I was going to throw up, and without that hot chemical smell worming up my nostrils and down my throat. And I'm glad I can go back to eating and drinking normal amounts. It'll be nice to go to bed without my stomach growling. It'll make it easier to focus on writing my rap—it's getting better, and I think it's almost done. I'll tell you when it is.

Love,
D.

JULY 8, 2018
Tornillo

Querida Tía:

Even though we just had dinner and it's almost time for bed, they're sending me to a new tent. Alpha 13. I've been in Tornillo for around a month, so I've been through a bunch of tents by now: Alpha 8, Alpha 4, Alpha 11 . . . I can't remember them all.

Usually, when I change tents, I talk to the boys who are already there. Some are sent here right after crossing the border, and others have passed through a few other kinds of jails like I have. You can usually tell from what they're wearing. Kids who were sent straight here are usually wearing the clothes they crossed the border in, but kids who have been through other albergues get new clothes. When I got here, I met some boys named Gabriel, Gustavo, Raphael, Rene, and Enrique. I asked if they saw Miguelito or Elías at any of the albergues they were in before, but none of them have. I was about to ask if I could join their card game, but before I had the chance, the night tíchers said it was time for bed.

Love,
D.

JULY 10, 2018
Tornillo

Querida Tía:

Nothing ever changes. I'm in a new tent, but it doesn't make much of a difference. It looks the same, smells the same. But I'm so bored, and when I'm bored, I worry about Elías and Miguelito. I never saw them at El Albergue, and I've never seen them here either. I guess that doesn't really mean anything. Maybe they brought them to a different detention center. Whatever happened, I just hope they didn't separate them from each other. Elías is pretty resilient, but I feel bad being away from Miguelito, and thinking about him being stuck, alone, in one of these places . . .

I don't want to think about it. That's why I sat down to write, actually, but I couldn't think of anything to write . . .

My foot is getting better, I think. For a long time it looked horrible—it was all kinds of different colors of black and blue and red and purple, and it was oozing this slightly pink stuff that wasn't blood, but I don't know what it was. It hurt to walk on, too, but now it hurts less. I still hobble a little bit, although not nearly as bad. I took all the pills that they gave me a few weeks ago at El Albergue, but nobody has given me any more, and they haven't rubbed any more ointment on it. I guess that in Tornillo, they don't know that anything was ever wrong with it. It still looks pretty bad, but it's better than before.

Anyway, writing about my foot isn't a great distraction. Maybe I'll just go back to sleep. At least when I'm asleep, I'm not worrying about Miguelito and Elías.

Love,
D.

JULY 13, 2018 (FRIDAY THE 13TH!)

Tornillo

Querida Tía:

I have a little bit of time before they take us to the campo de fútbol, so I want to tell you about something that happened. I don't usually write from the tent in the middle of the day, but I'm feeling so . . . just, like, excited and happy that I'm gonna do it anyway.

So . . . this morning we got new tíchers. When I was waking up, I heard someone, an adult, speaking Spanish. A tícher. A male voice. Since I got here, I don't think I've encountered any male tíchers who are native Spanish-speakers. I heard him saying "Buenos días, buenos días" as we were waking up. Usually I hate waking up here—at least when I'm asleep, I can dream I'm somewhere nicer—but I had to pee, so I jumped out of bed. But before I asked if we could go to the toilet trailers, I wanted to know who our new daytime tíchers were. If one of them spoke Spanish, at least that was something.

I looked around, and I saw two female tíchers, but I didn't see the man who had woken us up. Then, after a second, I realized that he was right in front of me, across the tent: he was standing with some of the other boys, and he blended in because he was so short. He's even shorter than me, and shorter than lots of the other boys here. And he's got brown skin like us. And he was smiling.

He started to talk.

"Hola chicos, ¡buenos días! My name is Iván, I just got assigned to this tent," he said in Spanish. "I'm from México, which is why I speak Spanish. I'm an immigrant like you. I came here because I really want to support you guys. I know you've all been through a lot. Whatever you need, tell me. And over here are your two other new teachers, Nancy and Yuli."

At first, I thought that Iván looked a lot like Elías, but when I looked closer, that wasn't really true at all. Elías is way taller, and their faces are different. But there's something about Iván's energy that makes them seem similar.

Nancy and Yuli introduced themselves. They spoke really good Spanish too. Three tíchers who speak Spanish: this, at least, is something to be grateful for in this place.

Everyone started getting ready to go to breakfast. I still really had to pee, so I went up to the new tícher, the man, to ask if I could go even though it wasn't an official bathroom break. He seemed more friendly than most of the tíchers here, so I hoped he'd let me.

"Tícher, can I go to the bathroom? It's an emergency."

"Of course. Come on, I'll walk with you," he said. "What's your name?"

I told him.

"Nice to meet you," he said. We started walking toward the bathroom. He seemed lost in thought. Then he said, "One thing, D. You don't have to call me 'tícher.' My name is Iván."

I couldn't believe it, honestly. After all these weeks of no adults telling me their name, he just came out and shared his with me.

Not long after I got back from the bathroom, they took us to breakfast. The food here has been getting worse, but an even bigger problem is that they're serving us way less of it than before: they give us fewer nuggets, fewer eggs, and watch us to make sure we grab only one cereal—they always watch closely, even though the grown-ups are allowed to have as many cereals as they want. They haven't ever explained why we're getting less food. Not that we expect them to. One of the kids I was playing conquian with this morning, Gabriel—who has the top bunk just beside me—says he thinks it's because they got the toilet trailers, so kids are eating a normal amount now, and that means on average we're going through more food.

At the table this morning, one of the other boys I was playing cards with, Chato, looked kind of sick. He turned to Iván and said: "Iván, me siento mal comiendo huevos. ¿Puedo tener otro cereal?"

Usually, the tíchers wouldn't let us have an extra cereal because it's against the rules. Iván seemed different, but still, I expected him to do the same stuff other tíchers do.

But he didn't. He just said, "Claro que sí, Chato, ¿cuál quieres?"

Chato said he wanted Frosted Flakes, obviously, because they're the best.

Then Gabriel asked if he could have another cereal, too, and so did another kid whose name I don't know. I thought for sure that Iván was going to say no, that it was way too many, that he couldn't bend the rules for all of us. But instead he just smiled and said, "Okay, ¡levanten la mano los que quieran otro cereal!"

Eight or nine boys raised their hands (including me).

"¿Y todos quieren Frosted Flakes?"

Eight or nine boys nodded (including me).

He went up to the box of cereals, smiled at the lady handing them out, and brought them back for us. We leaped on them like they were gold. Cereal was already the best part of the day, but double cereal . . . ? That made today the best day ever, or at least the best day since we got the toilet trailers.

A few minutes later, a fat, sweaty white man wearing a button-up shirt came up to our table and asked in English to speak to Iván. They walked a few meters away from the table. We could still hear them, but it didn't matter, because we can't understand them much, as far as we could tell, the sweaty man called Iván by the name of Gerardo and told him something about kids and one cereal. They exchanged a few more words, until Iván said, "*English english english* one cereal? *English english* boys *english english* and you *english english*? *English english*! *English english* Frosted Flakes!"

He wasn't yelling, but he was clearly upset and giving the sweaty man a hard time. The man looked surprised, and I think he was about to say something, but before he could, Iván turned and walked back to the table. He grabbed a few more boxes of cereal on the way.

The man stood there for a second, trying to figure out what to do, then turned and left.

I want to keep writing, but we have to run for fútbol! I'm not done writing about this, though, so I'll tell you more tonight.

—D.

JULY 13, 2018 (SAME DAY AS THE LAST LETTER, JUST LATER!)

Tornillo

Querida Tía:

Okay, I'm in bed now, and I have some time to write before lights out, so I'll pick up where I left off . . .

I can't describe how good it felt when Iván gave us that cereal. I was smiling so wide that it was hard to chew my second box of Frosted Flakes. I hadn't had an adult stand up for me, really, since before I came to Tornillo . . . or since before I crossed the border . . . or since before I left Naranjito . . . or, really, since you died.

Ever since this morning, I've been thinking a lot about a story in the Biblia that Padre Juan talked about at church once in Naranjito. It's about a man who gets beat up and thrown in a ditch by a gang, just like what happened to Damián. He's hurt and lying in this ditch, and a priest walks past without helping him, because it'd be too much work or he's afraid it's a trap or he doesn't want to get his clothes bloody or whatever. The man only gets saved when a buen Samaritano stops to help him. In a way, even though the priest didn't do anything, he was just as bad, or almost as bad, as the gang that beat the man up. Padre Juan says the priest in the story was bad *because* he didn't do anything. I thought it was interesting that Padre Juan told us about it, even though the bad person is a priest like him.

The point is, there are two ways you can hurt people. You can hurt a person actively, like by punching them or stealing from them or whatever. But you can also hurt a person passively, by refusing to give them help when they need it, or by pretending you don't see them, or by acting like they don't exist.

Since leaving Naranjito, there have been a few adults who have tried to hurt me actively—like the hombres del cartel who shot at us while we were riding La Bestia, or the pissed-off Migra guys who put me and my cousins in a refrigerator to freeze half to death. And all that was horrible, obviously. But in a way, when someone hurts you actively, the damage is mostly just physical. Back home, gangs are a fact of life, and even though I was always lucky—I was never directly targeted until the cartel chased me off La Bestia—there's always a risk that someone will hurt you in an active way. But that doesn't give me this horrible, whole-body feeling of worthlessness. In Naranjito, I never saw anyone get passively hurt. I'm sure some kids had parents and family who were bad to them, but in some ways, anyone's kids were like everyone's kids. If a kid was hungry, obviously it was their parents' job to feed them, but if their parents were missing for some reason, the rest of the pueblo wouldn't just let the kid starve to death.

Since crossing the border though, until breakfast this morning, I don't think a single adult in los Estados Unidos would have cared if I'd starved. In los Estados Unidos, the passive pain has been the worst feeling of all. Passive pain is a little harder to explain than active pain, but I'll try:

It hurts in a different way. The adults who have tried to actively hurt me aren't as bad as all the adults who stand around, seeing what's happening, doing nothing. Looking bored. This has been everywhere since I got to el Norte. There have been a million examples: the woman behind the desk at oficina de la Migra who called Papá and filled out my registration on her computer before her buddies in green uniforms stuck me in a refrigerator. The bus drivers who shuttled me and a vehicle full of innocent kids from one kind of jail to another and never stopped to ask what we did to deserve this, why we weren't in school, why we weren't with our parents, why we were crying, why we were dirty, why my foot was oozing blood and pus and stinking up the entire bus like roadkill. The servers in the cafeteria who see this food is making us sick but won't do anything about it, who won't let us grab another box of Frosted Flakes. The worst of all are the tíchers, these useless tíchers who call us by our bed numbers, these grown-ups who speak fluent English and could really do something to help us, but who just stand around looking tired and annoyed while kids like me are kept from our parents for no reason, tíchers who don't sound any alarms when nine- and ten-year-olds are passing out on the campo de fútbol because they're afraid to drink water, because they're afraid to use the bathroom.

Sometimes it makes me want to grab a piece of cardboard and write *I'm a kid, do something* on it. It makes me want to grab a megaphone and scream "I'm a person! I'm supposed to matter!" But more often, it makes me wonder if maybe I don't matter, it makes me want to collapse, it makes me want to give up, it makes me want to melt into my bunk, it makes me want to climb down the porta-potty pit and dissolve in the chemicals. It makes me never want to look anyone in the eye again. It makes me embarrassed to think what you or Felipe would say if you saw me now. It gives me an itchy-jumpy feeling in my chest when I think about seeing my parents, when I think about trying to join their lives. What if I don't matter to them, either?

When I was with my cousins, or with Roomie, it helped so much. It was like having another person standing beside me every day, silently repeating, "You and me are real, you and me matter." And that kind of warded off the pain caused by these adults who don't give a crap about us. It has been hard to get this kind of support only from other kids, but it also makes me feel mature, like a grown-up. Like Miguelito and Elías and Damián and Roomie and me have what it takes to look out for each other. It's only since they've been gone that the feelings have gotten really bad.

And that's why I couldn't stop smiling when this tícher, Iván, spoke Spanish to us and gave us those extra cereals. It was like for the first time in a long time, I was a kid again, and I could fall back on an adult who was looking out for me.

Love,
D.

JULY 16, 2018
Tornillo

Querida Tía:

I wasn't expecting it, but lately, I've been feeling really grateful. I wish I could stay in Alpha 13 forever. Or, I mean, not forever, but until they let me go to my parents.

There are always three tíchers during the day and three at night, and *all three of our day tíchers speak Spanish*! I can't even describe how freeing it is to be able to speak to an adult who can speak back to you.

There's Iván, the tícher who gave us our cereal. He's so much more fun than all the other tíchers in the other tents put together, and based on the things he says, it seems like this is more than just a job for him. I don't think he even thinks of being here as a job. There's also Nancy and Yuli, who are both really nice to us. Nancy is a little bit more organized—she's the one who's always paying attention to the schedule. And Yuli feels more like a mamá . . . she's kind of a calming person to be around.

Having tíchers who care enough to actually talk to us is even better than having tíchers who speak Spanish. Iván asks us about our families, and how we're doing, and how our fútbol games are going. All three of them actually learned our names instead of just calling us by our bed numbers, and they say we should call them by their names, too, instead of just saying *tícher*. And they play cards with us, too. We like to play conquian, and even though we don't have anything to bet with or any prize to give the winner, we've invented a way to make it feel more like gambling: after every round, the losers have to chug a whole plastic water bottle in one go. It's just a regular-size water bottle, so it's not that hard. It's just funny. Since we're in the desert, the tíchers make sure there are always a lot of water bottles around (even though nobody drank them very much until we got the toilet trailers). Iván and Nancy and Yuli actually join us for our games sometimes, and when they lose (which is almost every time), Gabriel tells them that they have to chug a bottle of water. Just like the rest of us. Nancy and Yuli always refuse—they try to laugh it off—but Iván actually does it! He chugs every time he loses—so he must have to pee all the time, because he loses a lot.

Iván, Nancy, and Yuli seem to get along well with each other, too. They're always talking and laughing. Before I came to Alpha 13, I don't think I'd ever seen anyone laugh in Tornillo, except during the funny scenes the first few times we watched the movies with Buddy the dog.

If I had to pick between having tíchers who speak Spanish and tíchers who actually take an interest in us, I'd pick tíchers who take an interest in us. I feel so lucky that we get to have both.

Love,
D.

JULY 23, 2018

Tornillo

Querida Tía:

This is the longest I've stayed in any tent since I got here, and I'm starting to wonder if they're done making us change tents. Whenever we ask about it, Iván says we don't have to worry, the changes are over, all of us are going to stay here together. I hope he's right—it would be like an answer to my prayers. I've been here with the same kids and with Iván and Nancy and Yuli ever since the morning with the cereals, and that was over a week ago. The night tíchers aren't nice—they threaten to report us all the time, and they don't let us go to the bathroom when it isn't an official bathroom break, even if we really have to go—but we're asleep for most of the night anyway, and Iván and Nancy and Yuli are always back in the morning.

Iván is funny—he's always goofing around or singing or dancing or giving us pep talks and trying to prepare us for life in los Estados Unidos. He also encourages us to get to know each other—to actually talk about our homes and our families and where we're going. "Para ustedes, puede ser muy difícil aquí," he's always saying, "pero juntos somos más fuertes." We're stronger together.

That's really true in Alpha 13. In the other tents, at most, we just made shy small talk and played cards. But here, I have my best friend, Juan Manuel (more on him soon), and my big brother, Iván, plus a whole cast of characters from different countries. A lot of them have really big personalities.

First, there's a group of three boys named Gabriel, Raphael, and Gustavo, and as a trio they call themselves "Los Compadres." They were in a different tent together before they came to Alpha 13, so when they got here, they'd already known each other for about a week. But based on the way they act, you'd think they were three brothers who have known each other for their whole lives. They're pretty sarcastic, and they're always telling jokes. It actually makes me miss Miguelito a little bit, to see the way they joke around with each other. Even though things have been way better since Iván and Nancy and Yuli came here, I can't stop worrying about him.

But anyway, Los Compadres set the vibe for the whole tent, probably because Gabriel is the tallest and oldest boy in here. He's seventeen years old and almost two meters tall, way taller than Iván. He has sort of become the leader, not just of Los Compadres, but of all the boys in Alpha 13. He's the biggest clown in the tent by far. He loves to dance. At least once a day, he asks Yuli to turn on the radio so he can dance to his two favorite kinds of music, banda and rap. Usually, Gabriel can convince a few of us to join him, but if he can't, he'll just dance alone like a chicken with its head cut off. And he's always playing pranks, too.

The second Compadre, Raphael, also has a big personality, even if he isn't as loud and silly as Gabriel. He's sixteen years old, and from Honduras like me. He's is a total fútbol fanatic. However much Gabriel likes banda music and dancing, that's how much Raphael loves fútbol. When I asked his name, he didn't just tell me his name like a normal person. He said, "It's Raphael, spelled and pronounced the same as Raphael Tessaro Schettino, the Brazilian goalkeeper." Every day he asks if we're going to get to play fútbol and, obviously, he's the best player in Alpha 13.

But the third Compadre, Gustavo, is completely different. He's not shy, but he's way quieter than the other two, and a lot more serious. He's sort of, like, the brains of the operation. Sometimes I'll see him whispering with Gabriel and Raphael before one of them pulls one of their pranks. He's also from Honduras, but his skin is way darker than mine, the darkest of anyone in Alpha 13. He's not embarrassed about it. He says it's because he's Garifuna, who are native people who don't speak Spanish. Sort of like Roomie, except it's confusing because Gustavo speaks Spanish way better than Roomie did. Gustavo is really proud of being Garifuna. Whenever they take us to play fútbol, all the rest of us put on long-sleeve shirts so we don't get any darker, but Gustavo never does. I guess he figures that he's so dark already, there's no point.

Los Compadres are the silliest group in the tent, but there are other interesting kids too. There's Rene and Enrique, who are the youngest boys here, and also literally the smallest. Sometimes Gabriel makes fun of Enrique for being so short, he's always calling him "chaparrito," which makes Enrique really mad. It's funny, because he's so young that he hasn't learned how to brush off a joke yet. He's only twelve years old, the same as Miguelito. But he isn't timid at all—he's always eager to make friends.

There's also a boy named Chapín, but he says we all have to call him McQueen. "Like in *Cars*," he says. I've never seen that movie, but if he wants to be called McQueen, that's fine. He's really thoughtful. He's always asking people about their families and trying to get to know everyone. I think he's really sensitive, too. He's in a bunk close to mine, and one night, I heard him crying softly, with his head under his pillow, so it wouldn't make too much noise. The night tíchers get mad and threaten to report you if you cry too loudly, and McQueen is even more scared of the night tíchers than the rest of us. I couldn't talk to him at night without getting in trouble, but the next day, I saw him looking depressed, and I asked him what was wrong. He said he missed his mamá. He said they rode La Bestia from Guatemala together, and crossed the border together, but then at La Perrera, he got separated from her, the same as I got separated from Miguelito and Elías. When they let him out of La Perrera and brought him to Tornillo, he thought she would be here, but it's just kids here, there are no adult migrantes. So he has no idea where she is, and he's scared for himself and scared for her. It reminds me of how I'm scared for my cousins, and how they're probably scared for me, too. When we get to make phone calls, he calls his tíos, but they haven't heard anything about where she is. He started crying again when we were talking about it, and I hugged him and told him it would be okay until he stopped.

The whole time we were hugging, I was thinking about how you hugged me and Miguelito when you told us you were sick. We think of hugs as a nice, simple, small thing you give to people you love. But I don't think that gives them enough credit. I'm starting to realize that sometimes, hugs are the only tool for survival that they can't take away from you.

Love,
D.

JULY 24, 2018
Tornillo

Querida Tía:

Now I want to tell you about Juan Manuel.

Juan Manuel is the boy who sleeps in bed 13, the bunk underneath mine. During my first few days in Alpha 13, he didn't say a word to me—or to anyone, really. He always looked really pale. I never even knew his name. Whenever the rest of us in the tent were playing a game or something, he'd almost always be sleeping. Every once in a while, he'd come and watch us play, but he never joined in. I've been getting to know the other boys, and I figured that if he doesn't want to talk, that's fine.

But one day in the cafeteria, we started talking. I was eating a blueberry muffin. The blueberry muffins are really tasty—they have this crackly sugar on top that I like to crunch between my teeth. But they don't serve them very often. Once a week at most. I was chewing on my muffin and drawing a character from *Naruto* when Iván came over and started talking to me.

"D., you're really into anime, right?" he asked, pointing at my notebook.

"Yeah, I love it. Do you watch anime?"

"Ha, no. I play a little bit of Pokémon Go sometimes, but I don't know about anime or manga or any of that stuff. But do you know who else loves anime? Juan Manuel," he said, tilting his head down the bench, toward where Juan Manuel was eating alone. I nodded. Iván explained that Juan Manuel has been sad a lot lately, and he asked if I would try to be his friend and give him some encouragement, since I'm friendly and extroverted. "Plus, you both love anime," he said.

He gave me a fist bump and walked away.

I've never really thought of myself as extroverted, but you and Felipe always used to call me that, too. I felt a little weird about just approaching this boy out of the blue, and I wasn't exactly sure what Iván meant by "give him some encouragement." But since they assigned me to Alpha 13, Iván has changed everything about Tornillo for me. I trust him. If he thinks something is a good idea, I'm going to do it.

I slid down the bench, so I was sitting next to Juan Manuel. He looked up, and I felt my heart start to race a little bit. I didn't know what to say, so I just blurted out the first thing that came to mind:

"Do you like *Naruto*?" I asked. I sort of tapped the drawing I'd been making of Sasuke Uchiha.

His eyes got big, and he gave me a sort of suspicious smile.

"I love *Naruto*. What's your name?"

"D. You're Juan Manuel?"

"Yeah. What's your favorite arc?"

I thought back to all the episodes I'd watched in Naranjito. "Have you seen one where Jiraiya is trying to gather information about Akatsuki? With the flashbacks to Orochimaru and Tsunade?"

We spent the rest of breakfast talking about anime—not just *Naruto*, but about other animes, too. Juan Manuel knows everything about anime and manga, and he suggested a bunch more series that I should watch. I'm going to try to remember them when I get to Nashville.

Since then, for the past week, we've been together constantly. Both of us have seen most of *Naruto* and *Tokyo Ghoul*, and we can talk about our favorite arcs and characters for hours. Now, when they take us to watch the movies about Buddy, we always sit together and talk about animes.

It's funny, because when I first got here, I was so glad to watch a movie for half an hour to get out of my head. But now that I have a real friend to talk to, the movies don't matter as much. It's nice to use a movie to sort of check out of reality for a few hours, but we wish they'd let us watch an anime or at least a superhero movie or something, but we know that the tícher with the big butt will say they're not appropriate.

Even though Juan Manuel is a little older than me, and he's from El Salvador and that's a really different culture from Honduras, we have gotten close really quickly. We're like Los Compadres, except there are only two of us. This has been happening a lot—the other kids are also pairing up into duos, or sometimes trios. All of us in the tent are still family. We all think of each other as brothers. But we spend a lot of time with our best friends.

Juan Manuel reminds me a lot of Miguelito. They're both really sensitive, and they're shy around new people, but once you get them talking, they bubble over with all the jokes and ideas they want to tell you. In a way, that makes me miss Miguelito, and it stirs up all the worry that I have about where he is an what's happening to him. But it also feels like a relief to be able to interact with someone in a similar way. It's easier.

He has been telling me about something that anime fans in los Estados Unidos do. Iván told him about it. It's called cosplay, he read about it online, on his neighbor's computer in El Salvador. Apparently, there are whole conventions for kids to dress up like their favorite characters from different anime series. We're not really sure what they do once they're together—talk about anime? Reenact their favorite scenes? But Juan Manuel says that according to Iván, anime fans in los Estados Unidos spend hours and hours making their costumes. He says that once he gets out of here, the first convention he goes to, he's going to cosplay as Kaneki Ken by painting his nails black and wearing all black with a white wig. I told him I'll go with him, I just have to figure out who I'll dress up as. Maybe Hideyoshi Nagachika.

I've never thought about dressing up as someone before. I didn't even know that was something people did. But if someone did dress up that way back in Naranjito, especially a boy, I think people would make fun of him and call him a goth.

Anyway, back to Juan Manuel . . . I don't think his isolation is something that started here in Tornillo. We haven't talked a whole lot about our lives back home yet, but I sort of suspect that he's never met a lot of other kids like him. When he's with me, he is always enthusiastic about anime, but I can tell that he used to be embarrassed for liking it so much. It's funny: you can be secretly ashamed of liking something when you think you're the only person in the world who likes it, but as soon as you find someone else who cares about that thing . . . it's like your excitement explodes times ten, and you feel super close to that person. It's like you've shared this secret passion with each other for your whole life, and now you finally get to talk about it.

That's how it is with me and Juan Manuel—it feels like we're making up for lost time.

Love,
D.

JULY 26, 2018
Tornillo

Querida Tía:

Sorry I haven't written in a while. The days keep flying by, and I've been spending so much time getting to know the other boys that by the end of the day, I sometimes don't feel like I need to write. There are twenty of us in here, and every day I end up playing cards or talking to a boy I hadn't interacted with much before. Like today, I played Uno with a boy named Mano. He's from Nicaragua. He has short, curly, black hair, band braces on his teeth. Mano says he doesn't like them, because they tear up the inside of his mouth. He says that when they let him out of here, he hopes the first thing his parents do is take him to get them removed.

Iván keeps trying to get everyone to talk to each other and be friends, but there are still some kids who aren't really talking. I don't know if it's because they're shy or sad or what. There's a boy we call Yarn Master from Guatemala, who's one or two years older than me. He spends most of his time sitting on the floor, playing with some yarn that he somehow attaches to his bed and then ties into knots to make bracelets. It looks like a slow process, but he's laser-focused the whole time. Even if the rest of us are playing cards or checkers or something, he just sits on the floor, silently working. What's crazy is that even though he's working for hours and hours, he probably only makes one bracelet every two days, at most. But the bracelets are beautiful.

Anyway, I really hope that since we haven't changed tents in so long, that really does mean we're here for good. The whole time I was at El Albergue, and the whole time I was here in Tornillo before they transferred me to Alpha 13, I'd completely forgotten what it felt like to belong in a family. But now, here, weirdly, I feel more like a kid than I have in a long time . . . not just since I began traveling north, but since Felipe and you died. It has been years since I have felt like I can just relax and make stupid jokes. I definitely laughed a ton with Miguelito and Elías and Damián, but on the journey north, even though Miguelito and Damián joked constantly, survival was our first priority. It felt like we were playing grown-ups on TV. We had to be serious almost all the time, because when you're trying to jump off a moving train or outrun grown men with guns, you don't always feel like joking. And I loved Roomie at El Albergue, and he had a great sense of humor, but because we didn't have a language in common, it was harder to bond with him.

Here, in Alpha 13, for the first time in a long time, I feel like I can relax, like I can be a kid who's hanging out with other kids. It feels really, really good, and I keep praying that they won't take it away. I've been trying to figure out what makes Alpha 13 different, and really, I think that it's mostly two things. The first one is Juan Manuel: he's like the brother I never had, and I'm so grateful that by the grace of God, we got to meet here. The second one is Iván: I think it's thanks to him that all of us here feel less . . . broken than we felt before. It's like we can come out as who we really are: kids. I've been wondering for a while why he's not like the tíchers in the other tents. I was a little nervous, but today I tried to ask him about it.

"Iván, why are you . . . " I couldn't figure out how to say it. But Iván understood. It felt like he had a speech all ready, like he's been asked this before.

"Why am I different from the other teachers here?"

I nodded.

"So, D. It's hard to be hispano en los Estados Unidos. But our community here is also incredibly strong and resilient and courageous. And I see those qualities in all of you boys. You're all superheroes to me. It's criminal that they've locked you up here." He said a lot about how us kids haven't done anything wrong. (It's so nice to hear someone say that! It feels like it's the opposite all the time.) He also told me how we should be with our families. He said he doesn't work here just as a job, but because he sees himself in all of us. He said he's a migrante, too, from México, and supporting us is important to him. At one point, he said, "I'm here for you, to fight for your rights against the pendejos who run this prison," and that made me laugh, and also smile, because the adults here never use words like *pendejo*.

But what I remember most from that conversation isn't that Iván used a bad word, it was the thing about "our community here." *Here* is los Estados Unidos, and *our* community, I guess, means hispanos (or migrantes?) in los Estados Unidos. In Naranjito, I never really thought about hispanos as a community. In Naranjito, pretty much everyone was hondureño, so it didn't make sense to think of ourselves as a community separate from any other community. The whole pueblo was its own community, obviously, but not in the same way. I guess that here, in los Estados Unidos, hispanos form a community *because* there are lots of other kinds of people around. And Iván is so great to us because he's part of our community, too. If other grown-up gringos in los Estados Unidos treat our community the same way the mostly gringo adults here treat us kids, then I'm worried that even after I get out of here, my future in Nashville isn't going to be as bright as I'd imagined. But then again, if our community is as fun as Alpha 13, and the adults in our community are as kind and loving and supportive as Iván and Nancy and Yuli . . . then I think I have a lot to look forward to.

I want to talk about it more with Iván, though, because I want to make sure I understand what he was talking about. I might've misunderstood. I'll fill you in.

Love,
D.

JULY 29, 2018
Tornillo

Querida Tía:

I've been in Alpha 13 for over four weeks. It's a billion times better than any of the other tents, but that doesn't mean the days here aren't boring and repetitive. Even if we're lucky enough to have kind adults in Alpha 13 who treat us like real human beings, this place is still basically a prison (just like Iván said in the conversation I mentioned in my last letter). Each day is exactly the same as the day before it. There are a few exceptions, though. Occasionally, we do something out of the ordinary, or something from the outside world finds its way into Tornillo. There are two special things on the schedule that we do once a week, and then there's also one weird thing that happens at random times every once in a while.

The first special thing is really nice: On Sundays, there's a worship service where they send some people from a church in another part of Texas, including a priest, to come and lead a service. Or, actually, I don't think he is a priest exactly. He doesn't dress like Padre Juan or any of the other priests back in Honduras, and there's no comunión or anything, but still, we sing songs about Jesús y la Virgen and there's readings from the Biblia. When they read from the Biblia, at least I get to hear stories that way. And singing together with everyone makes us feel close. There's this one song we sing every week, "Sumérgeme," about Jesús healing us after we've been through a lot of suffering. The verses repeat like a million times, so everyone knows all the words, and a lot of the kids get really into it when they sing. The worship service is optional, but everyone goes. Our tent is empty on Sunday mornings. For a lot of the kids, like Gustavo, the service is really meaningful—you see them praying and crying and singing the songs with a lot of emotion. For me, my faith is more of a personal thing: I like being together with everyone as a community for the service, and I pray all the time, but for me, it isn't all Padrenuestros and Avemarías, it's more like a conversation I have with Jesús. It's like a constant conversation, actually. I feel like I'm always talking to him in the back of my mind.

To be honest, my favorite thing about Sundays is that when the service is over, we get to eat pan dulce and conchas and doughnuts. It's probably the only part of the week when things feel normal, like it could be a regular Sunday anywhere, in Honduras or Guatemala or los Estados Unidos or Japón or Francia, where you come together with your community at church to eat pan dulce.

The second special thing that happens twice a week is the chance for us to call our parents. You'd think that would make us happy, but actually, for a lot of kids, it's kind of heartbreaking. For me, too. Let me explain. Once a week, they bring us to a tent where we're allowed to talk on the phone for ten minutes: we can either have one ten-minute call or two five-minute calls. You're in there with a bunch of other boys, and when you look around, about half of them are crying. Sometimes it's tears of joy because they're so happy to be talking to their families, but other kids are crying and panting and looking at the floor, and you can tell that it's too painful for them to speak. It's like they'd almost rather not talk to their families at all.

The tícher who dials the phone isn't one of the tíchers from your tent, it's an adult who you've never seen before, and they stick around for your whole conversation. I know that doesn't matter, because most of the time they don't speak Spanish, and even if they did, they wouldn't care enough about you to really listen. But, still, it makes you feel like you can't speak openly. That's how it makes me feel, anyway, like I can't talk naturally to my parents. We always end up having these weirdly formal conversations: they ask me if I'm okay, and I say yes and tell them they don't need to worry. They keep asking the government why their fingerprints are taking so long to "process," and they can't get anyone to answer. No one will tell them how long it might take. Talking to my parents is really frustrating in a way, because it seems so stupid that we can't see each other even though we're in the same country. It seems stupid that I have to stay here in this weird desert prison for kids, and it seems stupid that they're not allowed to be reunited with their own son. The tícher gives you a ten-second warning when your time is almost up. Then they hang up the phone, even if you were in the middle of saying goodbye. It's a rough experience.

During my first two weeks at this campamento, I was always so depressed after the phone call that I couldn't even write about it. I just wished I could fall asleep and not wake up until it was time to go home. I still feel weird and lonely afterward, but now that I'm in Alpha 13, when I go back to the tent, there's usually something else I can focus on. All the guys in our tent try to keep each other from getting too upset. One of the most important things friends can do is force you to tear your brain away from its saddest thoughts. Iván does a lot to help us too—he's almost like Dory in *Buscando a Nemo*, he always has this, like, unrelentingly positive attitude. Whenever someone's sad after the phone calls, Iván gives a whole pep talk about how strong we are. He says there's "fuerte historia de resiliencia hispana en los Estados Unidos." We don't always totally understand what he's talking about, but he makes us feel better anyway.

The third out-of-the-ordinary thing that happens in Tornillo is the weirdest. And it's the only one that's not on the schedule. We know it's something that isn't supposed to happen, because all the tíchers always freak out about it. Every few days, these flying . . . things show up in the sky. Even though they fly, and they have propellers, they're not airplanes or helicopters. They fly way too close to the ground, just a few meters above the top of the tents, and they're only around half a meter long and half a meter wide. Sometimes only one shows up, but other times there are two or three, and they fly above all the tents. They didn't start showing up until my second or third week in Tornillo, but they've been appearing more frequently as more kids have arrived. If someone spots one while we're walking around the camp—like, between the campo de fútbol and the cafeteria—the tíchers immediately walkie-talkie to each other and tell all the kids to get inside the closest tent, even if it's a tent we never go in, it doesn't matter, they just tell us we can't let the flying things "see us." It's a little scary because the adults all seem threatened by the flying things, but I don't really see how they could hurt us.

One time, Rene and Enrique asked Nancy and Iván what these things are. Iván said it's because this is an important moment in history, so people are sending these flying things to take pictures of Tornillo. He says that the whole world is watching and fighting to get us out of here. Apparently, because of Donel Tromp, there has been a lot of negative feeling and violence toward migrantes, but also a lot of hispanos and aliados trying to defend migrantes like me. I would never doubt anything Iván says, but after the way so many adult gringos have treated me since I crossed the border, it's hard to believe that the "the whole world" is fighting for us. Since getting to los Estados Unidos, it's has seemed like no one will ever notice your suffering unless they are suffering, too.

Maybe I'm wrong. If there's one thing I've learned from Iván, it's that there are exceptions to that rule.

More soon.

Love,
D.

JULY 30, 2018
Tornillo

Querida Tía:

Last night, for the first time since I arrived in Tornillo, someone from my tent left to join his parents.

It was Mano, the boy with braces from Nicaragua. A few days ago, after a phone call with his parents, he seemed to think that he was about to get out, so we were expecting it. Still, since we were getting so close as a tent, it was sad to see him go. Now there's just nineteen of us, and one empty bottom bunk. He's the first one to leave from Alpha 13, but not from camp. Kids have been leaving from other tents, too, and the cafeteria isn't as crowded anymore, so there's more food for us. After this place just kept growing for weeks and weeks, all of a sudden, the total number of kids has started dropping. It never even leveled out: last week they were busing tons of kids in, and this week they've started busing kids out. Iván says it's because Tornillo is a temporary shelter, it's not meant to be permanent. He always tries to keep us clued in on what's going on with our cases and with the camp.

Anyway, back to Mano. They came to get him in the middle of the night. I was awake, just by chance—it was dark, and I was trying to sleep, but when I heard some tíchers come in, I sat up in bed. They told him to gather his stuff and to meet them outside the tent in ten minutes. He asked if he could say goodbye to any of us, and they said no, he shouldn't wake anyone up. That made me so mad—why do they have to whisk us away in the middle of the night? Why do they never let us say goodbye to our friends?

Mano saw that I was awake, and he gave me a goodbye letter and told me to ask Iván to read it to all of Alpha 13 in the morning. He was in a weird state emotionally, and I guess that isn't surprising: and they said he was going to see his family, which is good, but they weren't letting him say goodbye to all of us, which felt like a final slap in the face after all the other things we've had to put up with. Not to mention, you never know when they're lying to you. Weeks ago, when I was leaving La Perrera, they said they were flying me to see my family, but instead they just brought me to El Albergue. So I think Mano was a little nervous, too. He seemed happy and sleepy and nervous and sad all at once. But he wrote a letter as quick as he could, folded it, and gave it to me. He almost didn't have the chance, because Bertha, one of the night tíchers, was shushing us and almost wouldn't let him hand it to me. I wanted to hug him goodbye, but Bertha would have gotten me in trouble—she might have put it on a report, and that might affect my immigration case. She might have even blocked Mano from leaving.

I didn't read the note myself. I wanted to give it to Iván so he could read it to the whole tent at the same time. The next morning, we told him and Nancy and Yuli that Mano was gone. The two of them and Iván really liked Mano, and they seemed bothered that no one gave them a chance to say goodbye, either. Yuli got teary-eyed. All the other boys were a little depressed too. But Yuli told us not to worry. She said Mano is with his family now, just like all of us will be before too long, we just have to stay strong in the meantime.

I think we're all a little bit jealous of him, too. We all hope we don't have too much time left here.

I gave Iván the letter from Mano, and he was surprised to see it. "Should I read it now?" he asked. Everyone nodded. In the letter, Mano thanked God, and thanked us, and said he knows the rest of us will be out of here soon.

* * *

When Iván finished reading, we all sat quietly for a second. Finally, Catracho said: "When the rest of us leave, if we don't have the chance to say goodbye, can we be sure to leave notes like Mano's? I don't want to think about any of us just disappearing."

We all nodded. And I asked Iván if I could take a look at the note, so I could copy it down in my notebook. I guess that it's so I can share it with you . . . but if I'm being honest with myself, I think it's because I'm worried I'm never going to see Mano again, and I want to have his letter preserved somewhere, written down, where I'll always have it.

Love,
D.

AUGUST 2, 2018

Tornillo

Querida Tía:

I've been in Alpha 13 for a long time now, and they still haven't sent me anywhere else or replaced Nancy, Yuli, and Iván. I'd be heartbroken if they made us move to different tents. It would be like losing Miguelito and Elías all over again. Me and Juan Manuel have been swapping clothes—mostly with each other, but also with the other boys. It's something we do a lot in Alpha 13. We all have clothes from different places: some of us got clothes at the albergues we were at before we came to Tornillo, or we have clothes they gave us here. All of it is really simple stuff, none of us have anything fancy. A lot of the other guys have clothes they brought with them from Honduras or Guatemala or wherever they came from. Sometimes, someone else might have pants or a hat or something that looks cool, and he'll trade it for something you've got. Or he'll just give it to you. It's sort of like a sign of friendship. After they take us to shower and get dressed, a lot of us will put on our best new clothes, and every day we'll tweak our outfits so we look as good as we can. At first, I thought it was just something to do to ward off the boredom, but soon I started getting really into finding the best combination of garments to look good, and the other guys give me feedback about which outfits work and which ones don't. We help each other plan what we'll wear the first time we see our families, after they let us out of here. I traded with Raphael to get a blue fabric belt that I want to wear when I finally meet my parents in Nashville.

Most of the boys have started believing (and hoping) they won't change our tent again. I have, too. Getting comfortable is scary. Things could change at any minute, and then we'll regret letting ourselves feel at home here. It would be safer to sit around waiting for them to take everything away from us again. But you can't live like that. I like the other kids here, and I like Iván and Nancy and Yuli, and I want to believe I'll get to stay with them until I leave.

To help us feel at home, Yuli suggested that we decorate the walls with drawings. This one boy from Guatemala, Flaco, has been drawing nonstop to try to cover the walls, and it has really helped Alpha 13 feel like home.

Some of the other boys, Catracho and Chato, also finished a jigsaw puzzle that Iván glued together and put on the wall. Me and Juan Manuel have been drawing scenes from *Naruto* and *Tokyo Ghoul.* We caption them with trademark lines from the show, like "It's my ninja way" and "Believe it!" and "I'm gonna be Hokage!" None of the other boys get it, but we don't care. We just want to make sure we get them up before Flaco claims all the wall space.

I'll let you know if there are any updates.

Love,
D.

AUGUST 8, 2018

Tornillo

Tía:

Another boy, Rene, left last night. He was best friends with Enrique, and now Enrique is pretty sad. But we're also all happy for him, since (we hope, if they're not lying) he gets to be with his family now. I hope I get to leave next, but it's weird, because I'm seeing how sad Enrique is, and it makes me think that Juan Manuel will be that sad if I leave before him. And I'll be that sad if Juan Manuel leaves before me.

* * *

Rene left a beautiful goodbye note too. Maybe I only think the letters are beautiful because I've started caring about writing, but it seems like one of the most . . . happy and sad things. It's like a way of leaving a part of yourself behind. It's not just a way of saying goodbye, though. It's like a way of saying, "Hey, I'm okay now, and all of you are going to be okay soon, too."

Love,
D.

AUGUST 11, 2018

Tornillo

Querida Tía:

Most days, they take us out of the tent for different activities, but on some days, we have to stay in the tent all day, except for when we go to meals, because it's either too hot outside or there's a loud thunderstorm. When that happens, the ground outside the tents gets all wet, and they don't want us tracking mud everywhere. Mud ends up getting all over the place anyway, though.

We spend those days making bracelets.

Yarn Master, the shy boy around my age from Guatemala, makes them with a bunch of different colors, and they look really cool. He never shows them off, but he wears them, and we're all fascinated by them. So before long, me and Juan Manuel and McQueen and a few other boys asked him to show us how to make them ourselves.

He was happy to show us—I think he was grateful to have a way of joining in with the tent that didn't involve too much talking.

Here's how he makes the bracelets: he takes eleven pieces of lana and snaps the ends of them under the cap of the mini sticks of deodorant the tíchers give us here so we don't smell too bad. He puts that closed stick of deodorant under the mattress of an upper bunk and lets the thread dangle under the metal bars that hold up the bed, then he sits on the floor and weaves the eleven stretches of thread together in a specific pattern.

It takes a long time to learn, but Yarn Master has been super patient with all of us. By now, we've all gotten good enough to make basic bracelets without his help. My first one was really simple, but it still took me two days, and I was spending at least three hours a day working on it. It's nice to have something to do. Nearly everyone in the tent spends at least some of the day making bracelets. We try to make letters to spell things or make emojis or other designs. Nancy and Yuli and Iván are glad to have us occupied doing this, and they have been trying to convince the people in charge to buy us more lana, in more colors, so we can make more complicated designs. They keep saying they're bringing us lana that the camp buys, but I think they might be buying it with their own money, because they always get our favorite colors.

We trade our bracelets with each other and wear them wherever we go. When we go to the cafeteria, all the other tents can tell when someone is from Alpha 13 because we have four or five colorful bracelets on our wrists. Me and Juan Manuel made matching green ones. We want to make bracelets based on the theme of one of our favorite animes, but we haven't figured out exactly how yet—and to be honest, we aren't that good yet. It's not a competition, not at all, but everyone tries to make the coolest designs.

Nobody is ever going to do better than Yarn Master, though. He's a master. He knows how to do tricks, like frame the letters on the bracelet with different colors and add extra layers of thread on top of the bracelet. He's also way faster than the rest of us, and sometimes he uses more than eleven lengths of thread—a few days ago I think he was making one with twenty.

A few days ago, Iván was asking about my bracelet, and he seemed kind of curious, so I offered to teach him how, just like Yarn Master taught me. I've been giving him lessons. He stands beside me while I'm working on my bunny rabbit bracelet, and he works on his first one. He really doesn't know what he's doing. It's cute, it's like I'm teaching the tícher. At one point, I told him that the bracelets remind me of the bracelets that you used to wear before you died. Iván asked how you died, and before long, I was telling him my whole life story, from Felipe and you dying up until I arrived in Tornillo. Now, whenever we're working on bracelets, he asks me all kinds of questions about Naranjito and my journey here on La Bestia, and being put in La Hielera with my cousins, and being put in La Perrera without them—all that. He is genuinely interested in my story. And he has been telling me about himself. About his own story of migration from México, and how his parents brought him to el Norte when he was five years old, and even though he has been allowed to stay here for his whole life, he isn't a citizen of los Estados Unidos, and they could still possibly deport him at some point. He says that he has always had an uncertain life in that way, but things have gotten worse lately because of Donel Tromp, and how because of him lots of people in los Estados Unidos don't want to let migrantes in, or even let the migrantes who have already been here for their whole lives stay. Iván is such a good person. He's always so good to us, and I wonder if it's because, like us, he's also living in this sort of middle space.

I'm a talkative person, but I don't usually open up with other people about stuff like how you and Felipe died. When I'm making bracelets, though, somehow the words just come out easier, like I don't even have to think about them. It's like the bracelet occupies the part of my brain that usually stops me from talking about personal stuff, and I can just talk. And with Iván, talking just feels natural, like I'm opening up to an older brother. So that's something else that's nice about the bracelets.

Love,
D.

Here is a picture of some of my favorite yarn bracelets I mastered making! P.S. The emoji one took me forever. *Photo taken by Iván Morales.*

AUGUST 15, 2018
Tornillo

Querida Tía:

Today we got to play fútbol. They always tell us when we're scheduled to play, but the schedule they give us is useless. Nancy reads it off in the morning, but she tells us not to get our hopes up too high about anything it says. Some days, it says we'll get to play fútbol, but instead we'll call our parents. Some days, it says we'll get to call our parents, but instead we go to watch the Buddy movies. I try to start every day fresh, without expecting anything.

I try to focus on being grateful that I'm here with my Alpha 13 family, instead of still in La Perrera, or in one of the sad, other tents here in Tornillo. Now, whenever I see kids from other tents in the cafeteria or at the worship service, I think they seem so dead-eyed. I probably looked like that just a few weeks ago. Whenever I get discouraged because the schedule changed at the last minute and I won't get to talk to Papá or play fútbol, I just talk to Iván or Juan Manuel, and I remember how lucky I am to be in Alpha 13. Being here, with my brothers, is a thousand times better than being alone anywhere else. Just because the kids in the other tents are surrounded by other people, that doesn't mean they aren't alone.

Kids keep leaving, and the good news is that means we get access to the campo de fútbol more, because we don't have to share it as much. Playing fútbol is great—we get to run around and all that. My favorite part is that when we play, they give us cold Gatorades from a cooler. It's hot in Tornillo to start with, but after running around for half an hour or forty-five minutes in our long sleeves, we're drenched in sweat.

Today, on the campo de fútbol, when me and Juan Manuel were grabbing our Gatorades—Iván always saves us the red ones, our favorite flavor—Iván asked Juan Manuel why all of us were dressed "like that."

We asked him, like what?

"In your long-sleeve sweatshirts. I don't get it. This is the desert, it's hot out already, why don't you play in T-shirts?"

"Because we don't want our skin to get darker!" Juan Manuel said.

"All of us wear sweatshirts or jackets when we play," I said, pointing to the rest of Alpha 13.

Iván seemed to think this over. I could tell he had some kind of strong feeling about that. Whenever one of us says something that shocks him, he's always really careful to keep a neutral expression on his face. Which is a dead giveaway because he's really expressive all the rest of the time. The only time he *isn't* expressive is when he's trying not to react negatively.

I started to feel a little funny when he didn't say anything, so I kept talking. "Gustavo doesn't wear one, though. He doesn't care." It's true, which gives him an advantage during the game, because he doesn't get overheated like the rest of us.

Yuli isn't as good as Iván at keeping a straight face. Whenever we play poker with her, she's terrible at bluffing. When she heard me talk about covering our arms in long sleeves, right away, she got a look on her face that seems sad or disappointed. She made eye contact with Iván for a few seconds, then turned back to me and said something like, "D., you have to love your skin. It doesn't matter if you're dark. People in this country actually pay a lot of money to get beautiful tan skin like yours. If you wear that sweater, you'll die of heatstroke. Did you ever wear long sleeves when you played fútbol back home? Por favor, por Dios, take it off."

Then Iván finally spoke. I don't remember what he said word-for-word, but it was something like: "You know how I'm always saying 'juntos somos más fuertes,' D.? You know, how we're stronger together? We need to be proud of the things that we share together. You have the same color skin as your abuela and your tío and you mamá and papá, right? The color of your skin is something you share, and that's beautiful." He paused for a second. "I know I'm proud to have the same color skin as all of you."

Juan Manuel kept his sweatshirt on, but I dropped mine on the ground and went back to the game. Obviously they were right. I was way cooler that way, and that made running around more fun. But I felt weird after having that conversation. I've never thought about the color of my skin like that before. Since getting to los Estados Unidos, at the permanent shelter and here in Tornillo, whenever we've spent a lot of time outside, I've always worn long sleeves. I just started doing it automatically, and so did everyone else. Everyone except for Gustavo, anyway. The only time before this conversation that I'd thought about it was when I noticed Gustavo always wore short sleeves, and I figured it was because he was already so dark that it didn't matter. But Yuli is right. In Naranjito I never wore long sleeves when I played outside.

Later, back in the tent, Juan Manuel asked me what I thought about what Iván and Yuli said. He said he didn't believe Yuli about people paying to get skin like ours. He thinks that their skin is like ours, but all the high-up people's skin is lighter.

From what I can tell, it seems like he's right. Even though the adults

I've seen en el Norte have all different colors of skin, all the most powerful people, like most of the Migra guys and the tíchers' bosses in Tornillo, are super-light-skinned. And besides, Juan Manuel asked me, why would they pay to get darker skin, how would that even work?

I don't know if it helped us understand things any better, but we both laughed a lot when he said that.

Love,
D.

AUGUST 17, 2018
Tornillo

Querida Tía:

I've been working on my rap a lot lately. I keep getting ideas while I'm working on my bracelet, while I'm talking to Iván about my journey. Talking about the trip has reminded me of a lot of things. I have been in survival mode since the first time I jumped onto La Bestia, so I haven't thought very much about what I've been through. But when I started talking about it, I realized that I have experienced a lot for a fourteen-year-old. So I've been trying to incorporate some of those experiences into my rap.

I've also been thinking about what Yuli said, about us wearing long sleeves when we play fútbol so we don't get darker. She's right, it's messed up, but I don't think it's all our fault that we think that way. Ever since I crossed the border, people have been treating me in a way that makes me feel like my life isn't worth as much as lighter-skinned people's. I cover up to avoid getting darker because I don't want to make things even worse for myself. When you turn a kid into a prisoner, and you separate him from his cousins, and you stick him in a room with no chairs or windows for three days, and you don't let him go to the bathroom when he needs to, and all that . . . how do you expect him to act? These aren't really developed thoughts yet, but I've been trying to add some of these ideas into my rap, too, to help me figure out what I think about them.

And I've been thinking about the other boys here, especially Juan Manuel and McQueen. Juan Manuel talks to me all the time, but whenever we talk about his life in El Salvador, he just says he left because of "the gangs," then changes the subject. I don't know what he went through, but I can tell it was bad. And I've been thinking about McQueen, who got separated from his mamá and cries himself to sleep every night. I think about the other kids and parents who were locked up in La Perrera with me for days, where no one ever talked, where we all just sat on the hard floor in silence.

Writing the rap has been like an escape from all the stress. I'm not claustrophobic, but ever since they've started transferring so many kids out of here, I've felt like the walls of the tent are closing tighter every day. It's the opposite of what you'd expect: the fewer kids there are here, the more claustrophobic I feel. But writing has always been like a refuge for me, even before I came to Alpha. It's the place where I feel comfortable. It's a way for me to express myself, even though no one ever reads what I write except for you.

I'll show it to you soon.

Love,
D.

AUGUST 20, 2018

Tornillo

Querida Tía:

Okay, I think I finally feel good enough about the rap to show it to you. But I have to be honest, you're not the first person to see it. Earlier, I was on my bunk writing when Iván walked by and asked me what I was drawing. I draw a lot, and so do some of the other kids in Alpha 13, but at that moment, I was working on my rap. I told him about it, and even though I was shy about it, I asked if he'd like to see it. I was a little nervous to share something I've been working on (I haven't even shown it to Juan Manuel yet), but it always feels so easy to talk to Iván, and I knew he wouldn't judge me or make fun of me. And to be honest, I was curious what someone else would think of it. So I handed over my notebook, and Iván started reading. As of today, here's how the rap looks:

"We Are Immigrants"

We are undocumented immigrants
Not even Donald Trump has found
United we are many and we are
In all states
Some praying
And me rhyming
We are strong
We are independent
Climbing on all the trains
Seeing how cartels
They kidnap people
Freezing breeze and cold rain
On days, only sun, without water, dries your throat
And in some cases to the grave it sends you, in some cases life is a risk and there are times that life takes you on "La Bestia"
Chihuahua and Guadalajara are the bad cities where all immigrants die from bullets
In that road there is betrayal and more come from Immigration, that's why I sing this song
You have to run from Immigration
We are strong and united and our plan is to reach the United States
American dream, we all crave it
But very few of us reach our destination, dying along the way
Elderly and children, we all live the same, we are worth the same life, one organism
We suffer deeply on the way with hunger
So we remain hungry
We get on top of trains
We are poor people but immigrants, all those who come here, nothing stops us

D. Esperanza with "La Paz de Oró"
[Translated from Spanish by Gerardo Iván Morales]

CALADRA

Somos hemigrantes

Somos hemigrantes idocumentados ni
Donal TromP nos a emcontrado
unidos Somos muchos y estamos
en todos los estados unos llorando
y llo rimando somos fuertes somos
idePendientes Subiendo en todos los
trenes ciendo como los carteles
Secuestran ala gente sentiendo
brisa y llubia fria y se cienten
los dias sol sin agua te
reseca la gargganta y en algunos
Casos ala tumba te manda en
algunos casos la vida se griessga
y hay beses qe te lleva la bestia
Chigua gua y guadalajara son las
Siudades males donde todo hemigrante
muere Por las balas en ese camino
hay traicion y mas la son la
emigracion Por eso canto esta
Cancion tienes correr Por emigracion
Somos fuertes y unidos y nuestro
Plan es llegar alos estados
unidos sueño americano todos lo vivimos

CALADRA

Pero muy Pocos llegamos a
nuestro destino muriendo
en el camino ancianos y
niños todos vivimos lo mismo
balemos lo mismo su bida y
organismo como sufrimos en el
camino qe con Hambre así seguimos
con hambre subimos alos trenes.

hay pobres somos los hemigrantes
Pero todos los qe llegan aqui
lla nada nos Para
repartando con la Paz de
oro

Calandra

"Somos inmigrantes," a poem written by me in 2018 dedicated to all immigrants.
Photo taken by Iván Morales.

Iván was reading for a long time. I wasn't sure if I should be watching him or not, so I just sat on the bed, pretending to be really interested in my pillowcase. Presenting someone else with something you've written gives me this weird mix of anxiety and eagerness. I'm proud of what I've written. I think it's pretty good, and when I showed Iván, I really wanted him to like it. But also, I don't know, I'm only fourteen, how good of a writer could I really be? I was worried about how he might react. If he didn't like it, he wouldn't want to hurt my feelings by being critical. But in that case, if he said he did like it, would I even be able to believe him? What if he faked it so he wouldn't hurt my feelings?

The rap is two pages long, and after he finished reading it, he flipped to the first page and read the whole thing again from the beginning. When he looked up, he had tears in his eyes.

"D., this is so beautiful. It's even more beautiful because I know what you've gone through," he said. "You really have a gift for writing. Has anyone ever told you that? You express things so clearly. This rap would resonate with so many immigrants. Like, I'm an immigrant, too, and it really gets me. What prompted you to write this? How long have you been working on it?"

Okay, so I could definitely tell that Iván wasn't faking it. He can't cry on command. He was genuinely moved by my rap. Which felt great—I spent weeks refining it, and that was exactly the effect I was hoping for. I quickly looked around to make sure none of the other kids could see Iván tearing up, because if they did, they might come over to see what was happening, and I still didn't feel ready to share my rap with anyone else.

I thanked him, and I told him a little bit about how writing—and writing to you, especially—helps me to think stuff through. How writing helps me understand things better.

He thanked me again, and talked about how he knew life in Tornillo was hard, and how he can't even imagine how difficult it must have been for me to lose you and Felipe, and now to be separated from Miguelito and Elías and Damián. When he said that, my eyes started getting teary, too. Sometimes, just hearing someone else acknowledging that you're having a hard time can make you cry.

He told me I was brave for writing about my experience and I should keep doing it. "Everyone will want to hear your story. I hope that one day, you'll be able to share your story with the world. You're going to change the world one day, D., I promise."

So, yeah, that was a huge reaction. It's really nice when an adult appreciates you like that. Everything Iván said really encouraged me. I don't know if he's right about me changing the world or anything, but I can tell he really believes in me, and that makes me want to try.

This whole time, I've just been writing letters to you because I miss you, and because it helps me process things, and it keeps my mind busy. I never thought I'd do anything with them. But I wonder if now that I have an archive of what has happened to me, I ought to use them to write something longer, like the books I read at el albergue. Iván was so enthusiastic about my writing that it feels like I ought to at least give it a shot. What do you think?

Love,
D.

Esto qe llo escribo en este cuaderno es
Parà qe conoscan mi istoria lo leeran y
lo Conserbara mi gran amigo esconca.

le agradesco a ustedes tres mis mejores
amigos qe llo tube Iuan, esconca

gracias Por darme apoyo animo Para yo
poder seguir fuerte me isieron reir
y les agradesco Por darme esas risas
llo conte mi istoria de cuando llo me
bine de Honduras Pero saben qe tienen el
Pribilejio de Saber toda mi istoria asiqe
en estos ultimos dias yo boy a estar
escribiendo mi istoria asta donde los
Conosi bueno aca les ba.

CALANDRA
Calandra

"What I write in this journal is for you to get to know my story . . .
I write my story from when I started my journey in Honduras, but
know that you have the privilege to know my entire story."
D. Esperanza's words
Photo by Iván Morales

AUGUST 22, 2018
Tornillo

Querida Tía:

This morning, Nancy, Yuli, and Iván told us all to sit in a circle, because they had to tell us something. Tornillo is closing. Apparently, lots of people in los Estados Unidos are upset about how the government built this place and put a lot of kids here without their parents. It has something to do with the flying things that keep appearing above the tents. I don't really understand the reason, exactly, but that's why they've started busing kids out of here. Yuli says that in the next few weeks, we're all going to get transferred. They'll either send us to our parents or, more likely, they'll send us to another detention center that's somewhere else in the country. They say that the whole immigration system is in chaos, because even though a lot of kids crossed the border with their parents, the government separated them and now they can't find them. And right now there are lots of kids like us in different shelters, and it's making it really difficult for them to reunite us with our families. That really doesn't make any sense to me. I don't understand it. They said some stuff about politics and Donel Tromp, but to be honest, I couldn't follow it. I don't see what any of that has to do with me. Yuli and Iván keep telling us that they're relaying all of the information that they're getting from their bosses, but also, that they can't really guarantee whether it's true or not.

I don't want to leave Alpha 13. For months, the gringo adults everywhere have been telling me, "You are safe here," but this tent is the first place where I have felt safe for real. I was depressed before I came to Alpha 13. It was hard for me to eat, and it felt like some part of myself was starting to fade, like a core part of me was dying. Because this place is a prison. It's a hard feeling to describe, but here, I'm a prisoner. I can't even eat or sleep or shit without permission. I'm treated like a criminal even though I'm a fourteen-year-old kid. If they send me away from here, I won't know what I'll do.

Juan Manuel gave me a sad look. A few of the boys were crying, and everyone looked sad. No one said anything. I didn't cry at the time, because it didn't feel real. I guess I was shocked. But now that I've had a few hours to process it, I feel sort of heartbroken. It's not fair. We're real people. They can't just move us wherever they want, whenever they want, and expect us to go along with it. But what power do we have? We're kids, they're adults. They have a whole government and la Migra and money and trucks, and what do we have? Nothing. Literally the clothes on our backs. It feels like leaving here and being sent to another detention center will be stripping something away. Like when I'm separated from my brothers in Alpha 13, the whole world will fall apart. All of us have been through a whole lot, and all of us miss our families. It feels like our parents' fingerprints will be "processing" forever. A lot of the other kids here probably had even more painful journeys north than I did. La Migra took away McQueen's mamá without giving him any warning, and he still hasn't heard anything about where she is. He probably isn't the only one—he cries at night, and during the day, but so do a lot of the other boys, and not all of them are able to open up about what's wrong. They don't have to. We do the best we can to comfort each other—we say "Todo va a estar bien" and "Ánimo, ya queda poco." We all know that there isn't much else we can do. We're prisoners, we're powerless. We can support each other, and we can pray, and we can sit tight. Like we always say, "Juntos somos más fuertes."

Actually, there's one other thing we can do to feel better. When Iván and Nancy and Yuli gave us the news, we all sat there silently. For a minute, there was just the sound of sniffling. Then Gabriel said, "Iván, can I turn on the radio?"

Iván nodded.

Gabriel scanned for a station that was playing music. Finally, he came to one: it was "Te boté," the version with Bad Bunny. Gabriel's favorite. He turned the radio up as loud as it goes and started dancing. A few seconds later, the other Compadres joined him. And a few seconds after that, all of us were on our feet. No one talked. We just danced and danced and danced, to every song on the radio, until it was time to go to breakfast.

Love,
D.

AUGUST 26, 2018
Tornillo

Querida Tía:

More and more guys have been leaving. Last night, it was Gabriel—Los Compadres won't be the same without him. The tent won't be the same without him. Iván read the note to all of us, just like he did with every goodbye letter that was left behind.

* * *

Whenever someone leaves Alpha 13, eventually they send in more boys from other tents to replace them. If there are five boys left in another tent and five empty beds here, they'll consolidate all of us in here. I guess that's so they don't have to pay as many tíchers. We've been welcoming the new boys, but it's a little different, because we know they won't be here long. None of us will.

When I think about leaving, I get an itchy feeling in my chest, under my heart. I worry that Iván will be fired, and we'll be sent to another tent with the same crappy kind of tícher we had before. I don't want to have other crappy, mean gringo adults in charge of me, I want my big brother, I want Iván. More than anything else, I worry about losing Juan Manuel. In my head, in a way, I feel like I've been taking care of him in the same way I took care of Miguelito. I feel guilty about not knowing where Miguelito is, so every morning, I wake up and check the bunk underneath mine to make sure Juan Manuel wasn't transferred out in the night. Like, at least I can take care of him, keep track of him. Sometimes I even have dreams that they're taking him away, and I wake up sweating and have to squint in the dark to make sure he's still there. He says he does something similar: he'll stare up at the bunk above him and wait till he sees the blankets hanging over the side move, so he knows I'm still sleeping there.

Iván says that at the end of this week, they're going to have a carnival to celebrate the closing of camp. He says there'll be pizza and cotton candy and games, and then we'll get to go to other shelters where we'll have more comfortable beds and privacy and air-conditioning. A few weeks ago, that would have been the answer to all of our prayers: something fun to break up the monotony, and a more comfortable place to live. But now, none of us can really get excited about it. We don't care about being comfortable, we just want to stay together.

Love,
D.

AUGUST 30, 2018—EARLY, EARLY, EARLY MORNING

Outside Tornillo

Querida Tía:

Well, I guess this is it. I'm . . . on a bus.

They woke me up at two or three in the morning. Now they're taking me somewhere else. They wouldn't say if it was to see my parents or to go to another detention center, they just said I needed to meet them outside the tent in ten minutes. But last time I asked, my parents' fingerprints were still "processing," so I wasn't optimistic. I was still half asleep. And nauseated. And scared. And heartbroken. I had been hoping this wouldn't happen, that by some miracle we'd be able to stay together in Alpha 13. I asked the night teacher if I could wake up Juan Manuel to say goodbye—just to Juan Manuel, no one else!—but of course she said no. I thought about waking him up anyway. I felt so guilty about not saying goodbye to Roomie before, I didn't want to repeat that same mistake. But I didn't break the rules once the whole time I was at Tornillo.

I gathered the few things I have as fast as I could—it only took about two minutes. I hadn't thought about what I would write in my goodbye letter. I'd been hoping, stupidly, that I wouldn't have to write one. So I grabbed a piece of pink construction paper I had been planning to draw on and started to write everything that came to mind with a green gel pen, as fast as I could, hoping my handwriting would be readable. I didn't have time to copy it down, but I think I remember it pretty well. It was something like this:

Hi friends,

This isn't how I wanted to say goodbye. But I believe in you guys, and I know you will be okay! I'm so grateful to God for bringing us together. For giving me such good friends, even in a place like this.

Nancy, Yuli, and Iván, it makes me so sad that I can't say goodbye to you, either. I'm grateful to God for giving me the chance to meet three incredible people like you.

Juan Manuel, best friend, hugs and kisses. They won't let me say goodbye.

I love you all,
D. Esperanza

I folded the paper in half, and then on the outside, in big letters, I wrote

Para mis amigos: los kiero mucho.
D.

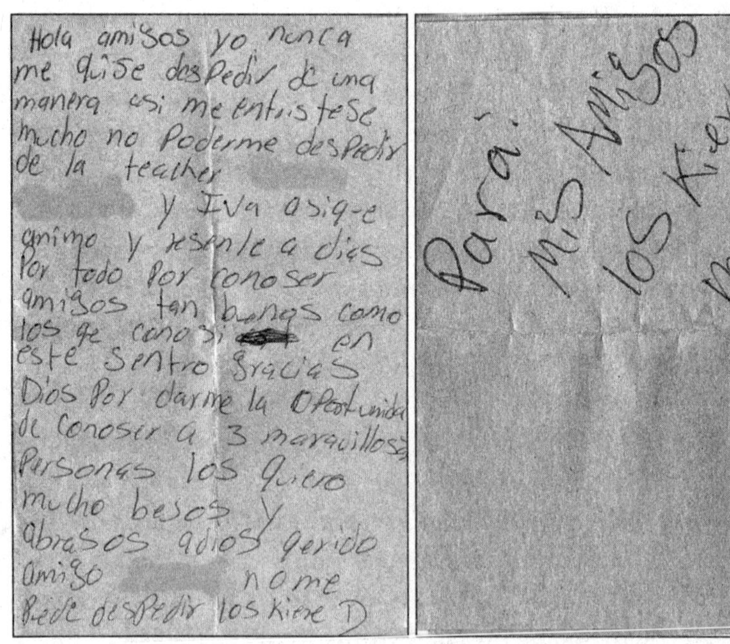

Hola amigos yo nunca
me quise despedir de una
manera asi me entristese
mucho no poderme despedir
de la teacher
y Iva asi que
animo y resenle a dios
por todo por conoser
amigos tan buenos como
los que conosi en
este Sentro gracias
Dios por darme la oportunidad
de conoser a 3 maravillosas
personas los quiero
mucho besos y
abrasos adios querido
amigo no me
puede despedir los kiere D

Para: mis Amigos los kiero mucho. D

"To my friends: I love you so much, D." A photo of my goodbye letter to my brothers in Alpha 13. Written on the only piece of paper I could find In such a short amount of time while I was being rushed out.
Photos taken by Iván Morales.

I left the note on my bed, where they'd know to look for it. I put it underneath a pile of all the bracelets I've made. I left them behind as a goodbye gift to the tent. Taking them with me felt like it would be wrong, somehow.

I was almost finished with the bracelet I've been making, the one I have to keep starting over because the lana always breaks, with the bunny rabbits and the heart. I snapped the ends of the threads into the cap of my mini deodorant, and I stuck the deodorant between the metal bars underneath my mattress so that the unfinished bracelet was all set up for someone to work on it. I left it dangling just a few inches above Juan Manuel's head. It'll be the first thing he sees when he wakes up. I hope he understands.

They took me to the cafeteria tent, where there were seventy, maybe eighty other kids, boys and girls. A lot of kids were rubbing their eyes, either because they were sleepy or because they were crying. Why do they always move us at night? It seems doubly cruel: it makes it impossible for us to say goodbye to our friends, and it throws us into this weird state of confusion. One minute we're dreaming, and the next, some adult we've never met, never seen, is saying, "Get up, get your stuff, and come with me." And we have to follow them. In Naranjito, I knew a lot of the grown-ups in my neighborhood, and we almost never saw outsiders in town. Even then, you and Felipe told me never to go anywhere with a stranger. Here, though, ever since crossing the border, I've just been expected to trust every adult I see. If an adult says "Come with me," I'm required to go with them. It doesn't matter who they are. If I ask who they are or where they're taking me or what's happening, they don't even have to answer.

Once all us kids were sitting down, another tícher, a man I'd never seen before, stood in front of us and started talking in a confusing mix of Spanish and English. His accent was so bad that the Spanish parts were almost harder to understand than the English parts. "Okay, niños, tienen que salir porque Tornillo is closing. Cerrar. Vamos a cerrar. So vamos a transfer you to a centro permanente de el albergue while we keep trying to reunir you with you families. Con tus familias. You'll be safe there. Van en dos autobuses. Cuando you get on the autobuses, decir tu número de cama al tícher so we can asegurar que todos están aquí."

So clearly, Tía, they aren't sending me to my parents. I'm stuck. They're going to keep me trapped, but alone. I have to be alone. I'm going to be alone forever.

I got dizzy when he said all this. It felt like I was sinking into my chair, and I wondered if it was a bad dream. I wondered if all of this has been a bad dream, ever since they took Miguelito and Elías away from me. Ever since I crossed the border. Ever since you died, Tía. I have no family, no friends, no one. Alpha 13 was too good to be true. Maybe that was the part I dreamed up. They could tell I was feeling too good in Alpha 13, that "juntos somos más fuertes," so they're picking us off one by one. They probably aren't even trying to send me to my family. If they were really trying to reunite me with Mamá and Papá, I'd be in Nashville by now. They want to tear us away from our families and from each other. They want us to be alone. They want to leave me without anyone to rely on, without Juan Manuel, without Iván, without Roomie, without Miguelito and Elías. They're going to make us so alone that we don't want to be in this country anymore, so that we beg them to send us back. But even then, they won't do it, they won't send us back, they'll keep us locked up forever. I don't know what they're getting out of this, but they're just going to keep lying. I don't know why they're treating us like this. These adults don't even seem to hate us, they don't seem evil, they just seem bored, tired, like what they're doing is no different from cleaning up cow dung. Just another annoying job. I don't know how they hide what they're doing from their own eyes. They're cruel in a way that's somehow invisible even to themselves, in a way that's invisible to everyone except their victims.

Anyway, it's still dark, it's the middle of the night on whatever road we're on. I'm going to try to sleep on the bus. Maybe I'll dream I'm someplace better.

Love,
D.

AUGUST 30, 2018

Bus

Querida Tía:

I woke up with the sun rising in my eyes. We're still driving. I don't even remember getting on the bus, but here I am. When I look out the window, I see the border wall again, the same one I saw when they drove me to Tornillo. I assume it's the same one, anyway. I guess it could just be a long wall in the desert.

I don't know how long we've been driving. Probably a few hours. My neck hurts from leaning against the window, and I drooled on it a little in my sleep. The other guys in Alpha 13 will probably be waking up soon and see my empty bed. I hope they find my note and the bracelets. Juan Manuel is going to cry. I keep imagining him waking up in the middle of the night and watching the bunk above him, waiting for the blankets to move. How long will he look before he gets out of bed and checks? I guess he'll notice the half-finished bracelet I left for him. I hope that's enough of a goodbye. I know Iván and Nancy and Yuli will take care of him, but we had something special, and now I'll never see him again, just like I'm never going to see Roomie again. I hope—I really hope and pray, and if there are any strings you can pull up there, Tía, I hope you will—that I'll see Miguelito again.

The other guys will be happy for me. First thing when Iván, Nancy, and Yuli show up in the morning, they'll tell Iván that I'm gone, that I'm going home to my parents. Iván will read my note out loud, and even if they'll miss me, the whole tent will be happy, because they'll think it means I'm free. Is this what happened to all the other boys who got sent away? When Mano and Rene and Catracho and Gabriel left, we were happy for them because we thought they went home. But had they actually just been sent to different prisons, far away from Alpha 13? And where—I'm sorry for saying this over and over again, but I can never get it off my mind—where did they send Miguelito and Elías?

I don't know what kind of prison they're sending me to. Maybe it'll be another campamento like Tornillo, or another albergue with air-conditioning and history classes. Or maybe they're sending me back to La Perrera. Maybe there are too many kids coming to los Estados Unidos and there's no room for all of us, so they're just going to drive across the border and dump us in México. Maybe they've decided that they don't want to keep us here, or maybe, even though I don't think I've done anything wrong, Bertha and the other night tíchers didn't think I was behaving well enough, so they reported me and now I'm getting deported. Maybe my parents weren't expecting me, because I didn't tell them I was coming, and there's no room in their life for me right now.

Thinking about this stuff is making my stomach hurt. I'm just going to close my eyes and try to sleep again.

Love,
D.

AUGUST 30, 2018

El Albergue

Querida Tía:

I wasn't even that surprised when I woke up and saw that we were parking at the same albergue where they sent me after La Perrera. The permanent shelter where I met Roomie.

Two women climbed onto the bus.

"Have you all eaten yet?" one of the women asked. It felt like I'd traveled back in time, to the moment I arrived at El Albergue the first time.

Everyone was shy, but a few of the other kids shook their heads.

"All right, let's get you some lunch, then," she said. "When you hear your name, come to the front for your group and bed number."

They gave me a number and led us to the cafeteria. I looked around and everything was the same: same lines, same campo de fútbol, same buildings. In the cafeteria, same rice and beans, same mixed vegetables. The only thing that was different was the faces.

While we were eating, we got the same presentation that they gave when I was here months ago. Possibly from the same woman as before—I don't remember what she looked like, but I remembered that she spoke

Spanish just as well as me. And she sounded just as bored then as she does now:

"Welcome to El Albergue. You are safe here. We are working hard to reunite you with your families . . . "

It was the same. Everything is the same. Except now, without Roomie. I know I should look for him. I know I should be looking for Miguelito and Elías, too, in case they're here. But it's hopeless. When they have us walk in a line between buildings, I look at my feet.

Love,
D.

SEPTEMBER 3, 2018

El Albergue

Querida Tía:

Fourth day here. I think.

I say "I think," because a day in this place is like a year, and that makes it hard to keep track of time.

Wherever we go, whatever we do, I just follow the line. Vamos en fila. We go to the cafeteria, I follow the line, I eat a little. We go to the campo de fútbol, I follow the line, I stand on the touchline. We go to class, I follow the line, I sit at a desk. I don't even know if we're learning history or English or what. I don't care. I remember sitting in a classroom here the first time, when I was so engaged in what the teacher was saying, and I didn't understand why there were kids in the back who weren't paying attention. Now I'm one of those kids.

In this permanent shelter, I have air-conditioning and a comfy bed and a bathroom I only have to share with my new roommate. The food isn't good, but it's better. I should be glad I'm here. When they brought me here the first time, straight from La Perrera, it felt like a dream come true. It was like during Semana Santa in Naranjito, when I'd go fishing and camping with my friends and we wouldn't work a single day. Compared to being held by the agentes de la Migra, that's how good it felt.

But I don't feel anything like that now. It's like I'm not really here.

I'm physically present, obviously, but my brain is still in Tornillo, with my brothers in Alpha 13. By now, the place should be almost completely shut down. More of the guys are probably leaving, either to their families or to other prisons. Some of them might even end up here, but it doesn't matter, because this place is so big that I wouldn't see them.

If I've been keeping track of the days right, today was going to be the day of the carnival.

Not that it matters. Not sure anything does anymore. Sorry, Tía.

Love,
D.

SEPTEMBER . . . 17 OR 20 OR SOMETHING
El Albergue

Querida Tía:

Day sixteen or seventeen here. Or eight or nine or twelve or thirty-seven. My new roommate is quiet. He doesn't seem to want to talk. That works fine. I don't want to talk either. I don't remember his name.

We got to do phone calls today. Papá asked how I was doing. I didn't tell him they sent me back to El Albergue. He would want to know—like, I'm his kid, he wants to know where I am—but I just . . . don't see what difference it makes. Mamá sounded worried. She could tell something was different in my voice. She asked if I was okay, and I just said what I always say, that I'm impatient for the fingerprints to finish processing so I can see them. But whatever. I couldn't think of anything to say besides that, so I pretended the tícher said we were out of time, even though we probably had one or two minutes left.

There are still books here. I've been taking them to bed with me. But it's not like before, the words don't stick in my brain. I run my eyes along the lines until I fall asleep. The good news is that I don't have bad dreams, like I did the first time I was here. I don't have dreams at all, or at least not any that I remember.

Tornillo should be closed by now. Alpha 13 will be empty. They've probably torn down the tent. I wonder what Iván and Nancy and Yuli are going to do. I wish I'd kept a bracelet.

Love,
D.

SEPTEMBER . . .
El Albergue

Querida Tía:

Day eleven, or something.

Every day is the same. I've gotten used to the idea that I could be here for . . . not the rest of my life, but . . . I'm not going to expect anything else. I've stopped expecting. I've stopped fighting, if that makes sense. In Alpha 13, we kept saying juntos somos más fuertes, but we never talked about what that means cuando estamos divididos.

I always thought that giving up would mean everything was over. Like in a video game, if you lose, you go back to the beginning of the level. It felt like if I gave up, I'd somehow end up transported back to Naranjito, working to survive, unloading boxes, taking care of cattle, whatever. Things would go back to the way things were before me and Miguelito left, because we'd have failed to reach el Norte. Either that or I'd lose the video game completely and die: I'd fall off La Bestia, freeze in La Hielera, get beaten to death by a gang or la Migra.

But that isn't how it works. Life isn't like a video game at all. When you fail, when you give up, when you lose, you stay right where you are. Nothing is different. You don't go back to where you were when you started. You don't die. When you give up, the world keeps turning. You just stop watching it turn.

I've stopped caring, stopped trying, stopped watching the world turn. I wish I'd never bothered trying to keep my spirits up. Why did I lie awake crying all those nights? It didn't make me any less lonely. Why did I keep hoping, every day, that they'd let me go to Nashville? It didn't matter how hard I hoped. I'm still here.

Because caring doesn't make a difference. If you recorded a video of me the first time I was here at El Albergue and you recorded another video of me today, it would look exactly the same. I don't waste my time wishing for anything different. I could wish I lived on the moon, but that wouldn't make it any more realistic.

Maybe the videos wouldn't be exactly identical. A few things have been different ever since I decided to give up. I don't try to win at fútbol anymore, I just stand on the field and watch. I eat less. I take a book to bed, but I don't remember anything. I don't talk to the other boys very much, and they don't talk to me. Were they this quiet the first time I was here? Probably. When you give up, you suddenly realize how many of the people around you have given up, too.

I talked to Papá again today. I didn't try to sound enthusiastic for him, either. He said I sounded strange and asked if anything was wrong, but I said I was fine. They're still feeding me three meals a day, Papá. The other boys are nice, Papá. You don't have to worry about me, Papá.

I wish I could've said: I love you, Papá. I miss you, Papá. When will you get me out of here, Papá?

And that's all true. But I don't have it in me.

The closest I managed to say was: I'm safe here, Papá.

I don't like myself when I'm this way, Tía.

Love,
D.

SEPTEMBER . . . 20, 2018, I THINK

Bus

Querida Tía:

Time for another transfer. Three-ish weeks here, I think, and now I'm off to someplace else. I guess I haven't completely given up hope, because when they woke me up in the middle of the night, I asked if I was finally going to my family. The tícher said she didn't know, but later, sitting on the floor of the gym with a few dozen other boys, they told us we were being transferred to another center. "More kids are coming," the man in charge told us before we got on the buses. "To make space for those who are arriving, we're going to transfer you to another one of our shelters."

I felt dumb for thinking I might see my parents. After I'd just decided I wasn't going to care anymore. Stupid.

At least this time I didn't feel as bad about leaving without saying goodbye to my roommate. Still, there's a kind of sadness in leaving. At least things were predictable here. At least I'd gotten used to it.

The transfers are like climbing on top of La Bestia. The first few times, it was scary and exhilarating and uncertain, but I've gotten pretty good at it by now. A few hours ago, as soon as I heard someone's voice in the middle of the night, before I even opened my eyes, I knew it meant they were shipping me someplace else. But just because I've gotten used to it, that doesn't mean it's any less brutal.

I should really be getting used to sitting on these buses. Fabric seats that recline, red emergency-exit levers, TVs they never turn on, a bathroom that's cramped and smelly but still way better than the Tornillo porta-potties. Border walls just on the other side of the window.

There is something I'm worried about. I've stopped caring—and I've stopped caring for real, I swear. I don't give a shit anymore—but that doesn't mean I have no survival instincts. I'm a little scared that they're just going to abandon us here, in the desert. Like, they won't even bother dropping us on the other side of the border in Juárez, they'll just get rid of us. They said they need to make space for "more kids," but how does sending us to fill different beds someplace else increase the total number of beds? Maybe they figure they gathered all the kids whose parents don't want them and they're just going to ditch us somewhere. Because there's something I still don't understand: why is it so hard for them to send me to my parents? It's not like I have no family in the country and they have to find someone to adopt me. My parents are here, in los Estados Unidos. I talk to them on the phone. Why can't Papá just come pick me up in his truck? When I ask, he says they're trying. He says the lady on the phone keeps telling him that there's nothing they can do. And they don't know who else they can talk to, because they're scared of getting deported themselves. Apparently stuff about migrantes is on TV and the radio all the time now, for the same reasons Iván always mentioned, the Donel Tromp stuff, and they're nervous that if they try to challenge the government to get me released, they might just make things worse, both for themselves and for me.

I don't think this is really going to happen. I don't think these tíchers would do something that cruel. At worst, I think they'll make us all go back to México. But still, I can't totally shake the thought. And I don't exactly like the idea of being abandoned in Juárez with no money and no cousins, either. But I'm trying to stick to my plan: Don't fight for anything, don't hope for anything. This is my life now. I'll just take things as they come.

Love,
D.

STILL SEPTEMBER 20, 2018, I THINK

Bus, but . . . parked in . . .

Tía:

So, holy crap. I don't know what's going on. We're back in Tornillo? They parked the bus and we've just been sitting here for like twenty minutes. I'm so confused. They said they were shutting Tornillo down, but it isn't shut down at all, it's actually way bigger than it was when I left. When the bus pulled in, there were dozens of new tents in areas that were just empty lots when I left. And there are tons of workers and pickup trucks and other vehicles all over the place, and they're putting up tents and hauling around materials, and there are lots of staff walking around in neon-green and orange and blue shirts that they never wore when I was here just a few weeks ago.

I have no idea what's happening. Did they lie to us? Were they ever planning on closing it? Or were they just trying to mess with our heads somehow by saying that?

Obviously, I'm thinking about Alpha 13. My heart literally starts to beat faster when I think about possibly going back. Will everyone still be there? Will anyone still be there? So many guys had already left by the time I left, I'd assumed more and more left until Tornillo closed. But maybe they decided not to shut the detention center down just after I left, and they didn't make anyone else leave? What if Juan Manuel is still here? Even if he isn't, if the campamento is still open, then Iván and Nancy and Yuli must still be working here, right? If I could be back in Alpha 13, even for just a few days, see my friends, my brothers . . . everything would be different. I've been praying: *Dios, María, Jesús, quién sea, that's all I want, por favor, let me go back, let me see Iván and Juan Manuel again, I didn't even have the chance to say goodbye. If I can go back there, I'll be able to survive for as long as I'm here. I can't go back to that loneliness again, I can't. Juntos somos más fuertes, por favor, permítenos volver a estar juntos.*

So much for not caring.

D.

STILL SEPTEMBER 20, 2018—NIGHTTIME
Tornillo

Querida Tía:

Okay, today was . . . long. There's a lot to catch you up on.

After we got here, when they finally let us off the bus, a tícher led us en fila to the biggest tent. But as we walk across the grounds, everything was chaos. This place is a mess. There are half-built tents and piles of trash everywhere. When we walked through the camp, tíchers were yelling instructions to each other instead of using their walkie-talkies like they did when I was here before. And the porta-potties are back, but they aren't right outside the tents anymore, they're all over the place, they're just in random spots throughout the camp. Some of them are wrapped up in yellow tape. I saw one tipped on its side. I hate to think how that happened. There are bathroom trailers, too, por suerte.

They didn't take me to the same tent as they did the first time I was here, it was a new one. The sun had set by the time they gave us our orientation meeting. They told us to sit in plastic chairs and gave us yellow Gatorade in plastic cups. Then a woman started talking to us in Spanish.

"Welcome to Tornillo. This is a temporary overflow facility where we will keep you safe as the government attempts to reunite you with your sponsors. Each of you will be assigned a tent and bed number. There will be three adult teachers in your tent at all times . . . "

It was the same speech as before. She didn't say anything about how this prison was supposed to be closed, how there were just a few hundred kids left by the time they took me to El Albergue.

But the good news—what seemed at the time to be the great news, the spectacular news—was that when they gave out tent assignments, they sent me right back where I belonged: Alpha 13, bed number 12. A safe haven in a prison.

I wanted to sprint to the tent, but I had to let the tícher lead me, even though I knew exactly where to run.

Finally, we got to Alpha 13. As soon as they opened the door, I looked straight toward the bunk I shared with Juan Manuel. He was lying in bed. He rolled over and looked up when he heard us coming in. He saw me, blinked a few times, and crinkled his eyebrows. It was as if he was seeing some kind of an illusion, like now it wasn't just the adults but also his eyes that were lying to him, like he expected me to vanish into a puff of smoke.

I ran over to our bunk and grabbed him by the shoulders and yelled, "Juan Manuel!"

He blinked one more time, then jumped out of bed and hugged me hard. We pulled back to try to talk, but before I could get a word out, he pulled me into the hug again. We stayed like that, holding each other tight until each of us was sure the other one was real. We knew we weren't supposed to be hugging, but we didn't care.

Finally, when we let go, we started to talk.

Behind him, I could see Gustavo. So I knew he was still here, too. He saw that I was back, and I could tell he wanted to say hi, but he was giving me and Juan Manuel a second together first.

Our conversation went something like this:

JUAN MANUEL: What are you doing here? I thought you were in Nashville! They didn't send you to your family?

ME: No, they just took me back to the same albergue, the one I came from before they sent me here . . . before they sent me here the first time.

JUAN MANUEL: You mean you didn't see your parents at all? Why not?

(*He started tearing up a little. I could tell he was having the same thought that I did when they sent me back to El Albergue:*

What if no one has ever been reunited with their families, what if it's all a lie?)

ME: I don't know . . . But, wait, what happened here? Why didn't they close the camp?

JUAN MANUEL: It was crazy. The campamento kept getting smaller and smaller, and they were taking down the tents and everything. Iván kept trying to tell us that it was going to be okay, that there was a good chance we'd get to see our families and, if not, they'd send us to nicer shelters where we could take classes and have normal bathrooms and stuff.

ME: But that didn't happen?

It turns out that no, it didn't happen. They had the carnival and everything, but the next day, Nancy told them that the people in charge of the camp had changed their minds. Juan Manuel said it had something to do with the Donel Tromp stuff and the flying things we'd been seeing. Instead, they started putting up way more tents, and thousands of kids kept coming in, with more buses full of kids showing up every day.

I was about to ask which other boys from Alpha 13 got sent away and if anyone besides me had come back, but just then, a redheaded teacher who I'd never seen before came up beside us. She was standing next to the same kid I was sitting next to on the bus, Tigre.

"*English english*, D. Esperanza?" she said. She's speaking English, but as slowly as possible so I can understand.

I said yes, I'm D. Esperanza.

"*English english* mistake, I'm sorry. You were *english english english* Alpha 11, but because you were here before *english english english english* we sent *english english*. *English english* assigned *english english*. Come with me."

I looked at Juan Manuel. Then I looked at Tigre. I don't think either of them understood her better than I did. But clearly, I was supposed to follow her. I didn't want to leave yet. I wished Iván were around to help me figure out what was happening, but it was after dinner, so there was no one in the tent except the night tíchers, and they've never been helpful.

"I'll see you in a minute," I said to Juan Manuel. Then I followed the tícher out of the tent. She took me two tents away, to Alpha 11. It looked exactly like Alpha 13, except without all the drawings and posters and completed puzzles on the walls. There they were just plain, khaki-colored tent walls. And the boys all looked way sadder, but that was normal, everyone who isn't in Alpha 13 always looks sad. Or, maybe not sad, but dead-eyed. It looked like they felt the same way I felt in El Albergue. The tícher tapped an empty bottom bunk with her hand, then she started walking away. The bad feeling in my chest began to get worse, it almost made me feel heavier, like the middle of my body was weighing me down. I asked her what was going on, so she called over one of the Alpha 11 night tíchers to translate. His Spanish wasn't very good either, but it was decent enough for me to understand.

"She says this is your bed assignment," he said.

I explained that when I got to Tornillo, they assigned me to Alpha 13, bunk 12. My bed.

He turned to the first tícher and said a bunch of stuff I couldn't understand. The only words I could make out were *Alpha 13*.

"Okay," the night tícher said to me, switching to Spanish. "She says there was a mix-up. They sent you to Alpha Thirteen by mistake because that's where you were before. But another boy has your bed now. Welcome to Alpha Eleven."

Both of them walked away: the first tícher exited the tent and went back to wherever she came from, and the night tícher went back to the other end of the tent. I gripped the pole holding up the nearest bunk and tried to breathe. I told myself it's going to be okay. I could spend the night there. Then tomorrow, when Iván showed up, Juan Manuel would tell him I was there but that they took me away, and I'd disappeared, and then Iván would tell them to transfer me back to Alpha 13. Everything was going to be fine. I'd spent the past two weeks away from Alpha 13. I could handle one night in another tent. And it was an Alpha tent, too, just two rows away from Juan Manuel. I figured that I might even see him at breakfast, before Iván got me transferred back.

I sat on my bunk for about half an hour, trying to calm down and process everything that had just happened. Part of me was tempted to go back to not giving a crap, to act like nothing mattered, but I didn't want to. It was just going to be a small delay. I told myself that tomorrow, Iván would fix it. I knew he would. I tried to keep feeling the flood of joy I'd felt, because really, I was still going to be back with Juan Manuel, I just had to have a little patience first. I had to remember it was a miracle that there was even an Alpha 13 for me to come back to.

I was just about to go to sleep when the same redheaded tícher who made me move came back into the tent. Immediately, I perked up. Maybe I wouldn't even have to wait until the morning. Maybe they'd bring me back to Alpha 13 right away. Juan Manuel might have explained the situation to the night tíchers. Maybe the night tíchers had gotten nicer and started caring, and they'd asked for me to be transferred back. It was hard to imagine, but it could happen.

The tícher seemed annoyed to be back. She walked right up to me and called for the same night tícher to come back and translate again.

"*English english english english.* We weren't *english* to *english* him *english* tent *english english english. English english english english*?"

The night tícher turned to me and explained in Spanish: "She says she made a mistake about making a mistake, you weren't supposed to be in this tent after all. So grab your stuff and follow her." He saw me grinning wide, and he seemed to think all of this was a little bit funny. I wondered what was going through his head. "That's the attitude," he said.

I followed the redheaded tícher out of the tent, turned left, and headed toward Alpha 13. I knew where I was going, and I wanted to catch up with Juan Manuel a little more before silent hours, so I was walking pretty quickly. It wasn't a long walk. Maybe thirty seconds. When I got to the door to Alpha 13, the tícher stopped me.

"Oh, no," she said. "*English english.*" She gestured for me to keep walking.

"Alpha Thirteen," I said. I even said *thirteen* in English.

"No," she said. "*English english english.*" Whatever she said, she said it sharply—not in a mean way, exactly, but in a way that seemed to say, *Look, kid, I'm tired, it's the end of the day, and I can't keep finding someone to translate just because you don't speak English.*

I figured it was my fault for not paying attention in class the whole time we were in El Albergue. Maybe if I had, I'd have been able to understand her. Still, when she said no, the horrible feeling in my chest came back twice as strong as it had been before. I should've known it was too good to be true.

We walked right past Alpha 13 and all the other Alphas until we got to the paved road where the buses come in. There were a few big trucks parked here. The tícher walked so fast that I had to hurry to keep up with her. She had been muttering something for a few minutes. We turned right, walked a little, then turned left into the Bravo section. I'd never been here before. We passed row after row of tents. This section of camp is huge—there are at least twice as many tents here as there are in Alpha. Eventually, she stopped at one of the tents—this tent, the one I'm writing to you from—and opened the door.

"Bravo Forty-two," she said. I understood what she was saying. I went inside. It was already quiet in there, I guess silent hours had started. A night tícher in the tent was expecting me, and without saying anything, she showed me which bunk was mine.

It feels sort of cruel, how I keep expecting things to be okay, or even to get better, and then they just keep getting worse. But I'm not going to go back to not giving a crap, it'll be okay. Just because I'm a lot farther away from Alpha 13 now, that doesn't change anything. Tomorrow, Juan Manuel will still tell Iván that I'm here, and Iván will still get me transferred back. For now, I just have to close my eyes and try to sleep. Tomorrow I'll be back with my friends. Tomorrow will be better.

Love,
D.

SEPTEMBER 21, 2018—SUPER, SUPER EARLY IN THE MORNING, LIKE 1 A.M. OR SOMETHING

Tornillo

Querida Tía:

I don't know how long I'd been asleep, but it felt like it had been around an hour, when I heard a voice right by my ear. Someone was waking me up again. For the second night in a row. Even though last night feels like it was months ago.

By now, I know what getting woken up in the middle of the night means: they were going to put me on a bus. But the day after I got there? Why did they bother bringing me back to Tornillo at all? I didn't want to leave. I didn't want them to take me to El Albergue or anyplace else. I wanted to stay there and go back to Alpha 13 with Juan Manuel and Iván. I didn't think they were waking me up to finally send me to Nashville. At this point, I'm pretty sure they're never sending me to Nashville. I'm pretty sure that they really never send anyone to their families. They say they do, but really, they just move us around from prison to prison.

Even if they were sending me home right away, I wouldn't have wanted to go—not immediately, anyway, not until I had the chance to give Juan Manuel a real goodbye. I'm sick of being torn away from people without getting to say goodbye.

I expected this tícher to tell me to get my stuff together and meet him outside in five minutes so I could get on the bus.

"Get your stuff together," he said in Spanish, whispering so he wouldn't wake the other kids up, "and meet me outside in five minutes so I can take you to Charlie Camp."

He stepped outside, and even though I was still half asleep, I tried to make sense of what was happening. They were sending me to another tent again? Four tents in one day? But still not back to Alpha 13?

It took less than five minutes for me to gather my things, so I hurried outside to ask this tícher what was going on. A few weeks earlier, I wouldn't have even dared to ask a tícher other than Iván, Yuli, or Nancy a question like that. Most questions seem to annoy them, and I didn't want to get on their bad side and end up getting deported.

But I'm starting to feel like . . . like my instinct to not give a crap is coming back. So at that point, part of me was thinking, *Screw it, I don't even care if he reports me.*

Honestly, this tícher didn't look that much older than Gabriel. I wondered if he was still in school. He had skin like mine and he spoke good Spanish, and one of his ears was pierced. When I asked him what was going on, he didn't get mad.

"I don't know what's going on, Bed Eight, I just know they told me to take you to Charlie Twenty-five."

I'm sick of being called by my bed number. Before I got to Alpha 13 and met Iván, I didn't think about it much—I didn't like it, but whatever, it was the least of my worries. But ever since they transferred me out, I feel so upset whenever I hear it. I'm a person. I might be a migrante and I might be a kid, but I'm still a person. People have names, not numbers.

I asked the tícher if Charlie 25 was closer to Alpha 13. There weren't any Charlie tents the last time I was here. They must've built them in the past few weeks. He said that it wasn't. That it was actually in the opposite direction.

We turned left and walked down the same road the buses arrive on. Before long, we got to another, new block of tents and turned left.

"They keep sending me to new tents," I said. "This is the fourth one I've been in tonight. And I was in Tornillo before, two weeks ago, and they sent me away, but then brought me back. Why can't I just stay in the first tent?"

He rolled his eyes when I said this, but I don't think he was rolling them at me. It was like he was upset at someone else.

"Don't worry, there'll be new games and kids for you to play with in your new tent. And they're working real hard to find your family. You'll be totally safe and taken care of in Charlie Camp until then, though, don't worry."

We got to Charlie 25. He opened the door, and inside, one of the night tíchers was waiting to show me where I'd sleep. She held her finger over her lips to remind me to be quiet, as if I didn't know how this worked by now.

There's a little moonlight coming in, so I wanted to write to you now, even though it's the middle of the night. Or, honestly, I'm not even really trying to write to you. Sorry, Tía. I just wanted to write all this down so tomorrow I'll remember what happened. Otherwise, I might think it was a dream. A bad one.

Love,
D.

SEPTEMBER 21, 2018

Tornillo

Querida Tía:

When I woke up here, in Charlie 25, it felt, for a second, like I was in Alpha 13. I'm on the top bunk again, and of course the beds and the tents are all the same. It smells the same, too, like dirt and sweat. But a few seconds after I woke up, I remembered where I am when I saw that there are no drawings or posters on the walls here.

For the first time since they sent me back to Tornillo, I feel a different kind of sadness from the lonely way I felt in Tornillo before they put me in Alpha 13, and it's different from the feeling of being separated from Miguelito and Elías in La Perrera, or the feeling of losing you and Felipe.

It's a kind of sadness I haven't felt since I was a little kid. It reminds me of when Cami went to los Estados Unidos, and she kept having experiences without me, making memories I wouldn't be a part of.

This is that same feeling. I kept thinking that the whole time I was in El Albergue, Juan Manuel and Iván and Nancy and Yuli and Raphael and Gustavo and Enrique and . . . everyone was still together, keeping each other strong. They were stuck in this prison camp, but they had the magic of Alpha 13 to get them through. I wasn't part of that magic anymore.

It makes me doubly sad when I think that me being gone made things worse for Juan Manuel. He doesn't have any other close friends in Alpha 13, or at least he didn't when I left. Everyone was nice to him, but nobody else really knew how to make him laugh or distract him from his sad thoughts about El Salvador. I know he understood why I left—why I was forced to leave—but he still probably felt abandoned, or at least lonely. It reminds me of how I felt lonely in Naranjito without Mamá and Papá around, even though I understood why they were gone and I didn't blame them at all. It felt like I'd done something worse, like I just left Juan Manuel without even saying goodbye, the same as I did to Roomie. It's something I felt guilty about the whole time I was in El Albergue.

Anyway, thanks for listening.

Love,
D.

STILL SEPTEMBER 21, 2018

Tornillo

Querida Tía:

Okay, just got back to Charlie 25 after lunch. I'm feeling okay about things right now. I think I'll be able to fix things. This morning, I asked one of the tíchers to let me talk to Iván. I was a little nervous, but at this point I still feel like I have nothing to lose anymore. I knew that in any case, Juan Manuel would tell Iván that I'm back as soon as he saw him this morning. But I was too restless to just sit around waiting. I went up to one of the tíchers in the tent who looked like she spoke Spanish. She didn't seem too busy, she was just staring into space. I asked if I could talk to Iván.

She looked distracted while I was talking to her, but she responded in Spanish.

"Why, did you leave a bag or something? Who did you say you want to talk to?"

"Iván Morales? He's one of the daytime tíchers in Alpha Thirteen."

"You came from an Alpha? Umm . . . no, I can't talk to 'em. That's a whole other company. They're on a different payroll, so all I can do is send it up the chain."

I didn't know what she meant about "a whole other company" or "up the chain," but she had gone back to staring into space, so I figured that meant she wanted me to leave her alone. I went back to my bunk. I was pretty bummed at that point, but things were about to get better.

All morning, I followed Charlie 25's schedule. It was almost exactly the same as the schedule we followed in Alpha 13, except everything happened in different places. There's a Charlie cafeteria tent and a Charlie phone-call tent and Charlie toilet trailers and Charlie showers. The only space that's shared across the whole detention center is the campo de fútbol. There's only one of those.

After lunch, they took us for our bathroom break. When I was walking out of the toilet trailer, I spotted Iván walking fast through Charlie Camp.

"Iván!" I called out. A few kids and tíchers looked up, because even though you hear tíchers and staff yelling to each other all the time, you almost never hear a kid raising their voice. I guess in theory it could have gotten me in trouble, but I didn't want to miss the chance to flag him down.

He saw me and retraced his steps so we could talk.

"D.! It's so great to see you! I was just looking for you. I've been trying to figure out where they sent you all morning. How are you holding up? Are you all right?"

I told him, as quickly as I could, about being sent back to El Albergue, then back to Alpha 13, only to have them transfer me three times last night. I tried to explain how weird I've felt since I got here, when I found out that Tornillo never closed. And how I felt when they wouldn't let me stay in our tent.

He told me how sorry he was, then said something like: "But remember, you're strong, and you can overcome any challenge. You made it this far, right? Nancy, Yuli, and I are here for you. Juntos somos más fuertes, right? I'm going to talk to the case managers to see if we can get you transferred back to Alpha Thirteen. And I'll tell them to send a clinician to your tent. When they talk to you, you should tell them about how you've been feeling and how you want to move back to Alpha Thirteen. Okay? Juan Manuel really wants you to come back. All of us do."

Then they took me back to my tent, and I've been waiting for this clinician to come see me. I don't really know what a clinician is, but I can't wait to talk to one.

Love,
D.

STILL SEPTEMBER 21, 2018

Tornillo

Querida Tía:

I still don't really know what a "clinician" is, but I just talked to one. She was a nice woman who spoke Spanish with a weird accent—she must be from somewhere in South America or something. I told her about how I used to be in Alpha 13, and how I'm really sad without Juan Manuel. She smiled and said she's already spoken to Juan Manuel and that he's really sad without me, too. She says it's hard for him to know that I'm in Tornillo but we still can't see each other.

"Okay, I'm going to put in a request for you to be transferred," she said.

"Does that mean I can go back?"

"Soon, yes. We just have to wait for case management and the contractor to clear it. There's paperwork. They'll come get you when it's time."

"When will that happen?"

"Probably today, maybe tomorrow. It should be pretty easy."

Tía, I'm so relieved I could cry.

Love,
D.

SEPTEMBER 23, 2018

Tornillo

Querida Tía:

I still haven't been transferred. So, it'll be sometime today. I kept looking up at the tent door all day yesterday waiting for someone to come in and take me, which just made the day last forever.

I'm so glad I'm getting out. It sucks here. The kids are all sad, and no one ever talks or plays cards. I want to make bracelets to pass the time, but I'm too embarrassed because no one else here makes them. It's impossible to imagine all the boys in this tent dancing to Bad Bunny like Gabriel would get us to do in Alpha 13. When we're in the tent—which is still around three quarters of the day—most of the guys either sleep or lie awake in their bunks. I've been doing the same thing. At most, I'll draw some anime characters.

It's Sunday, so we had the option to go to the worship service. It was way different from the way it was before: the people and priest-type guy from the church weren't here this time. There wasn't anyone from outside Tornillo at all. Kids did everything: they read from the Bible and sang songs, and the words to the songs were projected onto a screen so everyone could sing along. There was even a boy playing guitar, and I wondered where he got it. The service was way better than it used to be. It felt more genuine. It was clear that kids got to pick the songs, because it was all our favorite worship music. Before, I mostly looked forward to the Sunday service because we got pan dulce at the end. Today, though, I felt like the service matched my real experience. It was more the way I liked to pray: not with like formal Avemarías or whatever, but just a conversation con Dios . . . I was glad that there was still pan dulce, though, bendito sea Dios.

At first, it seemed like there were no adults involved in the service at all. But after a few minutes, I noticed a tícher telling kids when to go to the front, changing the songs that were projected onto the screen, and doing other stuff to keep the service going . . . and that tícher was Iván. I had no idea what he was doing at the service. How did he end up running it? Tíchers never do anything besides watch their tents. So much has changed, which is weird, because nothing ever changes in Tornillo, except the kids in your tent.

While we ate pan dulce at the end of the serviec, everyone had time to talk. I spotted Iván across the tent.

"Iván, hey!" I called out. He heard me and walked over.

"D., how's it going?"

I had a lot to say about how it was going, but first I needed to ask why the church service had changed, and what happened to the priest that used to come.

"Oh, D., so much changed while you were gone."

When Iván said that, it stirred up that same sad feeling of missing out that I was describing before. "So, there have been a lot of protesters, and . . . well, long story short, the church stopped coming."

I wasn't expecting that to be the answer. It's true that when I was here before, Iván was always talking about how this is a moment in history or whatever, but I never totally understood what he meant. Still don't. I guess I'm glad the church wants the government to let us out of here? But taking away our worship service doesn't hurt the government, it just hurts us.

I think Iván could tell I was having trouble figuring out what to say, so he kept talking.

"Anyway, I knew how important the Sunday morning service was to all of you, so I asked the people in charge if I could take over. I started organizing a child-led service. What did you think of it?"

I was still processing everything Iván had said about protesters, and it took me a second to find the right words. I told him that I loved it, because the music was way better, and we still got to have pan dulce at the end.

"Okay, so," Iván said, changing the subject. "I talked to a case manager, and they said they're going to transfer you back to Alpha Thirteen. I asked them to send a clinician to talk to you, since that's also part of the process. Did she come?"

"Yeah, yesterday I talked to a lady with a weird accent, and she told me she'd get me sent back. I thought they were going to move me last night, since it feels like they always move us at night, but they didn't. I guess they'll do it tonight? I'm really excited to be back in Alpha Thirteen. It's depressing in Charlie Twenty-five."

He said he always admired my positive attitude, and told me he didn't want me to ever change. Standing there with Iván, I felt supported in a way that felt familiar, and it took me a second to realize that he was reminding me of Elías, when he kept encouraging me on our whole trip from Quetzaltenango all the way to the border. I'm still so worried about Elías and Miguelito—they weren't at El Albergue, and there's been no sign of them anywhere, and my parents have no idea where they are—but it's comforting to have another big-brother-type person again, this time in the form of Iván.

So now I just have to wait for them to transfer me. I know I'm still at this child prison or whatever, and it's true I can't wait to be in Nashville, but . . . things could be worse.

Love,
D.

SEPTEMBER 29, 2018

Tornillo

Querida Tía:

I've been back in Tornillo for about a week. I'm still in Charlie 25.

Iván always says to stay positive. But what is there to be positive about if I have no one to rely on? The only people around here I can really count on are in Alpha 13, way far way.

Felipe always said "Paso a paso se va lejos." But what's the next paso, Tío Felipe? If every day is the same, and you have absolutely no tools to help you change anything, what's the step forward you're supposed to take?

No, in Charlie 25, in Tornillo, in this country, if you're a migrante kid, there's no stepping forward and no stepping backward. They keep you pinned where you are. We have no control. We are controlled.

And I don't even think they're trying to hurt us, exactly. They do it because that's just how this system is built. They do it because that's how it's done here. They've created this prison camp where all of us are constantly told: you're a criminal, you're a pain in the ass, you don't matter. They don't say it out loud, but stay locked up here long enough, and you get the message, loud and clear.

Even after they tore me away from my cousins and made me abandon Roomie, eventually I *still* lucked into a way to survive because I found Alpha 13, where Iván got me talking to Juan Manuel and all the other boys. We became a family. I was surrounded by people who treated me like I mattered. In Alpha 13, it felt like even in detention, my life was worth something.

But of course, that couldn't last, they had to ship me off somewhere else, tell me Tornillo was closing, make me abandon Alpha 13 without even saying goodbye.

And then, by some absolute miracle, they sent me back to this camp *that wasn't even supposed to exist anymore* and assigned me to my *exact same bunk* above *the best friend I ever had.* And for a few minutes, it felt like the answer to my prayers, like all my dreams had come true, like the world was a magical place. Then, just when that teeny sniff of friendship was getting my spirits up, they plucked me out of there.

They told me I could go back. The clinician lady said, "It should be pretty easy." She said "Probably today, maybe tomorrow." I remember her exact words because it was such a relief. But then one night passed, and then another. For once, I was hoping someone would put a hand on my shoulder and shake me awake while I slept. But no one came to transfer me out. Why did she lie to me?

I asked my daytime tícher in Charlie 25 if I could talk to the clinician again. A man came and talked to me, and he said the same thing—he'd put in a request to get me transferred. But nothing happened.

Iván has come in to check on me a few times. As usual, he tries to encourage me to stay positive, but I can tell he's angry, too. He says that he keeps following up with the clinicians and trying to encourage them to move me as fast as possible. He says they keep telling him my case is "getting stuck" with the case managers, but they're working on it. I don't even really know what the difference is between a tícher and a clinician and a case manager. They're all adults to me, they just wear different color shirts.

I know I should be grateful that I'm not still on La Bestia. I know I should be grateful that I'm not still in La Hielera or La Perrera. But I don't care. For once in my life, I'm letting myself be angry. Not just upset. Not just annoyed or sad or a little bit mad for a second. I feel anger, real anger. I feel it in my legs and in my stomach. It's an exciting anger that makes my face hot and keeps me awake at night. I feel bitterness and resentment and hate and confusion.

And I want to feel it. I'm forcing myself to keep feeling it. Because if I weren't so angry, I'd have to admit that they're right, that I'm a criminal, I'm a pain in the ass, I don't matter.

Sorry for being so . . . I'm just sorry. Love you, Tía.

D.

OCTOBER 3, 2018

Tornillo

Querida Tía:

It feels claustrophobic in here. The air conditioner is broken. It has been breaking a lot recently, and because it's not as hot as it was a few weeks ago, I don't think they're in a big hurry to fix it. But I'd take summer heat with air-conditioning over October without it. This is still the desert. Without air-conditioning, the sun cooks the tent and the whole place smells like plastic and sweat.

Everything is chaos now, and it isn't just the air-conditioning. They weren't ready for this place to house thousands of kids. The schedule is a joke. Half the days we're in the tent all day except for when we go to meals, because all the other tents and the campo de fútbol are full of other kids. A lot of the time we'll get to the cafeteria tent and the workers there will tell us to come back later, either because there's no space or there's no food. The serving sizes there have gotten way smaller, too, but it doesn't make a difference, because I'm never hungry anymore. I still leave most of my food on the plate.

I probably don't have an appetite, because I'm moving so little. I barely even leave my bunk. There are cards and games here, but nobody ever suggests playing. We don't talk to each other in this tent. All the boys are just depressed in their beds. I asked the tíchers if they have any books. They didn't, but they brought me two magazines, one in Spanish and one in English. I've been trying to read them, but mostly I just spend the days sleeping. I'll sit in my bunk and try to write or draw or read the magazines, but I just end up staring at the page until my eyes fall shut. It's kind of amazing that I convinced myself to write to you right now. During the day, I try to sleep through the heat and the sadness. And then I lie awake for most of the night, when it's cooler, and I get riled up thinking about how they're treating me here.

The daytime is when I'm sad, the nighttime is when I'm angry. That's the real schedule in Charlie 25.

I saw Iván again at the worship service on Sunday, a few days ago. I thought that at least I could talk to him, and that would give me some sense of belonging here. I tried to disguise how I've been feeling, but he could tell immediately. He tried to encourage me and tell me to stay strong, but I couldn't bring myself to perk up for him. Staying strong is hard, and when you're alone, it's a thousand times harder. I stared at my feet and mumbled for most of our conversation.

I could tell he was really worried about me.

"Hey, hang tight just a little longer," he said. "I'm trying every day to get them to send you back to Alpha Thirteen. Nancy and Yuli are bugging the case managers too. For your sake and Juan Manuel's. I'm not going to stop trying until you're back where you belong, all right? You're like a little brother to me, I'm not going to leave you hanging."

Hearing how much he cared was exactly what I needed to make it through another few days. It was like a quick dip in Alpha 13, just enough to remember: I do matter, I'm not forgotten. It's this prison that's screwed up, not me.

"Thanks, Iván," I said, "I've never had a big brother before."

"Don't forget, D.," Iván said. "Your voice is powerful. This is hard for you now, I know. But you're going to do spectacular things one day. Don't lose hope. Trust in God and trust in yourself. If you do that, nothing can stop you."

I gave him a fist bump.

And for the past few days, I've been trying to ride that moment of encouragement for all it's worth.

Love,
D.

OCTOBER 9, 2018
Tornillo

Querida Tía:

I have a little bit more to go on today—I saw Juan Manuel. It was only for a second, but I'm hoping it'll be enough for me to get by . . . as long as I need to.

Today we actually got to use the campo de fútbol—a rare instance of the schedule being correct. I would've thought that I'd be better at playing fútbol after spending all day every day sleeping. I should be so well rested that I have lots of left over energy for the game. But actually, it's like my body has been sleeping for so long that it just wants to stay asleep, so whenever we play, I get tired and out of breath way faster than I used to. Which is why it was so helpful to see Juan Manuel, even if just for a minute.

After our game, I saw the next tent that was going to have a turn on the campo: Alpha 13. I saw McQueen and Enrique and Chato . . . and Iván and Juan Manuel.

"D. Esperanza!" Iván called out from across the field, "We miss you!"

I could barely hear him from so far away, but I could see him turning to the other boys, then saying something to Juan Manuel. I think he gave him permission to leave the group, because after they spoke for a second, Juan Manuel began walking toward me as fast as he could—he walked so fast that he might as well have been running, which is against the rules. I did the same—I started walking as fast as I possibly could. We probably made a funny sight, the two of us, rushing toward each other with this weird, artificially rigid posture, with our hands straight down at our sides, trying not to look like we were running.

I wrapped my arms around him and squeezed as hard as I could. We stood like that for a few seconds until one of the tíchers from my tent came up to us and said, "No physical contact, chicos." I'd forgotten about that rule—and in any case, I haven't been particularly motivated to have physical contact with any of the boys in Charlie 25.

"C'mon . . . " the tícher started saying to me. He clearly didn't know my name. "C'mon, hey, it's time to go back to the tent."

I looked around to see if Iván was nearby, thinking that maybe he could convince this tícher to let me and Juan Manuel talk for a minute—but he was already with Nancy and Yuli at the other end of the campo.

I took off my blue fabric belt and handed it to Juan Manuel. It was the belt I was going to wear to meet my family in Nashville. But I don't know when that will actually happen. Maybe it never will. But Juan Manuel is my family, too.

"Here," I said. "In case I don't see you again."

He started to tear up when I said that. He grabbed the belt and wrapped it around his waist, even though he wasn't wearing pants with belt loops. Then he took off his sweatshirt and handed it to me.

I took it. "Are you sure?"

"Definitely. I don't want to keep covering up when we play fútbol anyway. I want you to have it."

The tícher interrupted, "Okay, come on, it's time to go now, amigo."

At that moment, I was all caught up in the emotion of seeing Juan Manuel, but looking back on it now, I think it's funny how this tícher kept finding creative ways to address me.

"You're going to see me again, though," Juan Manuel said.

"How do you know?"

"It's my ninja way. Believe it."

So I'm hoping that the next time I feel like no one cares about me, at least Juan Manuel's sweatshirt will remind me that somewhere, somebody does.

Love,
D.

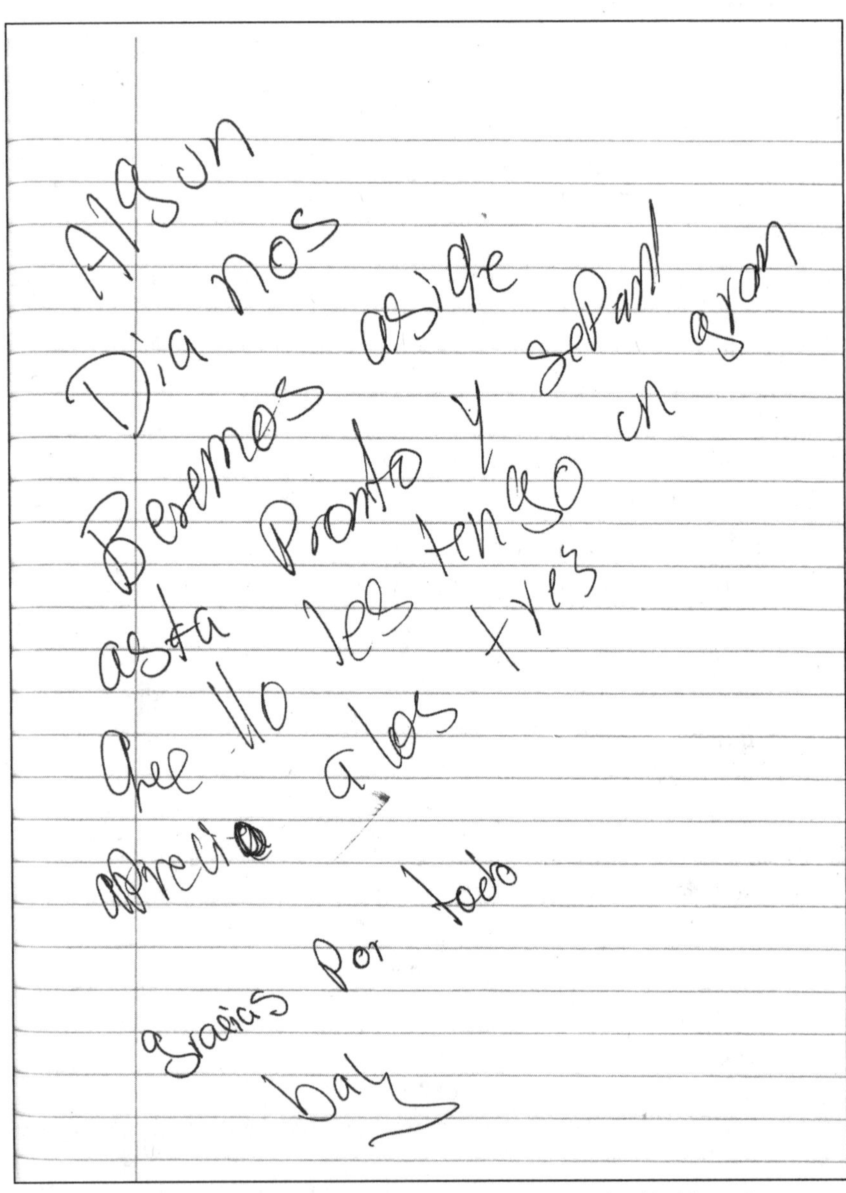

Algun Dia nos Beremos asiqe asta Pronto y sePan Qee llo les tengo un gran aprecio a los trez gracias por todo bay

"Someday we will meet again, so see you soon, and know that I hold you three very dear. Thank you for everything. Bye." A special note to my dearest friends.
Photo taken by Iván Morales

OCTOBER 13, 2018

El aeropuerto

Querida Tía:

Well. It's time for me to meet my parents.

I was just beginning to think this would never happen. And I'm still a little nervous that it won't, actually. But it feels so much realer than before, and I've never been in an airport before . . . I think it's finally happening.

There was a voice in my ear when I was sleeping, a few hours ago. It had to be two ro three in the morning. I flinched awake.

"¿Voy a Alpha Trece?" I asked the tícher who had just shaken me awake.

"No sé."

"¿Voy a otro centro?"

"No sé."

Very helpful, as usual. The tícher woke up one other boy from Charlie 25 and took us to the cafeteria tent. We walked past two buses, with the drivers waiting in their seats. So that meant we weren't changing tents. I figured they were sending me to another center. A different prison. It felt like my last hope of rejoining Alpha 13 was vanishing.

The tíchers handed out granola bars, then a man at the front of the cafeteria tent started giving us instructions. It was the same man who spoke to us the last time they transferred me out of Tornillo, who talks in a mix of Spanish and English that's hard to understand.

"Okay, niños, ahora vamos a hacer más fly-outs. Ustedes van a ir con sus assigned teachers al aeropuerto para irse. Muchos de ustedes van a hacer layovers. Es importante for you to follow las instrucciones that we give you. Los teachers van a darles más información. En el aeropuerto de destino, sus families van a pick you up."

I turned to the boy next to me and asked if they really just said we were going to see our families.

"I think so?"

A few other kids joined the conversation, and it seemed like we'd all heard the same thing: they were going to send us home.

At first, I wasn't sure I believed it. I was worried we might be misunderstanding what this guy was saying. But the more he talked, the clearer it became. I'd expected that I would've gotten excited, but actually, I just got nervous. I guess nervousness and excitement are like opposite sides of the same emotion.

It's all a little bit of a blur. They loaded us onto two buses. When we began to pull out of the campamento, I felt this gnawing feeling in my chest. Even though the whole reason I left Naranjito was to join my family in Nashville, my Alpha 13 family was still there, sleeping, and that bus was taking me away from them. They didn't even know that I was getting out. I don't even know if I'll see them again.

They drove us to an airport. It wasn't a long drive, less than an hour, but we drove through a city to get there. I never would have guessed that there was a whole city that close to Tornillo. Around the campamento, there's nothing except desert.

Part of me is still afraid they're lying to us again. I remember when they let me out of La Perrera and took me to the airport, and that agente de la Migra said we'd fly off to see our families, but instead they just put us on a bus to Tornillo. But this morning, the bus pulled up beside the airport and they took us inside.

Since we got here, I've been overwhelmed in every sense. I can't figure out what's happening: this place is noisy and huge, it's the biggest building I've ever been inside. It reminds me of Juárez. Or of a massive bus station. Maybe a massive bus station in Juárez.

When we were walking through the airport, I stayed close to the tícher because if I got lost, I thought I might be stuck in this building forever. The lights here are bright white even though the sun hasn't even risen yet. There are escalators and elevators and shops and restaurants and cars that drive *inside* the building. There are policemen walking dogs who look big and tough, like they could play fútbol americano like Buddy, and then there are regular people carrying crates with smaller dogs who look more like Caramelo. Everywhere I look, there are kids and parents and babies and old people and employees and cops. It's the first time I've seen gringos outside of the prisons I've been to, and they don't look like I expected. They aren't all white people. They aren't even mostly white people. There are Black people and Asian people and tons and tons and tons of people with skin like mine. Everywhere we go, I hear people speaking Spanish. I hear Americans speaking Spanish.

They made me put my backpack into a machine, then told me to stand inside another machine. The machines are supposed to scan us to make sure it's okay for us to fly. I was terrified that the machine would say *No, D. can't fly, don't let him on the airplane*, but the policeman on the other side just waved me through. He told me to have a nice flight. I wasn't expecting a cop to say something nice to me.

After spending so much time sitting in my bunk thinking about how sad and angry I am, and after going on this whole journey to be with my parents . . . I don't know how to feel. Obviously, I'm so happy to see Mamá and Papá. But I'm not relieved at all. I'm worried, actually. I don't know how I'll fit into their life. I don't know if they'll be disappointed when they get to know me. And I don't know if I'll feel at home in their house like I felt at home in Alpha 13. But I'm also so incredibly excited to see them, to meet them, to hug them for the first time. It's a complicated jumble of emotions.

And on top of all that, I'm super scared of being on an airplane. All of a sudden, I have a million questions about what keeps them in the air, how safe they are, how often they crash.

The more I let myself think about meeting my parents and about the airplane crashing, and about leaving Alpha 13 behind, the more nervous I get. So I'm just going to keep writing to you until they tell me to get on the plane, okay?

We're just sitting on metal benches. After they hurried us onto the bus and through the whole airport, the tícher we're with said we have to sit and wait for a few hours, because our flight is late. She seems to be really stressed about it, because when we get to wherever the airplane is going, we're supposed to switch onto other airplanes to go different places, and some of the other kids might miss their flights. But she says that in my case, I don't have to worry, because my second flight is leaving later than theirs.

So, after all that rushing through this weird, frenzied place, now I have some time to look around and think. We're sitting near a bar, and there's a man sitting by himself there, drinking a beer even though the sun hasn't even come up yet. He looks lonely. I recognize the look on his face—I think that's probably how I've looked recently. In the past ten months, I've felt the deepest loneliness. But at some points, I also felt the deepest love and gratitude and sense of family . . . even with people I have no blood relation to at all.

Is that weird? I'm going to see my parents, who're supposed to be the most important people in a kid's life, for the first time. But I guess I'm worried because, now that I'm thinking about it, my whole life has been a back-and-forth between feeling lonely and feeling like I belong. I was lonely without my parents, but I felt like I belonged with you and Felipe. I felt lonely when you and Felipe died, but like I belonged with Miguelito and Elías and Damián. I felt lonely when a gang and la Migra took them away from me, but I felt like I belonged with Roomie. I was lonely when they transferred me away from him, but then it felt like I belonged, more than ever, with Alpha 13. And I was lonely again when they transferred me back to El Albergue, and lonelier when they transferred me back to Tornillo but stuck me in Charlie 25. So now I'm wondering: Will I feel like I belong with my biological family in Nashville? Or will I just miss Juan Manuel and Iván and the family I adopted in Alpha 13?

The tícher says it's time to get on the plane, gotta go.

D.

OCTOBER 13, 2018

En el avión

Tía:

I'm in my seat. We walked through a tube-type thing to get on board. The airplane looks way more like a bus than I was expecting. The tícher told me to sit toward the back, by the window. The air-conditioning is blowing hard through a vent above me, and I can tell that I can twist it closed, but I'm not sure I'm allowed to. I don't want to do anything to get in trouble when I'm this close to being free.

Outside my window, the sun is just starting to rise. It's occuring to me, maybe for the first time, that I'm finally about to start my new life. This airplane isn't taking me back to Naranjito. It's not taking me to La Bestia or La Hielera or any of the bizarre in-between spaces where they put me after I crossed the border. After five months traveling from Honduras to el Norte, and five months in captivity here, this airplane is flying into my future.

If Iván were here, he'd ask, "D., ¿cuál es tu mayor illusion?" Now that I'm about to be free, what's my biggest dream? What am I looking forward to? That was one of his favorite conversation starters in Alpha 13: he'd ask what we wanted to do once we were out, and he'd tell us all about the opportunities we'd have in el Norte.

But honestly, right now . . . I don't have any dreams. When I think about everything that has happened in the past ten months, the first thing I think of is how incredibly close I felt with Miguelito, Elías, and Damián, and then with Roomie, and then with all of Alpha 13, especially Iván and Juan Manuel. I think about how Iván and Juan Manuel filled the big-brother and little-brother gaps left when I was separated from Elías and Miguelito. But the second thing I think is: this has been hell. Bendito sea Dios, because I'm going to be free. That thought eclipses everything else. I can't think about what I'm going to do next. I don't know what I'm looking forward to. Right now, I'm just relishing the fact that it's over. No more of La Bestia, no more gangs, no more Hielera, no more Perrera, no more monsters in green uniforms, no more prisons, neglect, hunger. I'm only fourteen, and I think I'm pretty mature for my age, but still, I know I've been through more pain than I'm supposed to.

This seat is comfy, but there was more room for my legs on the bus. It's making me think about the other kids who will sit here. Maybe not in this literal seat, but on a flight that will take them to their parents. If they ever close Tornillo for real, those kids'll have to go somewhere. And all the kids in El Albergue and in La Perrera and on La Bestia . . . eventually, hopefully, everyone has to go home. After such a long and hard journey, everything I've experienced is still just . . . one kid's journey. I don't know how many kids have sat here before me, and I don't know how many will sit here after me. But it must be thousands. Maybe millions, I have no idea. All of them going through what I've gone through, or worse. It's too much pain for me to wrap my head around. But also, maybe those kids will find new family that will help them through that pain, like I did in Alpha 13. If thousands or millions of kids get to feel that same sense of love and belonging . . . that's what I want to focus on. I hope that's what will happen. Maybe it's not realistic, but that's what I hope.

The airplane is cold. My arms are getting goose bumps. They turned on the engine and that made the air-conditioning blow even stronger than before. I just reached into my backpack, grabbed Juan Manuel's sweatshirt, and pulled it over my head.

I have to go now. The airplane is starting to move.

Love you forever,
D.

Gracias Por el tiempo de mi
atención ayudarme a tener
confiansa en si mismo los
regalos y Golodinas qe no
cualquiera lo ase.

Gracias Por todo Gracias
Por ser las mejores
Personas qe llo Pude conoser

Gracias Por todo cuenten
mi istoria alos amigo Para
qe sepa qe existen Personas
qe no son como los
demas.

"Thank you for your time and attention helping me gain confidence in myself . . . Thank you for everything. Share my story with your friends so they can know that people exist who are not like the others."
Photo taken by Iván Morales.

EPILOGUE

EN (UNA NUEVA) CASA

Everything you've just read takes place over the course of about ten months, between January and October 2018: five months traveling to the border, five months in detention. I'm writing this epilogue in January 2024, exactly six years after I began my journey. I'm guessing a lot of you are wondering about how I've changed since coming to the United States, but to be honest, I don't think I've changed at all. I'm pretty much the same kid, the only difference is now I'm nineteen, not thirteen. I still love writing and baleadas and dancing like an idiot to Bad Bunny, though, thankfully, these days, I dance to him in my kitchen instead of in a tent prison for migrante kids. I'm as hiperactivo as ever. I used to ride my bike all around Naranjito, now I ride it all over Nashville. I guess one thing is different: I've graduated to doing BMX. I go to the skatepark as often as I can, whenever I can get away from my work. Because of my status, I've only been able to find work in construction. Over time, I've gotten pretty good at carpentry. Interior carpentry. If you go into any new house in Nashville, take a look at all the wood fixtures: the floors, the door and window frames, closets, cabinets . . . if the house is only a few years old, there's a small chance I built it.

Let me bring you up to speed: After I was released from Tornillo, I unpaused my childhood. I became a teenager. I got to know my parents in person for the first time, and I got to meet my little sister. It has been really special for me. The mental image I'd had of my parents was of the photo I used to look at in Naranjito, when we were talking on the phone. Obviously, over a decade later, they looked very different, older, to the point that they almost could've been strangers. Even their voices were different than I was used to, because of course they were—everyone sounds different on the phone. I hadn't expected that, and the difference was jarring for a while. But at the same time, deep down, I recognized them instantly. How could I not?

I'll never forget the first time I saw them, when my heart was beating faster than it ever had before. Mamá was shorter than I realized, and wearing a floral dress. And Papá, tall and skinny, with long hair. The whole time I was gone, they had been kept in the dark about my whereabouts: they knew I was somewhere in Texas, and that I was being held by an organization that works for the government, but no more; I told them over the phone I was in a place called Tornillo, but the government wouldn't confirm it. My parents had to jump through more and more legal hoops before I could be released, all of which were complicated by the fact that they themselves were undocumented. But even if they had known where to find me and driven to Tornillo—even if they were standing outside the gates—I wouldn't have been released. It had been months of torture, and when they finally saw me, they both had enormous smiles on their faces.

Living with them for the first time was like being a child again—and it still feels that way to all of us. It's like we're reclaiming the time we lost. Mamá still says "mi pequeño niño" when she's talking about me or to me. And Papá is a fountain of wisdom, just like Felipe used to be. I hope I never take for granted the value of having an older person, with a life's worth of experiences, that I can turn to for advice.

My family and I have cobbled together a much safer life than we ever could have had in Naranjito, but living undocumented in Tennessee isn't easy either. La Migra exists beyond the border. They crack down on people who give work to undocumented folks. Not long after we were reunited, Papá had to go to another state for work. I miss him, and I've been lamenting the years we missed together. But I'm not the kind of person who says, *Oh no, things have changed, things aren't working out the way I'd hoped.* Change is part of life, and you have to embrace it. If you put your faith in God and stick close to the people you love, things will work out for the best. You have to acknowledge the incredible blessing of being alive, then carry on with your life. I stayed here in Nashville with Mamá. When I was still in school, she would wake me up every morning and make me breakfast. Every day, I had to remind myself—still do—that this is real life and not a dream, not a fantasy. I feel unspeakably lucky.

That blessing extends throughout the whole Hispanic community here in Tennessee. Through my family and community, I'm closest with the other hondureños, but there are lots of Spanish-speaking people here from all over: not just México, El Salvador, and Guatemala, but from places that used to seem unimaginably distant: Cuba, Venezuela, Colombia, Peru, República Dominicana. We speak with different accents and grew up eating different foods, but we all come here with the same purpose: to lead a better life in the United States. We've experienced the hardship of being far from our families, and that makes the Hispanic community in Nashville its own sort of family.

We have to stick together, just like I stuck with my cousins and with my brothers in Alpha 13, because being a migrante here is hard. Since arriving, I have had to learn about racism. It's something I never dealt with in Naranjito. Where I come from, no matter what someone looked like or how poor we were, we helped each other out. But here in Nashville, I've had the experience of being treated differently—of being treated worse—because I have darker skin and because I'm a migrante. Sometimes, there's a really shocking lack of empathy and generosity, and I have a hard time with it. Tío Felipe always used to say: *De un plato de comida comen dos personas cuando es necesario.* One plate of food can feed two (or five, or ten, or fifty) people if necessary. Sharing your one plato de comida doesn't solve world hunger, but it sure makes a difference to the starving person you're sharing it with. I'm grateful to live in Nashville and in Tennessee and in the United States. But when I first arrived, the inequality really slapped me in the face.

I enrolled in school. I was excited, because I hadn't been back to school since Tío Felipe died, and I'd gotten so interested in reading and writing and history and storytelling. But schools here are different. I loved seeing new faces and meeting new people, but because of the language barrier, it was difficult to keep up with the lessons.

At this point in the story, I should mention something important: Less than a year after I got to Nashville, I met a girl and, well . . . we're married now, and we have a beautiful son, la luz de mi vida. These have been the happiest five years of my life, and being a husband and a father has been the most rewarding, fulfilling experience I've ever had.

I know there are people who say that having kids is hard, that it's a burden. Maybe that's true for them, but for me, it has been the greatest blessing, the most fun, the best thing that has ever happened to me. Obviously it's difficult sometimes, but it's never a burden. For my mamá, who was heartbroken to miss most of my childhood, my son is like a second chance at mothering, but now as an abuela. Now I get to see, with my son, how she would've liked to be with me as a baby. When I'm sick or can't find work, Mamá has really come through. I feel bad for the parents who have to navigate the process of raising a child alone. I'm filled with gratitude for this humble life filled with family and community, and I wouldn't trade it for anything.

After you have a kid, lots of things change. You don't see the world through the same eyes anymore, because you have this little person following you around all the time, depending on you. And you get to introduce him to things. Sometimes we bring him to the skatepark, and we watch his eyes get wide at the other kids doing BMX. Obviously, he's way too young to even understand what he's watching, but still, my heart starts dancing reggaetón when I see the excitement on his face. I can't wait until he's old enough to learn.

Ever since becoming a father, I've seen my journey to this country in a different light. I have a new appreciation for why my parents migrated when they were about as old as I am now, and I have a new appreciation for how painful the decision to leave me in Naranjito must have been. People sometimes ask if I feel any resentment about my parents' absence during my childhood. Nothing could be further from the truth; despite the hardship, I feel a deep gratitude to them for staying strong and *not* coming back, no matter how difficult that was. They have told me how painful it was for them, and how conflicted they were, but ultimately, they knew that they were doing the responsible thing. They couldn't have provided for me, Tía, and Miguelito in Naranjito. I know that's true. And especially now that I have a son, I appreciate just how much of a sacrifice they made for me, and how deeply they believed that their absence was the best way to forge a better life for me.

Thanks to their sacrifice, now I am forging a better life for my own son. I grew up without my parents, but my son will have his. I had to drop out of school, but my son, I hope, will even get to go to college. I had to work from sunrise to sunset, but my son won't get a job until he's old enough, and instead of doing hard labor, he'll be able to follow his passions. I was sent to a prison camp, but my son will never have to set foot in a place like that; he was born in this country, and he will always be free. The United States is a land of opportunity, and my son will have a shot at a more dignified life than mine. Everything I endured in my childhood and on my ten-month journey north—the labor and the loneliness and the fear and the depression, the hunger and the blisters and the lacerations—all of it was worth it to give my future child a better life. It would be impossible to think any different.

I wasn't the only person in this book who was fighting for a better future, and if you've read this far, you probably want to know what happened to my cousins and brothers. As soon as I got out of detention, after I was reunited with my parents, the most important thing was finding out what happened to Miguelito and Elías, and to see if Damián made it back home safely. It took us a few weeks to hear anything about them . . . besides being cruel, the child migrant detention system is also profoundly dysfunctional, and in the chaos of Trump's child separation policy, it was practically impossible to track anyone down. Those weeks were full of conflicting emotions: I was so relieved to be out of detention and so excited but nervous about being with my parents for the first time, but my anxiety about my cousins' safety eclipsed it all.

Eventually, we did hear from Miguelito and Elías: they had been through a similar experience to mine—month after month of detention, confusion, and neglect—but they were okay, and they had been released to family in the United States. They're still here, working. Miguelito ended up living with family elsewhere in the United States, not in Nashville like we'd planned. I miss him, but we're always in touch, and I'm constantly sending photos of my son to him and Elías. Damián is back with his mamá, my tía Gloria, in Guatemala. He's living the life we all used to live: insecurity, constant threat of gangs, instability. But he's forging ahead as best he can.

I have no idea what happened to Roomie, and since I don't know his real name, I'm afraid he's gone from my life forever. But I treasure the time we had together, even if it was in abysmal circumstances. I still think he has one of the funniest senses of humor I've ever encountered. I've tried to find Juan Manuel. I haven't succeeded. I miss him terribly, and I have no idea where he is. I hope he's doing okay. Part of me is crossing my fingers that he'll hear about this book and get in touch. I'd love to continue our friendship.

I haven't been able to reconnect with any of the other boys from Alpha

13. I've tried, but people use different names, people get deported, people use different social media or set their profiles to private. And I never knew a lot of kids' last names in any case. There are so many parts of my journey north that I wish I could erase from my mind, but I never want to forget their faces and names. I don't miss that prison camp, but I do miss the powerful brotherhood that we formed. During my most difficult moments, it's something I feel an odd kind of nostalgia for. If I could, I would go back for just one day so I could say goodbye to everyone. And to make a plan so our brotherhood could endure outside of Tornillo.

But there's one person from Alpha 13 that I haven't lost touch with, my best big brother, Iván. We have a deep friendship now, a miraculous friendship. I'm grateful to God for bringing us together in the most unlikely, unsavory circumstances. We're always texting, and he's like an uncle to my son. Our bond is incredibly special to me. As time has gone by, I have forgotten some of the important things that happened in Tornillo, and working with Iván to publish this book has helped me resurrect so many memories.

Some of those are cherished memories of my brothers in Alpha 13, but there is no shortage of painful ones. Now that I'm an adult, I realize that I had to process far more trauma than a child ever should. I still get flashbacks to La Bestia, to being chased by the cartel, to La Hielera, and especially La Perrera. To six months as a child prisoner. I think of all the false hope I put in the first agente de la Migra I encountered in the United States, right after crossing the border. I trusted in him, and I was flung into emotional turmoil when that trust was betrayed, when I was funneled into the negligent, abusive (and for some people, very lucrative) migrant detention pipeline.

That kind of thing leaves a mark on you. It's not easy to explain, but sometimes I still fall quiet, close my eyes, and feel those moments like they're happening in the present. It doesn't pass quickly, it's serious, and I think it'll be with me for the rest of my life. It goes beyond the physical, it attacks your mind. You're not the person you were before. It's hard to be yourself again.

In Tornillo, there were thousands of kids whose voices were not heard. Countless instances where—I now know, after getting educated in this country and reading about the topic—our fundamental rights were violated. Because in this country, no matter what some people say on TV and on social media, undocumented people, asylum seekers from Central America, and especially asylum-seeking children have legal rights that are protected under the Constitution. But almost no one in that facility cared, and because we had such limited contact with the outside world, the full extent of the negligence went unnoticed.

Tornillo closed, but other detention centers for underaged migrantes remain. La Hielera and La Perrera still exist. Children in those places are still crying out for help; no one can hear them, and no one knows their stories. I hope that you read this book not as a story of something that happened a few years back, but as a story of what is happening right now, in this country. And then I hope you help do something about it.

At the beginning of this epilogue, I said that I haven't changed, that I'm still basically the same kid I used to be back in Naranjito. But the world around me has definitely changed *a lot*. A year and a half after I got to Nashville, the pandemic hit, and it impacted the Hispanic community—my community—especially hard. There was a presidential election. Child separation ended, but the new administration kept many of the previous one's most horrific anti-immigrant policies in place. By the time you read this, there will have been another election, and God knows what else will have happened. But if the experiences I describe in this book have taught me anything, it's that the authorities—cops, tíchers, administrators, agentes de la Migra, presidents—will never save us. We can expect nothing from them except cruel indifference at best and cruel abuse at worst. But the world is also full of Iváns and Nancys and Yulis; it's full of generous souls who give needy kids oranges, tamales, rosaries, and pineapple empanadas; women with septum piercings who volunteer at the Casa del Migrante; men with face tattoos who strap you onto the train so you don't fall off. It's full of brothers and sisters ready to stand in solidarity with you, like my brothers in Alpha 13. All we have is each other. Juntos somos más fuertes. If we put our faith in God and stick together, I know—from experience—that we can survive the unsurvivable.

NOTE BY GERARDO IVÁN MORALES

My name is Gerardo Iván Morales, and I am a DREAMer and a DACA recipient. I was born in Irapuato, Guanajuato, Mexico, in 1994. When I was five years old, my father made the difficult decision to move our family to the United States, in pursuit of a better life.

My uncertain legal status has plagued me all my life. Like most DREAMers, I have always lived as an American, and the United States is the only home I have ever known. But at any time, the government could banish me from that home. My only reassurance is the 2012 Deferred Action for Childhood Arrivals (DACA) policy, which President Obama established by executive order in response to Congress's failure to pass the Development, Relief, and Education for Alien Minors (DREAM) Act. DACA was intended as a temporary solution to shield me and my community of 800,000 young migrants from deportation. It has made a normal life possible for me, even if that normality could be snatched away at a moment's notice. Obama's executive order gave me a social security number, a driver's license, and the right to work. Needless to say, this has made me an outspoken advocate for long-overdue justice in our immigration system.

In the spring of 2018, the phrase *kids in cages* was everywhere: on the news and social media and college campuses, and at dinner tables and demonstrations across the country—everyone was talking about the Trump administration's horrific policy of family separation. Nursing babies as young as ten months were separated from their mothers. Families applying for asylum at official border crossings—in full compliance with all U.S. laws—were torn apart. Unaccompanied three-year-olds were given orders to participate in their own deportation hearings. Border Patrol instructed detained ten-year-old girls to care for detained two-year-old infants with leaky diapers. Although Trumps's broad "zero tolerance" child separation policy was unprecedented in U.S. history, it was a natural extension of the U.S. government's long-standing, bipartisan border-enforcement strategy known as "prevention through deterrence," which aims to reduce illegal crossings by selectively surveilling safer regions of the border, effectively pushing migrants into far more treacherous regions of the Sonoran Desert, where untold thousands have died since this policy was first implemented in 1994. Greater pain for migrants means a more effective policy—so the thinking goes. (Incidentally, this policy has been entirely ineffective at deterring migration.) The Trump administration's inhumane child separation policy operated according to a similar, sick logic: cause migrants unspeakable trauma by tearing children away from their parents, thereby disincentivizing future migration.

With the growing number of minors crossing the border and more children to house due to the child separation policy, in June of that year, the government resorted to opening an "emergency influx care facility"—i.e., a makeshift children's prison—in the middle of the desert in Tornillo, Texas. The American people were given almost no details about the inner workings of the center. But in keeping with the inhumane, almost Hitlerian logic of prevention through deterrence, the government used the pretext of bureaucratic protocols—FBI background checks that could take months, fingerprinting appointments that children's undocumented parents were scared to keep—to keep these families separated for far longer than necessary, if it had even been necessary in the first place. The greater the pain, the more effective the policy. When I read about the indignities these children faced, my stomach sank, my throat closed up, and tears filled my eyes. I knew in my heart that I had to take action. So, in July, only a few weeks after the Tornillo facility opened, I sought a way to become directly involved, and ultimately I was deployed as an "emergency service reservist" through a staffing agency, which was contracted by a nonprofit organization in San Antonio, which was contracted by the Office of Refugee Resettlement and Health and Human Services, which was in turn tasked with custody of unaccompanied Central American minors by the Trump administration. I was given a twelve-hour shift, from 7 a.m. to 7 p.m., seven days a week. My first day was Friday the 13th. I was assigned to Alpha 13. I stayed for six months.

What I witnessed there changed me forever. The Tornillo facility will go down as a dark period in U.S. history when asylum-seeking, vulnerable children spent months living in a slapdash tent city in the desert, in the care of unqualified, negligent personnel. Many of these children had endured unspeakable hardship and, in many cases, violence. They desperately needed psychological care and their family's loving embrace; instead, our government added another chapter to their stories of trauma. They came to the United States seeking stability and safety; we gave them uncertainty and imprisonment. These beautiful, unique, inspiring individuals were reduced to bed numbers. Their experiences in Tornillo will follow them for the rest of their lives.

Friends and family have asked me about my decision to work in such a horrible place. If the U.S. immigration system is so broken and morally bankrupt, doesn't working within it make me complicit? I have given this question a lot of thought and prayer, but to be honest, I never seriously doubted my decision. I was inspired by Dolores Huerta's famous words: "Every moment is an organizing opportunity, every person a potential activist, every minute a chance to change the world." I was driven by the concrete good that I was doing for those children; the benefit to them was so glaringly obvious that I couldn't imagine doing anything different. One obvious comparison is the foster care system: many people are aware that in the United States, that system is profoundly broken. Cases of neglect, mistreatment, and abuse abound. If a volunteer, social worker, or foster parent can make a difference in the life of just one child who is enduring that system . . . well, the system will remain as broken as ever, but it will make a whole lot of difference to that one child; it may even save their life. And—we can hope and pray—that one step at a time, those small differences will add up to systemic change. I see my work in Tornillo no differently. As soon as I arrived, I resolved to stay at the facility until it got shut down. I made that my purpose.

Although my heart broke every day, it was an honor and a privilege to meet so many courageous young people. In the face of unspeakable hardship, the boys of Alpha 13 embodied true strength, trust in God, and solidarity with one another. I admired their bravery, resilience, and desire to fight for a better future. We became like a family. I made it my sole priority to rectify the injustices I saw in Tornillo by supporting those children as much as I was able. As a Latino, I tried to empower them to be proud of our rich and diverse Hispanic community in the United States.

As one of the few adult immigrants present in Tornillo, I hoped to act as some sort of role model. I strove to build community and brotherhood in our tent. And I took charge of Sunday worship services, which gave me the chance to meet thousands of boys and girls who weren't in my assigned dorm. At those worship services, whenever one of the children led the community in prayer, I was reduced to tears.

In Alpha 13, I met one particularly inspiring individual, an unaccompanied minor from Honduras named D. Esperanza. He was an extremely talented young man with a passion for poetry and writing. I encouraged him to use this gift and continue writing. He wrote the story of his journey north in a wide-ruled composition book. It was a heart-wrenching tale of hardships that no thirteen-year-old should ever have to endure. I immediately told D. how much his words and talent moved me, and I urged him to continue writing.

In January 2019, the facility officially shut down. After all the children were gone, I took the time to salvage their incredible artwork and beautiful handmade bracelets, as well as some of their goodbye letters, all of which had ended up in the trash. I saved these treasures. Years later, I was moved to translate D.'s poem "Somos inmigrantes" into English and to share his story with the world. Together, we sought literary representation. And that is how this book ended up in your hands. Both of us consider it our mission to correct the narrative about immigrants in this country. There is this widespread, unfounded belief that we are bad people, gang members, criminals. This narrative keeps fear within the U.S. community, and many bad actors leverage that fear to further oppress and marginalize us, culminating in the abhorrent policies and practices that this book describes.

We hope that we have given a more realistic face—a face as charming as D.'s—to child immigration. The country needs to know the truth about what takes place inside American child detention centers. D.'s story is special, but tragically, it is not unique. Every year, more than 100,000 children cross into the United States to seek asylum. Like D., they are fleeing horrendous violence and debilitating poverty in their home countries. They travel thousands of miles in the hopes of receiving asylum. Americans have a duty to protect these children's basic human rights, and we must hold those who fail to do so accountable. Many facilities like Tornillo continue to operate, regardless of which way the political winds blow.

As a society, we have a moral obligation to dismantle this system of negligence and dehumanization. I think virtually everyone can agree that children must be protected at all costs; their human dignity must be preserved no matter what. And yet children remain, in my opinion, the most marginalized group in society. They have no rights, no voice. They can't vote or hire lobbyists or go on strike. It is their parents who are expected to advocate for them. So when children are torn from their parents—by ICE, by gangs, by Border Patrol, by the president, by the cartels, by dismal and degrading economic circumstances—who is left to defend their welfare?

The answer, I believe, is you and me. I hope you understand this book as a call to radical solidarity. We are, in fact, stronger together—juntos somos más fuertes—and together I know we can effect real change that will make a difference in the lives of these children. Radical solidarity is about more than a post on social media or the occasional donation. As Reverend Martin Luther King Jr. said, "True compassion is more than flinging a coin to a beggar; it comes to see that an edifice which produces beggars needs restructuring." I hope that after reading our story, people can come together to abolish these morally depraved child detention centers, which have no place in a nation that claims to be under God. I hope that we can summon our common humanity and finally discontinue the murderous policy of prevention through deterrence, which has gone unchallenged for the duration of the Clinton, Bush, Obama, Trump, and Biden administrations.

As I hold D.'s composition notebook in my hands and glance through the pages, I am in awe of his natural talent. His diary so powerfully, so eloquently depicts the dangers and pain he experienced, and the negligence and abuse that are built into our immigration system. The time he spent in Tornillo cannot be brushed off as an isolated moment in American history. Millions of other children are enduring the same thing today. They are enduring it right now. It is time to hear their stories, and it is time to act.

ABOUT THE AUTHOR

D. Esperanza was born in Naranjito, Honduras. When he was a baby, his parents migrated to the United States so they could provide him with a better life, and he was largely raised by his grandmother and uncle. At the age of thirteen, he and three cousins began traveling north to seek asylum in the United States. When they arrived at the border in 2018, at the height of the Trump administration's "zero tolerance" policy, D. was separated from his cousins and sent to a child detention center in Tornillo, Texas. After five months of excruciating uncertainty, he was released and reunited with his father. He now works in construction in Tennessee and is the proud father of a nine-month-old boy.